China and the Roman Orient

China and the Roman Orient

Researches into their Ancient and
Medieval Relations as Represented
in Old Chinese Records

Friedrich Hirth

With an Introduction by
Victor H. Mair

I.B.TAURIS
LONDON • NEW YORK • OXFORD • NEW DELHI • SYDNEY

I.B. TAURIS
Bloomsbury Publishing Plc
50 Bedford Square, London, WC1B 3DP, UK
1385 Broadway, New York, NY 10018, USA
29 Earlsfort Terrace, Dublin 2, Ireland

BLOOMSBURY, I.B. TAURIS and the I.B. Tauris logo are
trademarks of Bloomsbury Publishing Plc

First published in Great Britain 2021
This paperback edition published 2023

Originally published by Georg Hirth and Kelly & Walsh, 1885

Introduction © Victor H. Mair, 2021

Victor Mair has asserted his right under the Copyright,
Designs and Patents Act, 1988, to be identified as Author
of the Introduction of this work.

All rights reserved. No part of this publication may be reproduced or
transmitted in any form or by any means, electronic or mechanical,
including photocopying, recording, or any information storage or
retrieval system, without prior permission in writing from the publishers.

Bloomsbury Publishing Plc does not have any control over, or
responsibility for, any third-party websites referred to or in this book.
All internet addresses given in this book were correct at the time of
going to press. The author and publisher regret any inconvenience
caused if addresses have changed or sites have ceased to exist,
but can accept no responsibility for any such changes.

A catalogue record for this book is available from the British Library.

A catalog record for this book is available from the Library of Congress.

ISBN: HB: 978-0-7556-3937-3
PB: 978-0-7556-3941-0
ePDF: 978-1-7556-3938-0

To find out more about our authors and books visit
www.bloomsbury.com and sign up for our newsletters.

INTRODUCTION

VICTOR H. MAIR

There are a considerable number of books that attempt to deal with both China and Rome writ large. *China and the Roman Orient* by Friedrich Hirth, though first published in 1885, has stood the test of time as a work of scholarship that is still worthy of being consulted regularly today. It may truly be said to be a classic of its kind. There are not many books dealing with ancient Eurasian history written well over a century ago that are still regularly cited by the best scholars. What makes Hirth's *China and the Roman Orient* different? In my estimation, it is because the author sticks closely to the original Chinese sources and has the philological expertise to read them carefully and accurately. He does not add a lot of his own speculative interpretation, which makes his work all the more highly appreciated by critical scholars.

China and the Roman Orient is one of those rare works whose exceptional Sinological scholarship sets it apart from all but a small handful of others that will never grow old. It truly is in a class with Berthold Laufer's *Sino-Iranica* (1919; 2017) which has also recently been reissued.

***

The longevity of Hirth's *China and the Roman Orient* (henceforth *CRO*) is extraordinary. To what may we attribute its staying power? What are the strengths that have enabled it to remain relevant for well over a century? We have learned more about the relationship between Rome and China than was known 134 years ago in 1885 when Hirth finished his impressive volume. Yet scholars continue to consult *CRO* with assurance that it provides an enormous amount of fundamental, reliable information in a concentrated, easily accessible format. Why is this so?

First, a look at the man. Friedrich Hirth (1845–1927) was educated at the universities of Leipzig, Berlin, and

Greifswald (PhD, 1869). From 1870 to 1897, he served in the Chinese maritime customs service. Later, after teaching at the University of Munich, in 1902 Hirth was appointed as the first professor of Chinese in Columbia University and served as the head of the Chinese Department for fifteen years.

Hirth was an exceptionally versatile Sinologist. Above all, he carried out research on ancient Chinese texts through adopting the methods of classical philology. The topics and fields on which he lectured and wrote were astonishingly numerous: ancient Chinese history and early Chinese literature; Sinological sources for the history of the Turkic peoples; Chinese documentary style (on this he was one of the leading authorities); bronze drums and mirrors; foreign influences on Chinese art; Chinese painting; and so forth. Some of the subjects he wrote about are truly surprising, such as his paper on the origin of the mariner's compass in China (1906). In addition, Hirth assembled a distinguished collection of ancient Chinese porcelain and made illuminating observations about the pieces in it. Hirth has scores of publications to his name, including parts of the article on "China" in the acclaimed 11th edition (1911) of *Encyclopædia Britannica.*

One of the most outstanding features of Hirth's CRO is the identification of a great number of place names east and west, and he deserves tremendous credit for that achievement alone. We must remember that Hirth accomplished this in the days prior to Bernhard Karlgren (1889–1978), the Swedish historical phonologist, relying on the findings of Joseph Edkins (1823–1905) and utilizing various and sundry other sources to reconstruct the probable ancient sounds of Sinitic. There was no comprehensive, systematic presentation of early sounds of the Sinitic writing system as a whole. Instead, Sinologists in Hirth's time had to depend on ad hoc data, drawing on their knowledge of rhyme categories, topolectal comparanda, and so forth.

Other outstanding scholars who followed in the generation after Hirth, but still before Karlgren, became even more proficient in the ways and methods of reconstructing the sounds of Middle and Old Sinitic, utilizing their remarkable mastery of an astonishing range of Oriental and classical languages (Chinese, Japanese, Tibetan, Sanskrit, Arabic, Persian, Greek, Latin, etc.) as resources upon which to base their reconstructions. This, in fact, was what Hirth had both hoped for and predicted:

The Chinese ancient and mediaeval literature regarding the west is as yet an unworked mine; and I hope that, after years of patient research, we shall see the day when Western and Central Asiatic geography will be considered a rich source for the study of Chinese old sounds, and when this modest list [VHM: Hirth's "Linguistic Results," for which see item No. 7 below] will attain the size of the books of Sanscrit transliterations now on record. (*CRO*, pp. 309–10)

As such, I view Karlgren's achievement as a synthesis that built upon the outstanding scholarship of his predecessors such as Edkins, Hirth, Paul Pelliot, Laufer, and others. Yet there is an essential difference between the approach of a scholar like Karlgren and that of his predecessors such as Hirth. Whereas the latter were essentially philologists who plowed the fields of ancient texts and were dedicated to reading and understanding the literary, historical, geographical, and other remains they confronted, Karlgren—while still grounded in philology to a certain extent—made the leap to linguistics, especially historical phonology.

Hirth, situated in the Far East, declares that, in writing *CRO*, the chief challenge that preoccupied him was to clarify "The mystery connected with that country in the Far West, described by ancient Chinese authors under the name of Ta-ts'in (*CRO*, pp. xix)" (Da Qin in modern spelling [Hanyu Pinyin], Ta-ch'in in Wade-Giles Romanization). "Ta" means "great," with "ts'in" being the transcription in Latin letters of the name of the first bureaucratic empire in the East Asian heartland (Mair, 2004), whence we get the English name "China." The identification of "Ta-ts'in" ("Great Ts'in/Qin/Ch'in") was a puzzle that had captivated the world of Sinology for nearly two centuries.

Before Hirth's *CRO*, many Western scholars did not take the Chinese records concerning Ta-ts'in (the Chinese name for Rome) very seriously because they did not jibe well with what was known about Rome from Occidental sources. Indeed, some of them looked upon the Chinese notices as "puerile nonsense." Hirth was able to correct this erroneous judgement by showing that Ta-ts'in, which was called Fu-lin during the Middle Ages, did not refer to the Roman Empire with Rome as its capital, but only to its eastern portions, namely, Syria, Egypt, and Asia Minor, with Syria being of cardinal importance. To be sure, the designation Fu-lin, though it does not look like "Rome" in its Modern Standard

Mandarin garb, is actually the Sinitic transcription of that very illustrious name.

Earlier scholars who realized full well that Fu-lin referred to the eastern part of the Roman empire during the Middle Ages tried to connect it with "Franks," "Constantin*polin*" (accusative form of Constantinopolis in Greek), Bethlehem, and so forth (*CRO*, p. 287, esp. n. 2; p. 290). Hirth himself gave serious consideration to the latter two names, especially "Bethlehem," though none of these suggestions was fully convincing, neither from a phonological point of view nor from a historical and geographical stance. It is only in recent decades, with the discovery of new materials and significant advances in the historical reconstruction of Sinitic, that it has been possible to see that the medieval pronunciation of Fu-lin 拂菻, namely /pʰɨut lɨmX/, reflects the pronunciation of "Rome" in the relevant Central Asian Middle Iranian language Sogdian (frwm /frūm/), (βr'wm /frūm, frōm/, "Rome, Byzantium") or Chorasmian (frōm), which are akin to Parthian frwm (Frōm), Middle Persian (Hrōm, "Rome; Byzantium"), Bactrian (фромо), and Old Armenian (Hŕovm), all of which are ultimately from Ancient Greek Ῥώμη (Rhṓmē), also Runic writing pUrm with spellings like *pur(u)m or *pur(i)m. (A full philological and phonological exegesis of these equations would require a lengthy technical paper, the makings of which exist in personal communications from Diana Shuheng Zhang, South Coblin, and Peter Zieme.)

The case of Fu-lin = Rome is one example of how modern scholarship has gone beyond Hirth's contributions, but we may be certain that he would be pleased with these developments, particularly in light of the fact that current research rests solidly on the firm foundation provided by him.

Once we readjust our thinking about both Ta-ts'in and Fu-lin as referring only to the eastern portion of the Roman Empire, many of the observations of the old Chinese records about western Eurasia and the Middle East begin to make much more sense.

What makes *CRO* still worth reading well over a century after it was initially published? Above all, many of Hirth's identifications of names, places, people, and things, still stand. When there are doubts about their validity, Hirth's clear statements of evidence, and the reasoning behind them, make it easy to prove or disprove them on the basis of new data. Second, *CRO* amounts to an encyclopedia of plants, animals, minerals, manufactured goods, and all manner of other materials that were transmitted across the length and breadth of Eurasia. As always, what makes Hirth's book lastingly valuable over such a long period of time is the painstaking philological exactitude with which he arrived at his identifications and designations. Finally, though there is much more that could be said in defense of Hirth's methods, although he is relying on written texts that date from a period of roughly two millennia in length, he adopts a rigorous, fundamentally scientific, approach in assessing their worth. Consequently, researchers from a variety of backgrounds can still consult CRO with confidence that it offers a wide range of trustworthy information on the contacts and exchanges between east and west during the period of the contemporaneous Roman and Chinese empires.

Hirth considered himself above all a German philologist, a proud calling that he took very seriously. On the other hand, he was keenly aware of the lack of resources that confronted him in China. Consequently, he had to rely heavily on the Chinese texts that were available to him in Shanghai. Furthermore, he struggled over whether to write his book in English or in his native language, German. In the end, he decided to write it in English, because he realized that it would have to be published in Shanghai, where there were English presses but few facilities for publishing in German. Here he felicitously cites the familiar *bon mot* according to which German is the language in which we should think, and English the language in which we should write, commonly attributed to Madame de Staël.

In his quest to identify and explicate "Ta-ts'in," Hirth felt obliged to undertake the following tasks:

1. Collect all the Chinese texts on the subject.
2. Translate or retranslate all the relevant texts, some of which had been worked on by earlier Sinologists.
3. Clarify the facts available in the Chinese texts that he had collected and translated.

This he did with exemplary thoroughness and admirable precision. What we have in CRO, then, is a substantial volume divided into the following parts:

1. A succinct preface in which Hirth lays out the problems he wishes to solve and the goals that he hopes to achieve in his book.
2. A detailed table of contents that enables the reader readily to locate all the components of the volume.

3. Seventeen premodern (ancient, medieval, and late imperial) Chinese texts touching upon the question of Ta-ts'in, together with their translations into English and essential annotations. These texts are mostly taken from the official histories, plus two encyclopedic works, and the famous Nestorian inscription—all primary sources and relatively reliable.
4. Textual variants.
5. Index to the translations and Chinese texts.
6. Identifications of the kingdoms, cities, places, persons, and things mentioned in the texts. This is the heart of CRO (pp. 135–308) and constitutes the most daunting, demanding challenges Hirth faced in writing this book. It is also the part of CRO to which most readers will turn to again and again for assistance in trying to match up Chinese terms with the Occidental names to which they refer. Accuracy in making such identifications is one of the most excruciating aspects of Sinological research, and Hirth carried it off with meticulousness and exactitude.
7. A brief section on "Linguistic Results" (pp. 309–13), in which Hirth presents seventy-six Chinese morphosyllables arranged alphabetically according to their modern Mandarin pronunciations followed by his phonological reconstructions and examples of their application in specific names from the translated texts. These are like building blocks for the reconstruction of ancient Sinitic sounds, anchoring them in identifiable names and terms in western Eurasia.
8. A generous (fourteen pages) general index of the names of peoples, places, scholars, and topics mentioned throughout the book

Hirth's *CRO* contrasts with Frederick J. Teggart's *Rome and China: A Study of Correlations in Historical Events* (1939), written fifty-four years later. Superficially, the two books share similar titles and topics, but they could hardly be more different in their orientations and goals. Whereas Hirth was determined to identify the names of places, peoples, and things from the far west of Eurasia that were Sinographically transcribed in ancient Chinese—an extremely difficult philological task, Teggart's aim was far more theoretical. Teggart strove to demonstrate that the battles, movements of peoples, and other events that occurred in western Eurasia,

Central Asia, and East Asia for half a millennium during the Roman Empire, were intimately interrelated, although in *Rome and China*, he focuses intensely on the period from 58 BC to AD 107.

We may note that so much of the activity studied by Teggart centered on the Tarim Basin (the geographical hub of Central Eurasia) and the Tängri Tagh/Tianshan/Heavenly Mountains to the north, including Kucha and Turfan as key nexuses of east-west interaction along the so-called Silk Road. (Note especially that both Kucha and Turfan were major centers of Tocharian language and culture. Although, as the easternmost Indo-European group who, moreover, interacted with the Chinese already by BC times, the Tocharians have become essential for understanding the development of civilization in Eurasia, it would have been impossible for Hirth to know about them when he wrote *CRO* because the manuscripts and cultural remains associated with them had not yet been discovered.) Furthermore, it should be emphasized that, before the coming of the Turkic peoples in large numbers from the northeast beginning around the eighth century AD, most of the inhabitants of the Tarim Basin and surrounding areas were Indo-European speakers, primarily Iranians and Tocharians, plus Chinese military garrisons sporadically in place from the Han Dynasty (206 BC–220 AD) on. After reading Teggart's persuasive work of historical analysis and synthesis, it is impossible to view western, central, and eastern Asia as in any way isolated.

Relying on a massive accumulation of data concerning wars that took place across Eurasia, "for every country from Britain to Cambodia," close analysis of the times and results of their occurrences revealed that every "barbarian uprising in Europe followed the outbreak of war either on the eastern frontiers of the Roman empire or in the 'Western Regions' of the Chinese" (*Rome and China*, p. vii). Hence, we may say that Hirth established the raw data and Teggart accumulated, applied, and interpreted them. That is the difference between history and philology.

This, then, is the sum and substance of *CRO*: the philological determination of fundamental facts about the history of the Roman orient, and it explains why this extraordinary book has stood the test of time and is receiving a new edition now.

Another undying work of Hirth, written in collaboration with W. W. Rockhill and published by the Imperial Academy of Sciences in St Petersburg in 1911, is *Chau Ju-kua: His Work on the Chinese and Arab Trade in the Twelfth and Thirteenth*

Centuries, entitled Chu-fan-chï. This is the translation and annotation of *Zhufan zhi*諸蕃志 by Zhao Rugua趙汝适 (1170–1231), which Hirth and Rockhill refer to in English as *A Description of Barbarous Peoples* or *Records of Foreign Nations*. Although dating to a later period and dedicated to the translation and annotation of a single work, the *Zhufan zhi* of Hirth and Rockhill follows a similar pattern to that of CRO, namely, a strong emphasis on the identification of foreign names and terms as transcribed in Chinese characters. As befitting a volume that is devoted in large measure to sea trade involving sailors and merchants from Java, Southeast Asia, South Asia, and the Middle East, it pays greater attention to products that were shipped hither and thither on the sea routes linking these areas. Still, the fundamental method of philology employed in CRO is retained in *Zhufan zhi*, though requiring fewer formidable phonological reconstructions because the later time of the work meant that the sounds of Chinese characters in this work are closer to those of the foreign words in question and, moreover, far more familiar due to their geographical propinquity and frequency of mention than names and terms cited in CRO.

It is interesting that the two living scholars whose work most closely resembles and continues the investigations of Hirth in CRO are both independent scholars. They are John Hill, a researcher in Australia, and Chris Dorn'eich, a researcher in Germany. The former's magnum opus is *Through the Jade Gate: China to Rome* (2nd edition, 2015), while the distillation of the latter's monumental investigations may be found in his *Zhang Qian: The Secret Envoy of Han Emperor Wu in Search of the Arsi (Yuezhi) and the Fall of the Græco-Bactrian Kingdom* (2008). Though the conclusions they come to are not identical with those of Hirth, their methods are similar in that they comb every available bit of historical data in an effort to determine what happened between China and Rome, where, and when.

Hill has been working for many years translating and interpreting the accounts of the "Western Regions" in the *Hou Hanshu* (History of the Later Han) and the *Weilüe* (A Brief History of Wei), portions of which were also selected for close examination by Hirth. Like Hirth, Hill focusses on the identification of the many place names, routes, and products mentioned in the accounts. He highlights how the two Chinese texts, along with the many other Chinese and Western histories, mutually support and enhance each other. Together, combined with modern archaeological, genetic, and other scientific advances, they provide us with a far richer and more accurate picture of the incredible expansion of regular communications and trade right across Asia, Europe, and Africa during the early centuries of the present era than was hitherto available to scholars. For more than thirty years, Hirth's seminal work, CRO, has remained a constant and trusted companion for Hill, never far from reach, along with the works of Aurel Stein (1862–1943), and Édouard Chavannes (1865–1918).

Dorn'eich is an architect by profession. The starting point for his historical research was a remarkable monument of ancient architecture known as the "Minar-i Chakari" in the mountains southeast of Kabul, Afghanistan. Dorn'eich visited this enormous (28.5 meters in height), freestanding pillar in 1965, while still a student of architecture at Stuttgart University. In the following years, he wrote his first paper on this Buddhist column (stambha) with its Gandhara-style architecture and demonstrated that it belonged to Kushan times (late first to early second century CE). Heavily damaged during the Afghan Civil War, the "Minar-i Chakari" was subsequently destroyed by the Islamic fundamentalist Taliban regime in March 1998, three years before their destruction of the colossal Buddhas of Bamiyan, also in Afghanistan.

Just as Hirth concentrated on Ta-ts'in/Daqin ("Great Qin"), that is, the Roman Orient, Dorn'eich focuses on Daxia (lit., "Great Xia") and Da Yuezhi ("Great Yuezhi"). Hirth, and many other scholars before and after him up to the present day, identified "Daxia" with Bactria, but Dorn'eich, following De Groot (1926:10) and based on his own intensive, deep investigations, provides abundant evidence (including especially from the Greek geographer and historian Strabo [XI.8.2]) that it should in fact refer to the Tocharians. Dorn'eich identifies their conquerors, the "Great Yuezhi," whom many confuse with the Tocharians themselves, as the Arsi (there are many different renderings of this ethnonym), the true "Seres" or Silk People in Roman and later times, under their Kushan kings, all of whom were missing from CRO. Ironically, Hirth showed clearly that he did know about the Yuezhi/Kushans, but that was not until much later—in 1917 during World War I, while he was teaching at Columbia University—when he made the first English translation of Sima Qian's (ca. 140–ca. 86 BC) Shiji (The Grand Scribe's Records) 123 as "The Story of Chang K'ien, China's Pioneer in Western Asia," an excellent piece of work.

It is well known that Hirth himself planned a revised and enlarged second edition of *CRO*, as recounted by Franke (1926: 204):

Er hatte das Material für eine vollkommen neue, erweiterte und verbesserte Auflage des vergriffenen China and the Roman Orient zusammengestellt und nahm es bei seiner Rückkehr nach Deutschland im Sommer 1920 mit sich. Der Koffer, der alle in den Jahrzehnten gesammelten Auszüge, Notizen, Übersetzungen usw. enthielt, wurde mit vier anderen in Hamburg aus dem Lagerraum der Speditionsfirma gestohlen.

[He had compiled the material for a completely new, expanded and improved edition of the out-of-print *China and the Roman Orient*, and took it on his return to Germany in the summer of 1920. The suitcase, which contained all extracts, notes, translations, etc., collected over the decades, was stolen from the storage room of the forwarding company with four others in Hamburg.]

Based on his 1917 article on Chang K'ien and other things Hirth wrote after *CRO*, we may be confident that in the second edition of *CRO*, planned for the time after his return to Germany (around 1920), Hirth would have brought in plentiful materials on the Yuezhi/Arsi and the Kushans, and likely also a good deal on the *Periplus of the Erythrean Sea* and other texts dealing with the sea trade engaged in by the Kushans, whereby they circumvented the Parthians who blocked the way to the Middle East and Rome. Unfortunately, as Franke tells us, Hirth was frustrated when his trunk containing all the material he had collected was stolen from a Hamburg customs hall upon his return to Germany from America.

Hirth's own revised edition of *CRO* thus never became a reality, yet the labors of Hill and Dorn'eich, his able successors who have devoted the better part of their lives to the task, enable us to imagine what it would have been like, since they fill in the gaps that he was evidently aiming to plug. By consulting their exhaustive works and the research of scholars like Craig Benjamin (2018) and William H. Nienhauser (2019), we can supplement the original *CRO* of 134 years ago and, in a sense, realize Hirth's goal of a revised edition of his Sino-Roman masterpiece.

BIBLIOGRAPHY

Benjamin, Craig. *Empires of Ancient Eurasia: The First Silk Roads Era 100 BCE–250 CE*. Cambridge: Cambridge University Press, 2018.

Coblin, W. South. "Notes on the Western Han Initials," *Tsing Hua Journal of Chinese Studies*, 14 (1982), 111–33.

De Groot, Johann Jakob Maria (Otto Franke, ed.). *Chinesische Urkunden zur Geschichte Asiens. Erster Teil: Die Hunnen der vorchristlichen Zeit. Zweiter Teil: Die Westlande Chinas in der vorchristlichen Zeit*. Berlin: W. de Gruyter, 1921/1926.

Dorn'eich, Chris M. *Zhang Qian: The Secret Envoy of Han Emperor Wu in Search of the Arsi (Yuezhi) and the Fall of the Græco-Bactrian Kingdom*. Berlin: Christof Michael Dorn'eich, 2008.

Franke, Otto. "Friedrich Hirth," *Ostasiatische Zeitschrift*, Neue Folge, Dritter Jahrgang. Berlin and Leipzig: W. de Gruyter, 1926, 197–207.

Gharib, B. *Sogdian Dictionary: Sogdian-Persian-English*. Tehran: Farhangan, 1995.

Hill, John E. *Through the Jade Gate: China to Rome*. 2nd edition, 2 volumes. Scotts Valley: CreateSpace Independent Publishing Platform, 2015.

Hirth, Friedrich. *China and the Roman Orient: Researches into Their Ancient and Medieval Relations as Represented in Old Chinese Records*. Leipzig and Munich: Georg Hirth; Shanghai and Hongkong: Kelly and Walsh, 1885.

Hirth, Friedrich. "Origins of the Mariner's Compass in China." *Monist*, 16 (July 1906), 321–30.

Hirth, Friedrich. "The Story of Chang K'ien, China's Pioneer in Western Asia: Text and Translation of Chapter 123 of Ssi-Ma Ts'ien's Shi-Ki." *Journal of the American Oriental Society*, 37 (January 1, 1917), 89–152.

Hirth, Friedrich, and Rockhill, W. W. *Chau Ju-kua: His Work on the Chinese and Arab Trade in the Twelfth and Thirteenth Centuries, entitled* Chu-fan-chï. St. Petersburg: Imperial Academy of Sciences, 1911.

Laufer, Berthold. 2017, Brian Spooner, intro. *Sino-Iranica: China and Ancient Iran: Commodities and Cultural Exchange from 1000 BC to Medieval Times*. London: I.B. Tauris, 1917.

Mair, Victor H. "The North(west)ern Peoples and the Recurrent Origins of the 'Chinese' State." In Joshua A. Fogel, ed., *The Teleology of the Modern Nation-State: Japan and China*. Philadelphia: University of Pennsylvania Press, 2004, 48–84.

Mallory, J. P. "The Problem of Tocharian Origins: An Archaeological Perspective." *Sino-Platonic Papers*, 259 (November 2015), 1–63.

New York Times. "Prof. Friedrich Hirth, Chinese Scholar, Dies." *New York Times* (January 10, 1927).

Nienhauser, William H., Jr., trans. and annot. "Ta Yüan." *The Grand Scribe's Records. Volume XI: The Memoirs of Han China, Part IV*. Bloomington: Indiana University Press, 2019, 53–100.

Pulleyblank, Edwin G. "The Consonantal System of Old Chinese," *Asia Major* 9 (1962), 58–144.

Schuessler, Axel. *ABC Etymological Dictionary of Old Chinese*. Honolulu: University of Hawai'i Press, 2007.

Teggart, Frederick J. *Rome and China: A Study of Correlations in Historical Events*. Berkeley: University of California Press, 1939.

Witzel, Michael. "Loan Words in Western Central Asia: Indicators of Substrate Populations, Migrations, and Trade Relations." In Victor H. Mair, ed., *Contact and Exchange in the Ancient World*. Honolulu: University of Hawai'i Press, 2006, 158–90.

Yu Taishan. "The Earliest Tocharians in China." *Sino-Platonic Papers*, 204 (June 2010), 1–78.

PREFACE.

ALTHOUGH I may hope that the researches forming the subject of this volume will meet with some interest on the part of a few readers in various countries, I must confess that, in writing down the results of my studies, I have endeavoured to please the German critic rather than the learned of any other country. Having myself studied the method of philological research at the feet of masters like Ritschl and Haupt, I am keenly sensible of the shortcomings of these notes. Principal among these is the selection of authorities for facts connected with classical antiquity. I have only too often been obliged to draw from second-hand sources, which would be considered unpardonable in the case of authors fortunate enough to pursue their studies in the midst of one of the Imperial or Royal Libraries of Europe. I am therefore bound to urge that these sheets were written at Shanghai in the empire of China, amid the bustle of business life; and that in collecting the most necessary information required to prove my points, I had chiefly to depend upon the Chinese and western works of my own limited library. This is obviously a great drawback in the case of western authors; and it constitutes almost as great a difficulty where Chinese authors are concerned. For, whatever facilities life in China may offer to a western student in the way of personal encouragement, it would be a mistake to assume that it is easy for a foreigner in this Empire to obtain access to a great number of native books, especially rare books, which have to be collected as chances for purchasing them may offer. It is much easier to pursue such studies in the libraries of Paris, London, Berlin, Munich, or St. Petersburgh, where all the important and interesting works in Chinese literature are found together.

I owe yet another apology to the German critic. Why, my philological countrymen will ask, write your book in English as long as you can write your own language? why expose yourself to the risk of finding your bad English denounced as long as you are able to handle a German pen? I must admit that the choice between the two languages occupied my mind considerably at the outset; but, finally, practical reasons prevailed upon me to risk all the disadvantages to which writers in foreign languages are exposed. The book had to be printed somewhere; if in Germany, the absence of the author would have created insuperable difficulties in supervising the printing of Chinese passages; if in Shanghai, the printing of a German book would have obliged the author to learn more of the art of printing than the opportunities of life had hitherto taught him ; and as matters happen to be, it seemed best to follow the advice of Mme de Staël, who is credited with the authorship of the familiar *bon mot* according to which German is the language we should think in, and English the language we should write in. There is some sort of consolation in the idea that most sinological readers in Germany understand English. I regret to say that this is not generally the case with classical students, and that my notes will be lost to many a connoisseur of Roman oriental antiquities who might have elucidated difficulties now left in the dark for want of special study.

The mystery connected with that country in the Far West, described by ancient Chinese authors under the name of Ta-ts'in, has occupied the sinological world at intervals since the beginning of the last century. The task which I thought had still to be performed in connection with this interesting subject was—

1. The collection of all Chinese texts embodying information on the subject ;

2. The translation of these texts as far as they were new to the public, and the retranslation of portions already known but hitherto imperfectly rendered ;

3. The identification of facts contained in these Chinese texts.

My interpretation of these records leads to the conclusion that the ancient country of Ta-ts'in, called Fu-lin during the middle ages, was not the Roman Empire with Rome as its capital, but merely its oriental part, viz., Syria, Egypt and Asia Minor; and Syria in the first instance. If applied to the Roman Orient the greater part of the facts mentioned by the Chinese can be traced, and a reasonable explanation may be found for them without resorting to improbabilities; while, if applied to the whole empire, or to Italy, or to any other part of ancient Rome, the matter contained in the Chinese tradition does not agree with reality. As I read the Chinese notices they contain tolerably exact statements regarding the contemporaneous geography of western Asia; they would indeed be "puerile nonsense"—as I believe Colonel Yule calls them somewhere in his *Cathay*—if applied to any other part of the world.

Yule remarks with regard to the information possessed by ancient western geographers of the country of the Thinæ: "It is natural in such a state of imperfect knowledge both that the name of the remoter but dominant nation should sometimes be applied to its nearest subject races, and that the characteristics of these nearest races should sometimes be transferred to the governing nation. Something in a degree analogous has taken place in our own specific application of the term 'Dutch' only to our neighbours of the Netherlands." (*Cathay*, Vol. I, p. xliii). Quite a similar remark may be made with regard to the idea we find prevailing among Chinese ancient and mediæval writers about the characteristics of their Ta-ts'in and Fu-lin. But we have to add that, although many of the peculiarities of the governing nation (Rome) were found in the subject country (Syria), the Chinese were not aware that Ta-ts'in as known to them was subject to a larger Ta-ts'in yet. To them Antioch was the capital of the empire; for, the "queen of the east" possessed so much splendour of her own, that to the oriental traveller the distant grandeur of her superior rival was eclipsed. It struck Yule, "in spite of the 'confident identifications' of de Guignes and Visdelou, that the view entertained by the Chinese themselves of the Roman Empire and its inhabitants, had some striking points of analogy to those views of the Chinese which are indicated in the classical descriptions of the Seres." "There can be no mistaking the fact," he continues, "that in this case also the great object was within the horizon of vision, yet the details ascribed to it are often far from being true characteristics, being only the accidents of its outer borders towards the east." I am about to show that, as long as these details are not ascribed to the whole empire, but merely to its eastern borders, they are sufficiently accurate to be called true characteristics, and that the deficiency urged in the last sentence of Colonel Yule's remark is not one inherent in the Chinese notices themselves, but one which is artificially introduced by those who persist in applying them to the Roman Empire. As Syria and Egypt were Roman provinces we find, of course, traces of Roman life among the characteristic details placed on record by the Chinese historians; but we shall find that the oriental character prevails in all the main points, apart from the unmistakeable features of the topographical configuration of the country.

I have had the satisfaction of seeing the principal results of these researches, as far as they could be judged of by the perusal of advance sheets of the book, approved of by a number of sinological friends; and I may consider myself fortunate if they meet with a similar reception on the part of the general public. I am, of course, well aware that much remains to be done and that there is a fair chance for fellow-workers to treat with success quite a number of problems which I have either not taken up at all, or not attempted to solve definitively, because the range of my studies did not seem to qualify me for the question.

Mr. Phillips writes with regard to my identification of T'iao-chih: "this is the only part I cannot quite make up my mind to accept. There are two things that require research. Firstly, did the Rhinoceros thrive and flourish at Hira at the time mentioned? and, secondly, can the term *Hsi-hai*, western sea, be applied to the Bahr Nedjef? T'iao-chih is the pivot upon which the whole thing turns. I find that I, like yourself, have in my manuscript about Ta-ts'in made Ssŭ-pin and Ssŭ-lo Ktesiphon and Seleucia, etc."

As regards the Western Sea question, I hold that, as the periplus from east to west began or could begin in the Chaldaean Lake, it is quite possible that these waters were comprised under the name "western sea." A correspondent of the *China Review* (Vol. XIII, p. 358) quotes Herodotus (I, 184) to say that, before the reign of Semiramis, the Euphrates used to overflow the whole plain like a sea. Further, Mas'udi (transl. A. Sprenger, Vol. I, p. 246) says: "The greatest part of the water of the Euphrates had once its course through el-Hírah: the bed may still be traced, and it has the name of 'Atík (ancient). On it was fought the battle between the Moslims and Rostam (at the time of 'Omar), called the battle of el-Kádesíyah. The Euphrates fell at that time into the Abyssinian sea [*i.e.*, the Indian Ocean, here the Persian Gulf], at a place which is now called en-Najaf [Nedjef]; for the sea came up to this place, and thither resorted the ships of China and India, destined for the kings of el-Hírah." A few pages farther on, Mas'udi relates a dialogue between the Arab conqueror Kháled and a native of Hira. Kháled had asked that the people of the city should depute an intelligent aged man to his camp, that he might enquire of him about their affairs. The following colloquy then took place between Kháled and this aged man of Hira:

"Are you Arabs or Nabathaeans?

"We are Nabathized Arabs, and Arabized Nabathaeans.[1]

"How many years are come over thee?

"Three hundred and fifty.

"And what hast thou seen?

"I have seen the ships of the sea coming up to us in this deep country with the goods of es-Sind and India; the ground which is now under thy feet was covered with the waves of the sea. Look how far we are at present from the shore, etc."

Re the Rhinoceros: the difficulty arising from the mention in the *Hou-han-shu* of this animal as "coming from" T'iao-chih together with lions, zebus, peacocks and ostriches is not removed by placing T'iao-chih in any of the countries with which others have associated it, nor by giving it a position farther south on the coast of the Persian Gulf; the countries producing the rhinoceros at the present day are altogether out of the question. Dr. Bretschneider (*Notes and Queries on China*

---

[1] Cf. the remarks on p. 172 regarding the relationship between the Chaldaeans (T'iao-chih) and the Nabathaeans (Li-kan, Rekem).

and Japan, Vol. IV, p. 60 seq.), in trying to identify T'iao-chih with ancient Persia (Susa, Persepolis), assumes that, in this case, the term *hsi-niu* should be translated by *buffalo*; buffaloes being found in great numbers all over western Asia. But the difference between this animal and the rhinoceros is far too great; and I would certainly not credit the Chinese writer, who must have known the former from his own experience and the latter from detailed descriptions of the Annamese species occurring in contemporaneous and older Chinese works, with such a confusion. If we possess no positive proof of the rhinoceros having existed in Chaldaea, I am also not aware of ancient authors stating that it did *not* exist there; for, ancient literature, as it now exists, is mainly of an accidental nature and cannot fairly be expected to contain an exhaustive picture of the geographical range of each animal. Whether the rhinoceros did or did not occupy a prominent position in the Chaldaean fauna, there is no doubt that the low, swampy soil of the inundated fields near the lower course of the Euphrates must have been as good a habitat for this pachyderm as any other part of the world. Our knowledge in this respect is very incomplete, and the faith I place in the accuracy of ancient Chinese records has been so much strengthened in the course of my studies that I consider their mention of the rhinoceros in T'iao-chih quite as reliable as if the animal was stated by Ktesias, Pliny, or Strabo to have been seen in Chaldaea. Is not our knowledge of the old fauna of countries much nearer our own civilisation equally doubtful? Who would have looked for rhinoceros' bones in the caves of Mount Libanon near Beirût where they have actually been seen together with the relics of the ure-ox, the bear, the capricorn, the aboriginal goat (Urziege), the gazelle and the antelope? (Fraas, *Drei Monate im Libanon*, Stuttgart, 1876, p. 66.) Brehm (*Thierleben*, 2nd ed., Vol. III, p. 520) mentions a rhinoceros seen by Chardin at Ispahan, though I am not able to say how the animal had got to that place.

I have much pleasure in acknowledging the advice and assistance I have received in passing these sheets through the press from Messrs. H. A. Giles and E. H. Parker.

F. HIRTH.

Shanghai, June 1885.

CONTENTS.

PREFACE	pp.	iii–xii
CONTENTS	„	xiii–xvi
1.—INTRODUCTION	„	1–30.

Dynastic Histories—Daily Chronicles, p. 1; the *Shih-chi* 2; the *Ch'ien-han-shu* and *Hou-han-shu* 3; the Ta-ts'in account in the *Hou-han-shu* referred by some to Roman Empire 4; arguments against this theory; Nestorian Inscription as a witness 5; early editions of the *Hou-han-shu* 7; old Chinese texts compared with western classical texts 9; probable sources of information regarding western countries 10; the *San-kuo-chih* 13; the *Wei-lio* 14; the *Chin-shu, Liang-shu*, etc., 16; the *Wei-shu, Sui-shu* and the two *T'ang-shu* 17; the *Sung-shih* and *Ming-shih* 19; minor publications, cyclopedias, etc.; Ma Tuan-lin 20; the *Chu-fan-chih* 21; conjectures regarding the life of Chao Ju-kua 23; the *T'u-shu-chi-ch'êng* 25; Fa Hsien 26; mistranslations 27; von Richthofen misled by de Guignes 28; necessity for new translations 30.

2.—TRANSLATIONS AND CHINESE TEXT ... ... pp. 31–134.

Translations, Introductory Note 33; Synopsis of Extracts 34.

EXTRACTS.

		Translation:	Chinese Text:
A.	*Shih-chi*	p. 35	p. 97
B.	*Ch'ien-han-shu*	„ „	„ „
C.	*Hou-han-shu*	„ 36	„ „
D.	„	„ 37	„ 98
E.	„	„ 40	„ 99
F.	*Chin-shu*	„ 43	„ 101
G.	*Sung-shu*	„ 45	„ 102
H.	*Liang-shu*	„ 46	„ „
I.	*Wei-shu*	„ 48	„ 103

		Translation:	Chinese Text:
K.	*Chiu-t'ang-shu*	p. 51	p. 104
L.	*Hsin-t'ang-shu*	„ 56	„ 106
M.	Nestorian Inscription	„ 61	„ 108
N.	*Sung-shih*	„ 62	„ „
C.	*Ming-shih*	„ 64	„ 109
P.	*Wei-lio*	„ 67	„ 110
Q.	*Wên-hsien-t'ung-k'ao*	„ 77	„ 114
R.	*Chu-fan-chih*	„ 92	„ 120

Variants 122; Index to Translations or Chinese Text 123.

3.—IDENTIFICATIONS ... ... pp. 135–313.

Ancient route from Central Asia to Ta-ts'in 137; Li-kan and T'iao-chih; Kan Ying's mission 138; An-hsi identified with Parthia 139; the earliest account of An-hsi, *ibid.*; the later (*Hou-han-shu*) account of An-hsi; Hekatompylos 141; Mu-lu identified with Antiochia Margiana 142; T'iao-chih identified with Chaldaea 143; Li-kan T'iao-chih may be the Seleucid empire 146; the "western sea," *ibid.*; the "city of T'iao-chih" on the peninsula in the Chaldaean Lake 147; the kingdom of Hira 149; Yü-lo identified with Hira 151; overland route from Hekatompylos to Chaldaea 153; Acbatana, Ktesiphon, 154; the Euphrates and Tigris; Orchoë 155; "the port of Ta-ts'in," and the periplus of the Erythraean Sea; outlets of Roman trade in the Red Sea; Egyptian and Nabathaean ports, 156; Phœnician dyeing and weaving industries probably diverted the silk trade to Nabathaean ports 159; Aelana, Eceôn-geber; Petra or Rekem 160; Rekem, an old seat of oriental trade and civilisation 161; bifurcation of road at Rekem; Ta-ts'in lies between two seas 163; the terms *hai-hsi* and *hai-tung*, *ibid.*; the sea trade from Chaldaea to Rekem 164; Kan Ying's failure 166; speed of ancient navigation 167; Li-kan mentioned in early records 169; various explanations of the name 170; identified with Rekem 171; early relations between the Chaldaeans and the Nabathaeans and the joint name Li-kan T'iao-chih 172; alleged embassy to China of A.D. 166, p. 173; the silk trade through Parthia interrupted through war and disease 174; the alleged embassy may have been a commercial expedition sent in order to re-open trade with China 175; arrival of the first Ta-ts'in mission in China 176; sea-route to the coast of Pegu; route through Yün-nan 179; Roman trade through the Egyptian ports: the Nile route known in China 180; Alexandria in Egypt 181; sea passage on the Mediterranean from Alexandria to Antioch 182; overland-routes from Babylonia to Syria 184; the term *jao-hai*: ambiguousness of a passage in the *Hou-han-shu* 185; Mesopotamia 187; analysis of routes mentioned in the *Wei-lio* 188; dependent kingdoms 189; Tsê-san near the mouth of the Euphrates 190; Lü-fên may be the region of Osrhoëne 191; the flying bridge mentioned in Chinese records identified with the bridge of Zeugma 192; Ch'ieh-lan (Palmyra?) 193; Ssŭ-t'ao (Sittake?), Ssŭ-fu (Emesa?) 194; Hsien-tu (Damascus?), the "Stony Land" (Arabia Petræa?) 195; the Taurus and other ranges; difficulties in the text of the *Wei-lio* 196; Ssŭ-lo (Seleucia) 197; the city of Madain and the Tigris; the site of T'iao-chih 198; Ch'ih-san is Alexandria, and not Byzantium 199; the Amazons 200; information reaching China through Indian sources 201; the Pygmies 202; the Ichthyophagi 204; the city of Antioch identified as the capital of Ta-ts'in 207; size of Ta-ts'in and Fu-lin territories 214; the number of cities in Ta-ts'in 218; tigers and lions in Ta-ts'in 219; the Ts'ung (hyæna, jackal?) 220; roads and postal arrangements 221; the milliary system: parasangs, Arabian miles and stadia 222; distances of various places quoted 224; profit on trade with India and China 225; articles of trade in ancient China 226; balance of Roman oriental trade 227; Roman import trade in Chinese produce chiefly paid for in kind; glass industry 228; derivation of the word *liu-li* 230; the introduction of glass-making in China 231; glass considered a precious substance in ancient China 233; Syria, the centre of trade in precious stones 234; imitation gems 237; employment of crystal in decorating pillars, walls, etc., 238; crystal and glass confounded 239; the use of gems and precious stones in decorating walls, etc., is a local feature of ancient Syria 240; sources of information regarding precious stones in Chinese literature 241; the "jewel that shines at night" 242; gold, silver, amber 244; gems probably came from the factories of Alexandria 245; corals 246; pearls, textile fabrics 247; purple-dyeing; names of Ta-ts'in piece-goods 248; Chinese modern names for broadcloth and

Russian cloth; Asbestos cloth 249; the Roman Orient was the seat of the principal cloth industries 252; embroidered textures, gold embroideries; Attalicæ vestes 253; textures of several materials (silk, wool, linen, byssus) 254; musters and colours of Ta-ts'in rugs 255; silk industries in Ta-ts'in 256; Chinese silk imported to be unravelled and re-woven 257; Coicæ vestes 259; the water-sheep 260; Col. Yule's and Dr. Bretschneider's views regarding the water-sheep 261; storax (su-ho) a product of Syria 263; frankincense 266; the Henna plant 268; alleged introduction of papyrus rolls from Rome: the paper offered to China is Annam produce 272; realgar, orpiment, copper, gold and silver 275; theriac 276; barter trade in Ceylon: the spirit or devil market 279; analysis of records regarding Fu-lin 283; Mr. Phillips' view of Fu-lin the correct one: the king of Fu-lin an ecclesiastical ruler 284; Fu-lin as the country of the Nestorians 285; old sound of the name Fu-lin 287; the name Fu-lin represents the sound Bethlehem 290; the Jo-shui or Weak Water of Chinese legend-writers 291; the king of Fu-lin, Po-to-li, a Nestorian (?) patriarch 293; the capital of Fu-lin besieged by the Arabs 295; Fu-lin as a Seldjuk province 297; Milikshah, the Seldjuk Sultan; the titles Sultan and Melek 298; Mi-li-i-ling-kai-sa 299; Damask blades and saddlery; Fu-lin physicians: trepanning 301; Chinese embassies alleged to have arrived in Rome 304; the Indian embassy under Constantine; the alleged arrival of Seres under Augustus 305; no official mission was sent from China to the west before Kan Ying; the mission of Ts'in-lun, a merchant from Ta-ts'in 306; linguistic results 309.

I.—GENERAL INDEX ... ... p. 315.

INTRODUCTION.

INTRODUCTION.

It is well known that China is fortunate enough to possess a series of historical works comparing most favourably, in some of its parts, with the historical literature of any nation in the West. Since the Han, each dynasty has had its own history, compiled from its court chronicles or *Jih-li* (日 歷), during the succeeding reigns. The *Jih-li*, lit. "Daily Chronicles," must be considered the prime source of all the information contained in these histories. Whether these latter were impartial in the treatment of historical characters, whether they did not "turn black into white, or right into wrong," would, of course, depend greatly on the entries made in the *Jih-li*, but also upon the neutrality of the historian himself. If the assumption could be justified that a new dynasty, having by conquest gained the ascendency, regarded the succumbing dynasty as the enemy of its cause, we might perhaps expect but scant justice from those who had power over both the Chronicles and the compilers. There is, however, no ground for this suspicion when a lifetime has elapsed between the period described and that during which the history was written. One fact only strikes us as being possibly ascribable to prejudice on the part of historians, and that is, that the last ruler of a dynasty is generally described as either a very foolish or a very wicked character. Our present subject is, fortunately, scarcely affected at all by these considerations; and the less so, as, thanks to the uniform arrangement of these dynastic histories, the information regarding the various foreign nations with which the Court of China had come into contact has been extracted from the *Jih-li* and collected separately in special geographical divisions of the work.

The *Êrh-shih-ssŭ Shih* (二十四史) or "Twenty-four Dynastic Histories," contain in all over 3,000 books, and a European scholar who would think of extracting from them notes on a subject similar to ours, would find this to be a Herculean labour were it not that the methodical mind of the Chinese writers had carefully put aside all he wants into special chapters regarding foreign countries. Thus we find chapters on the Hsiung-nu; on the South-Western barbarians (Man); on the country of Ta-wan, generally identified with the present Ferghana, in the *Shih-chi* of Ssŭ-ma Ch'ien (司馬遷), whose work opens the series of the *Êrh-shih-ssŭ Shih*. Ssŭ-ma Ch'ien[1] did not

---

[1] This historian died about B.C. 85. He was the best known member of a family in which the talent for historiography was as hereditary as musical talent was in the Bach family.

attempt to carry his geographical notes farther than the countries with which China had then come into immediate contact. His successor, Pan Ku (班 固), who, with his sister Chao (昭), compiled the *Ch'ien-han-shu*, *i.e.*, "History of the Former Han Dynasty," and who died A.D. 92, knows considerably more about the countries of Central and Western Asia. His geographical chapters, of which we possess a translation,[1] betray the interest which had been taken in geographical enterprise since the death of Ssū-ma Ch'ien, and which must have naturally been increased in the author from the fact of his being the elder brother of Pan Ch'ao (班 超), the famous military traveller of that period. Pan Ku may have heard of his brother's expedition to the foreign territories in Western or Central Asia but he was no longer alive when Pan Ch'ao returned to China in A.D. 102. This may account for the fact that much of the information for which the Chinese must have been indebted to Pan Ch'ao's last expedition found its way into the *Hou-han-shu*, or "History of the After Han Dynasty," and not into Pan Ku's work.

The *Hou-han-shu*, compiled by Fan Yeh (范曄), of the earlier Sung Dynasty (A.D. 420-477), is the first authority which gives us a certain

---

[1] A. Wylie, in *Journ. Anthropol. Inst.*, "History of the Heung-noo in their Relations with China," Vol. III, pp. 401-452, Vol. V, pp. 41-80; "History of the South-Western Barbarians and Chaou-sēen," ibid., August 1879; "Notes on the Western Regions," ibid., August 1880 and November 1881.

number of details regarding the countries in the extreme west of Asia. The *Hsi-yü-chuan* (西域傳), *i.e.*, "Traditions regarding Western Countries," then became a regular feature in the dynastic histories, and is found under this or some similar designation in most of the subsequent Shih.

The Hsi-yü-chuan of the *Hou-han-shu* contains for the first time a description, consisting of 589 characters, of the westernmost amongst the countries described in Chinese literature previous to the Ming dynasty, the country of Ta-ts'in[1] (大秦國). In this description we find quite a number of facts regarding the situation of the country, its boundaries, capital, people, products, and industries, which would, apart from any collateral information derived from later histories, have furnished a sufficient basis for the identification of the country, had not an unfortunate prejudice at once taken possession of those European sinologues who investigated the subject, for they held to the opinion that Ta-ts'in, being the most powerful country described in the Far West, must necessarily be the Roman Empire in its full extent, with Rome as its capital. This theory has been especially defended by Visdelou and de Guignes, and recently by Bretschneider, Edkins, and von Richthofen. I must confess that I once shared

---

[1] The name is so well known in this orthography that I may be allowed this slight departure from Wade's system of transliteration, otherwise adhered to in this book. It should have been spelt Ta-ch'in. Visdelou spells Tacin.

INTRODUCTION.

that prejudice, and that when, two years ago, I commenced to collect the passages relating to this question, I did so for the purpose of supporting the arguments in favour of Rome and Italy. I soon found, however, that a close examination of the Chinese accounts, instead of substantiating my original views, induced me to abandon them altogether. In these records mention is made of the manufacture of storax, which has been shown by Hanbury to have been at all times confined to the Levant; of the use of crystal (glass) and precious stones as architectural ornaments; of foreign ambassadors being driven by post from the frontier to the capital; of the milliary system of the country, which was based on the division of ten and three; of the dangerous travelling, the roads being infested with tigers and lions, thus compelling wayfarers to resort to caravans. A consideration of this among other testimony forcibly suggested the idea that Ta-ts'in was not Rome itself, but one of its eastern provinces.

It is well known that the Nestorian missionaries, whose existence in China during the 7th and 8th centuries A.D. is witnessed by the celebrated stone inscription found near the city of Hsi-an-fu in A.D. 1625, declare Ta-ts'in to be their native country, and the country in which Christ was born. This clearly points to Syria; and on this evidence several of those who were familiar with the subject have been induced to abandon the idea of Rome being the country sought for, in favour of Syria or a part of Syria (Judæa, Palestine). Paravey,[1] adopted that view in 1836; so, some twenty years later, did. Wylie[2] and Pauthier.[3] But the reasons assigned by these three sinologues for their opinion rest mainly on the Nestorian inscription itself. They would not be valid in the eyes of those who consider this document a forgery as did Voltaire, and recently Renan, neither of whom were sinologues, supported by K. F. Neumann and St. Julien, who were, and might have formed a better opinion on the matter but for their prejudice against those who held the opposite view. I am personally perfectly satisfied as to the genuineness of this inscription, and think it superfluous to add any new arguments to those brought forward by Wylie and Pauthier. What I wish to do, however, is to fill the gap left by those two writers by collecting such of the arguments in favour of the identity of Ta-ts'in with Syria as may be derived from ancient and mediæval Chinese historical literature, altogether apart from the Nestorian inscription.

In giving an outline of my Chinese sources I had arrived at the *Hou-han-shu* of Fan Yeh. The text of this work, as it now appears in recognised editions, was not entirely written by Fan Yeh

---

[1] *Dissertation abrégée sur le Nom antique et hiéroglyphique de la Judée*, Paris, 1836.

[2] "On the Nestorian Tablet of Se-gan-foo," *North-China Herald*, 1854 and 1855; reprinted in the *Shanghai Miscellany*, 1855 and 1856, and in the *Journ. Am. Orient. Soc.*, Vol. V, Art. II, pp. 275-336.

[3] *De l'Authenticité de l'Inscription nestorienne de Si-ngan-fou*, Paris, 1857, and *L'Inscription syro-chinoise de Si-ngan-fou*, etc., Paris, 1858.

himself, the so-called *Chih* (志) being of another hand. The chapters on foreign countries, however, are assigned to him. The emperor Kao-tsung (A.D. 650-683) ordered a commentary to be written,[1] which is still printed with Fan Yeh's text. It must be understood, therefore, that the notes intended to explain certain difficulties in the text are written about two centuries after the latter. As regards the trustworthiness of the tradition we must consider that the *Hou-han-shu* was first printed during the Sung dynasty, and that none but manuscript copies existed for several centuries after the completion of the work. I have not seen the *editio princeps*[2]; but I have had before me one of the oldest editions, printed during the 3rd year of Ch'ien-tao (A.D. 1167)[3] together with the *Ch'ien-han-shu*. It was a magnificent print consisting of 64 volumes in large folio; the characters were of the largest size, printed on white paper, exhibiting, as it were, the characteristic water-mark, viz., the absence of the transparent horizontal lines found in all

---

[1] *Ma Tuan-lin*, ch. 191, p. 17.

[2] Printed in A.D. 1022. The first printed edition was edited by Sun Shih (孫奭), an official of rank in the Kuo-tzŭ-chien (國子監), or Imperial Academy of Learning (for which see Mayers, *The Chinese Government*, No. 247; also Imbault-Huart, *Recueil de Documents sur l'Asie centrale*, p. 47, note 2), and well known as an authority in the interpretation of the classics (see the *Ssŭ-k'u-ch'üan-shu-tsung-mu*, ch. 15, p. 24). He was entrusted with the responsibility of comparing the first printed text with the manuscript on record in the state archives.

[3] With leaves from an edition of the 2nd year of Ch'un-yu A.D. 1242).

Chinese paper manufactured after that period. Each page contained in the margin the name of the copyist whose handwriting had furnished the wood-cutter with the model from which it was printed, and each volume contained the vermilion seal of a former owner, Prince Kuo (果親王). The work was then for sale at the price of 700 taels (£175). I have compared that part of the text which relates to Ta-ts'in with a modern standard edition, and am satisfied that, excepting the omission of a final yeh (也) in one case and the correction of the character shih (師) "legion," into shih (獅) "lion," in the later edition, no change has been made in it since the Sung edition was printed.[1] Previous to the Sung period, as I have already remarked, probably only manuscript copies existed; but although it is impossible for us to trace back the text to its first origin, we have so much less reason to throw doubt on the tradition, as, owing to the distance of the country described, Chinese copyists could have no possible interest in making spurious additions. If any changes have been made in the text they can only be due to oversight; and such errors, though not absolutely excluded from a Chinese book, play a much less

---

[1] Through the kindness of Mr. Hsü Chia-kuang (徐嘉廣), the manager of the Chinese Publishing Company, T'ung-wên-shu-chü (同文書局), which has made a noble start in the reproduction, by means of photolithography, of the best and rare editions of the standard productions of Chinese literature, I am enabled to insert a facsimile copy of the two pages, printed in A.D. 1167 and 1242 respectively, containing the account of Ta-ts'in as appearing in the *Hou-han-shu* edition referred to.

important part in what we may call the "Text-kritik" of ancient Chinese authors than they do in the codices of our Greek and Roman classics. The reasons for this fact are obvious enough. The Chinese scholars to whom at various periods the state archives (which must include official manuscripts of former dynastic histories) were entrusted, were neither as ignorant or careless in what they copied as were the monks having furnished that treasury of Greek and Latin blunders which made philology such a useful science; nor did they have to contend with any difficulties similar to those arising from the fact that the study of classical literature had been dormant for centuries when its revival began in Europe; that the manuscripts then brought to the light were partly mutilated and thence unintelligible; and that the way of writing both Greek and Latin had undergone considerable changes. In China, such works as the *Han-shu* have during no period been entirely lost sight of; they were written in language understood by the educated classes at all times up to the present day; they were first copied in characters hardly different from those in use at present, and at a time when the present mode of writing the so-called Ch'ieh-shu (楷書), which was destined to become the orthodox style for the last fifteen hundred years, had been *en vogue* for more than a century. Wang Yu-chün (王右軍), whose handwriting became the pattern of elegant writing, died in A.D. 379; the characters he wrote are even now daily copied by those who wish to write well, and are as clear to any one conversant with modern literature as are those appearing on the Nestorian inscription of A.D. 781.[1]

The prime source of the text of the Hsi-yü-chuan should, like that of the chronological chapters, been sought for in the daily notes (*Jih-li*) made by the contemporaneous Court chroniclers (Shih-kuan, 史官)[2]. These, like the Tu-ch'a-yüan or Censors of the present dynasty, were allowed to have their own opinion on the actions of their government, and enjoyed the additional advantage of not having to openly remonstrate with their monarch, but keeping their historical records secret. When these were handed to the historian for publication, the monarchs whose actions were described were no longer alive or in power, and their family was excluded from government. Neither the Emperor nor any of his ministers had access to this part of the state archives. Such, at least,

---

[1] Neumann's doubts (*Zeitschr d. deutsch. Morgenl. Gesellsch.* IV, p. 38, seqq., 1850), shared by Renan and Julien, as regards the style of writing used in the Nestorian inscription, which he says is too modern to be credited with a thousand years' age, is utterly baseless. An untrained eye will scarcely notice the difference between that style and the style practised nowadays, and this may be said with regard to any other similiar text of the T'ang as of other former dynasties. A Chinese *connoisseur*, who had never heard of the Nestorian Tablet, and to whom I showed a tracing of it, declared it at once as "T'ang-pi," *i.e.*, written in the style of, and containing the slight varieties adopted during, the T'ang dynasty.

[2] *Ma Tuan-lin*, ch. 51, p. 15, seq.

was the principle on which the daily chronicles were based, whatever transgressions of the rule may have taken place.

The information regarding foreign countries, we must assume, was entered in the chronicles from depositions made by the various foreigners arriving at the Court of China. Whether these were in the possession of credentials from their own monarchs, and if so, whether their credentials were, or could be, properly scrutinized, is an open question. It appears that the Chinese Courts were only too much inclined to look upon the presents brought to the capital as the essential part of a foreign mission, and that foreigners, especially foreigners coming from distant countries and arriving with curiosities of a certain value, were readily received as tribute-bearers adding to the glory of the most powerful empire. The accounts of the countries of Central and Western Asia contained in the dynastic histories exhibit a certain uniformity inasmuch as certain classes of geographical facts are represented in them with some regularity. It looks as if the foreigner, on or before being introduced at Court, was subjected to a kind of cross-examination, and that a uniform set of questions was addressed to him by means of one or several interpreters (ch'ung-i 重譯). Thus, if a merchant came from Ceylon to Annam, accompanied by a Ceylonese interpreter who understood Greek, the trading language of the

Indian ports visited by western merchants,[1] and thence proceeded to Chang-an (or Hsi-an-fu) with an Annamese who was familiar with the language spoken at Ceylon, and another Annamese who understood Chinese, these three interpreters would have been able to mediate at the examination. The questions asked were, perhaps, of the following kind: (1) What is the name of your country? (2) Where is it situated? (3) How many li does it measure? (4) How many cities has it? (5) How many dependent states? (6) How is the capital built? (7) How many inhabitants live in the capital? (8) What are the products of your country? etc., etc., and finally, What else can you tell us about your country? This, I presume, is the origin of the notes in the *Jih-li*, which we must assume to have been the basis of our Hsi-yü accounts. The historical writers did not, of course, confine their work to copying these chronicles. They were men of literary merit and, as masters of the historical style, had to arrange the facts they found simply stated into a sort of narrative. This involved that reports derived from other sources should not be despised. Hence the occasional episode commencing with "yu-yün" (又元), "it is said by some that, etc." The Ta-ts'in account in the *Hou-han-shu* especially, as I have already suggested, may have been enlarged by what was

---

[1] Reinaud, *Relations Politiques et Commerciales de l'Empire Romain avec l'Asie Orientale*, Paris 1863, p. 161.

then known of the results of Kan Ying's enquiries, who had, in A.D. 97, been sent on a mission to Ta-ts'in by his chief, the general Pan Ch'ao. Kan Ying, it will be seen hereafter, only reached T'iao-chih, on the coast of the Persian Gulf, whence a regular traffic by sea was carried on to the Syrian port Aelana, in the Gulf of Akabah, at the head of the Red Sea. Kan Ying, who came into immediate contact with the sailors who were in the habit of making that journey, has certainly had the best opportunity for collecting information regarding the object of his mission. But apart from this, it is very likely that at the Court of Parthia which, prior to the Romans taking possession of Syria again in B.C. 38, *i.e.*, just 135 years before Kan Ying's journey, had ruled over that country for several years, information regarding Ta-ts'in could be easily obtained. This must have been prominently the case with Ta-ts'in products and articles of trade which came to China through Parthian hands.

The *San-kuo-chih* (三國志), "Memoir of the Three Kingdoms," compiled by Ch'ên Shou (陳壽), who died A.D. 297,[1] comprises the history of the three contemporaneous states of Wei, Shu, and Wu. That of Wei contains a meagre account of some of

---

[1] Mayers, *Chinese Reader's Manual*, p. 33. Note the discrepancy in representing Ch'ên Shou's position *vis-à-vis* the Wei dynasty whose part he took, in Mayers (l. c.) and Wylie, *Chinese Literature*, p. 14.

the less distant countries, the incompleteness of which, as that of the whole work, caused the Emperor Wên-ti of the earlier Sung dynasty to order P'ei Sung-chih (裴松之) to compile a new edition, embodying into Ch'ên Shou's text, which had been written but about 130 years prior to himself, whatever pertinent notes he could find in other contemporaneous authors. It is to this fact that we are indebted for the most detailed account we possess of the country of Ta-ts'in. P'ei Sung-chih's edition was submitted to the Emperor, as the Preface shows, in the 6th year of his reign, *i.e.*, A.D. 429. The work from which this geographical account is quoted is the *Wei-lio* (魏略), *i.e.*, "Abridged History of the Wei Dynasty," by *Yü Huan* (魚豢), which must have been written between the end of the Wei dynasty, *i.e.*, A.D. 264, and the time when P'ei Sung-chih prepared his commentary, *i.e.*, previous to A.D. 429. I am not prepared to say whether this work exists at the present day, but I am inclined to believe that it does not, and that we must be contented with the extracts given from it in other works. The catalogue of the Imperial Library at Peking (*Ssŭ-k'u-ch'üan-shu-ts'ung-mu*) is silent upon the subject, whereas works compiled during the Ming dynasty, like the *Pên-ts'ao-kang-mu*, mention the title as that of one of the authorities consulted, and the Lei-shu, or encyclopedical works, quote under its name passages (relating to Ta-ts'in, for instance) which deviate somewhat from the text inserted into P'ei Sung-chih's commentary so as to make me think that another text of the *Wei-lio* has existed not too long ago. This assumption is strengthened in so far as Ma Tuan-lin's account of Ta-ts'in (ch. 339), which is identical with that of the *Wei-lio* in numerous details, contains certain extensions in the text, thus suggesting the idea that either Ma Tuan-lin has had before him a text of the *Wei-lio* more complete than that quoted in the *San-kuo-chih* is at the present day, or that both Ma Tuan-lin and the *Wei-lio* drew from one common source anterior to the latter. I have to say that Ma Tuan-lin here, as in his other geographical accounts, refrains from stating the name of the work from which he has drawn his information. Such as it is, the enlarged edition of the *San-kuo-chih* furnishes information regarding Ta-ts'in which is not only quite as complete, but also quite as old, as that of the Hsi-yü chapter in the *Hou-han-shu*. The *Wei-lio* account abounds with statements not found in the other standard histories, the authors of which apparently despised this compilation, if they were at all aware of its existence; and yet, if we allow for some confusion made in the geography of dependent states, in the directions of the compass, distances, etc., we find no cause to look at these accounts with more suspicion than at any of the other early records. Regarding these we cannot possibly expect greater accuracy in an ancient Chinese work than we find in an ancient western authority, say Ptolemy, especially if we consider what monstrous deviations from reality may be seen in the sketches of India and the whole East in maps as recent even as Edrisi's (A.D. 1154; see Peschel, *Gesch. d. Erdk.*, ed. Ruge, München, 1877, p. 145). The fact of Ma Tuan-lin's text being partly based on either the *Wei-lio* or some other text very similar to that of the *Wei-lio* shows that Chinese critics of high reputation did not always follow the example set by court historians.

The next history in the Chinese standard list is the *Chin-shu* (晉書), compiled by Fang Ch'iao (房喬), who died A.D. 648. Its Ta-ts'in account is mainly a reproduction of what we have learned in the *Hou-han-shu;* nor do we find much novel information in the following Shih, the *Sung-shu* (宋書), which is probably a century older than the former, since its author Shên Yo (沈約) died in A.D. 513. The *Nan-ch'i-shu* (南齊書) contains a short account of foreign countries which does not, however, extend as far as Ta-ts'in. The same remark would apply to the *Liang-shu* (梁書), compiled early during the 7th century A.D., but for a few pertinent notes in a description of India (Chung T'ien-chu) and a short account of the reception of a merchant from Ta-ts'in at the court of Sun-ch'üan, the founder of the Wu dynasty, in A.D. 226. I have searched for further details regarding this traveller in the older *History of Wu* contained in the *San-kuo-chih*, but without result. In going through the minor histories I found the first account of some value in the *Wei-shu* (魏書), the history of the northern Wei dynasty (A.D. 386–556). Although this account repeats many of the statements of the *Hou-han-shu* and the *Wei-lio*, in accordance with the Chinese method observed up to the present day, by which all that was recognized as true hundreds of years ago must be true for ever, and thus may be quoted without further scrutiny, there are in it signs of independent information having been received in China since those earlier accounts were compiled. The history of the same dynasty (the northern Wei) is the subject of a later work, the *Pei-shih* (北史), which contains an almost literal reproduction of what we find in the *Wei-shu*. Of the histories preceding the *Pei-shih* I merely mention the *Sui-shu* (隋書), embracing the period A.D. 581–617, because I found in it the first trace of the new name under which the country of Ta-ts'in was known thereafter, viz., Fu-lin (拂菻)[1]. There is no description in this book of either Ta-ts'in or Fu-lin, but in an account of Persia (ch. 83), I found it stated that "Fu-lin is 4,500 li north-west of that country." The next important account is that of the *Ch'iu T'ang-shu* (舊唐書), *i.e.*, the "Old History

---

[1] The *Ta-t'ang-hsi-yü-chi* (translated by Julien in *Mémoires de Hiouen Thsang*, see Livre XI, p. 180) ch 11, p. 23, mentions the kingdom of Fu-lin (拂懍), which is merely another way of writing that name. The work referred to was completed in A.D. 646.

of the T'ang dynasty," which work was remodelled during the 11th century and republished under the name *Hsin T'ang-shu* (新唐書) or "New History of the T'ang dynasty." The account of Fu-lin—for under this name we have now to look for the ancient Ta-ts'in—contained in the latter supplements the former, and *vice versâ*, although many of the facts stated are identical apart from the difference in the style of language used in describing them. It may look pedantic to lay stress on two almost identical reports clothed in different language, but it is, in reality, quite necessary to make the most out of every Chinese sentence we can hunt up in ancient authors relating to one and the same fact. By pursuing this method we not only glean a number of minor facts which may be contained in one account while being omitted in the other, but we also succeed in overcoming many of the difficulties of the text. Many passages would be quite unintelligible to European and Chinese scholars alike, if we did not find the key for their correct meaning in parallel sentences conveying the same idea in different words. I could mention numerous instances of mistakes made in the translations relating to Ta-ts'in and Fu-lin by de Guignes, Visdelou, Pauthier and others, which they would perhaps have avoided had they adopted the method of eliminating the meaning of difficult passages by comparison with the corresponding passages in other accounts. This remark refers especially to the accounts of Fu-lin· contained in the Old and the New History of the T'ang dynasty. The *Sung-shih* (宋史), the work of T'ŏ-t'o (脫脫), a Chinese author of Mongol birth, is known amongst the literati for its want of accuracy; and we have to read its account of Fu-lin with a certain caution. This account is, however, otherwise very important to us, as it contains none but independent information, and does not, like the *T'ang-shu*, fall back on the tradition of former histories, thus leaving us entirely in doubt whether the facts stated refer to the period of the dynasty (T'ang) or to some former epoch lying 500 years farther back. The final account in the Twenty-four Shih is that in the *Ming Shih* 明史. Its main features are the tenor of a manifesto handed by the Emperor T'ai-tsu to a merchant from Fu-lin for transmission to his sovereign, and the mention of the first modern Christian missionary, Matthaeus Ricci, having arrived in China.

I am not aware of many descriptions of either Ta-ts'in or Fu-lin which may be considered authorities, having appeared apart from those contained in the twenty-four dynastic histories. The Nestorian inscription (A.D. 781) contains an account of Ta-ts'in, drawn up in truly lapidary style; and the various encyclopedical works (Leishu) frequently allude to the country in quotations derived from minor works which are either lost, or not procurable, or forming part of a Ts'ung-shu or "Collection of Reprints," such as the *Wu-shih-wai-kuo-chuan*, 吳時外國傳 ("Account of Foreign Countries at the Time of Wu,"— 3rd century A.D.), or the *Nan-fang-ts'ao-mu-chuang* 南方草木狀, a work on the plants, etc., of southern countries.

Foremost amongst the Cyclopedias (though not classed with the Lei-shu by the Chinese) is the *Wên-hsien-t'ung-k'ao* (文獻通考), the celebrated work of Ma Tuan-lin. Its chapters regarding foreign countries (ch. 324, seqq.) may be interesting enough to a Chinese reader who wishes to learn some of the wonderful tales told at one time or another of each country enumerated, but they are of little use to the critical student. Whatever the merits of this much-admired[1] compilation may be otherwise, its geographical section does not satisfy the foreign reader, and we cannot but wonder how a Chinese scholar like Rémusat could find no better authorities for his subject,[2] although he had spent

---

[1] *Vide* Rémusat's panegyric "Ma Touan-lin, savant Chinois" in *Nouv. Mélanges Asiatiques*, Vol. II, p. 166.

[2] "Sur quelques Peuples du Tibet et de la Boukharie, tiré de l ouvrage de Ma Touan-lin, et traduit du Chinois." *Nouv. Mélanges Asiatiques*, Vol. I, p. 186. The Marquis d'Hervey de St. Denys has lately commenced translating the geographical portion of Ma Touan-lin's work under the title "*Ethnographie des peuples étrangers à la Chine,—ouvrage composé au XIIIe siècle de notre ère par Ma Touan-lin, traduit pour la première fois du Chinois avec un commentaire perpetuel.*" I regret not having seen this work.

several years in studying it, according to his own saying. Like nearly all the material contained in the *Wên-hsien-t'ung-k'ao*, the notices of foreign countries, including accounts of Ta-ts'in and of Fu-lin, are compiled from the histories; but the author generally leaves us entirely in the dark as to the authority from which his text is drawn, which is, indeed, a great shortcoming to everyone anxious to know in what century it was written. A great part of Ma Tuan-lin's remarks anent Ta-ts'in is apparently derived from the *Wei-lio* or from some other records, perhaps even older than the *Wei-lio* but based on the same information as the latter, whereas other parts remind again of the *Hou-han-shu*. The wording of his text is often slightly altered from that of the text he copies as it may be traced in the literature now existing; it therefore serves in many cases as a sort of commentary to the texts of ancient records, for, as I have already intimated, many of the linguistic difficulties of the latter, which at first sight look quite unsurmountable, disappear if we see the same idea expressed in different words.

Some valuable information is contained in the *Chu-fan-chih* (諸番志), an account of various foreign countries, by Chao Ju-kua (趙汝适) of the Sung dynasty. I copied the text of the Fu-lin portion from an edition contained in a "collection of reprints" entitled *Hsiao-chin-chi-yüan* (學津討原). It is, no doubt, the identical text of which the extract quoted in Huc's

Le Christianisme en Chine, Vol. I, p. 74, and Pauthier's, pp. 51 to 53, in his work *De l'Authenticité de l'Inscription nestorienne*, etc., were meant to contain a translation. I cannot, as far as Ta-ts'in is concerned, agree with the Imperial Catalogue (*Ssŭ-k'u-ch'üan-shu-tsung-mu*, ch. 71, p. 9) in assuming that Chao Ju-kua collected all his information from personal inquiry while being employed as an official in the salt gabel in the province of Fu-kien. A superficial comparison of the *Chu-fan-chih* with what has been said about Ta-ts'in and Fu-lin in former records will show that by far the greater part of Ju-kua's notes is derived from the Han and T'ang records.[1] On the other hand, it must be admitted that certain notes look like independent statements, inasmuch as they cannot be discovered in any previous work. But even these we may suspect to have been copied from older books which may not

---

[1] The passages R 6, 10 to 15, and 20, 21 and 23 (*see* the translation following), for instance, are clearly derived from the *Hou-han-shu;* and the information contained in R 7, 27 and 31 can be easily traced to the *T'ang-shu* accounts. The author of the review of the *Chu-fan-chih* contained in the Imperial Catalogue, says himself that, owing to the great distance of Ta-ts'in and T'ien-chu, it should be assumed that Ju-kua did not come into immediate contact with natives of those countries; but he draws attention to a quotation from the *Ts'ê-fu-yüan-kuei* (冊府元龜, completed A.D. 1013, *see* Wylie, p. 147), according to which the adherents of the Yao (祆) religion, styled Ta-ts'in-shih (大秦寺, church of Ta-ts'in) during the T'ang period, are identical with the Hai-liao (海獠, lit. sea-hunters, sea-tribes) mentioned in the *T'ing-shih* (桯史, *see* Wylie, p. 158). This would insinuate that a foreign tribe on the coast of Kuang-tung, called Hai-liao, was in the possession of traditions regarding its native country, Ta-ts'in or Fu-lin.

exist now but may have been consulted by Chao Ju-kua. We possess no direct record as to the period during which this author lived or wrote, but in the *Imperial Catalogue*, l. c., reference is made to a genealogical table in the *Sung-shih*, which contains his name, and from which it appears that he was a descendant from a member of the Imperial family of the Sung, whose real name was Chao (趙), just as Hohenzollern is the name of the kings of Prussia. and that he was born after the eighth generation dating from T'ai-tsung, *i.e.*, after the middle of the twelfth century. The "Catalogue" further states that, foreign ships being allowed to trade at the southern ports under the southern Sung dynasty, his position as Inspector of Salt Gabel brought him into frequent contact with foreigners who supplied him with accounts of the countries they came from. The title given him was that of Shih-po (市舶), which may be translated by "Superintendent of Sea Trade." The *Hsü-wên-hsien-t'ung-k'ao* (續文獻通考), the continuation of Ma Tuan-lin's work, quoted in the *Yüan-chien-lei-han*, ch. 110, p. 33, states that the title Shih-po, in connection with the superintendence of salt and revenue matters, was first used in Fu-kien during the 14th year of Chih-yüan, and was abolished again in order to be replaced by the title Yen-yün-ssŭ, the term used at the present day for a Collector of Salt Taxes, in the 24th year of the same period. This may possibly give us a clue as to the time when Chao Ju-kua collected the information for his work; for the time during which alone the post said to have been held by him existed in Fu-kien, extends from A.D. 1277 to 1287. Both time and locality seem to be in favour of the theory here advanced, of the principal information collected with regard to foreign countries during the Sung and Yüan period originating there and then. An official of the class described would most probably have been stationed at the port of Chinchew or Ch'üan-chou-fu, for some time the provincial capital. Whether this city or Phillips' Geh-kong was the Zayton of Marco Polo's days (see *J. R. G. S.* XLIV, p. 97, seqq.), there seems to be evidence that just during the ten years A.D. 1277 to 1287,- the period when, owing to the change of dynasties and the weakness resulting from warfare in the interior the exclusive policy of the government could not be carried on with the usual energy,- foreign trade was flourishing there more than at other times. I quote from Yule's reply to Phillips' "Notices of Southern Mangi" in *J. R. G. S.*, l. c., p. 107:

"In 1282, envoys arrived from sundry kings of India, including one from Kulang, *i.e.*, Coilom of Polo, or Quilon (*Gaubil*, p. 196)."

"In 1286, vessels arrived at T'swanchau from more than 90 foreign states, the names of several of which that are given belong to Southern and Western India (*Gaubil*, p. 205)."

Marco Polo's visit to that neighbourhood must have taken place soon after that period. The ports of Fu-kien were then, however, no longer in the hands of the Sung, who were driven by the advancing Mongols into the Kuang-tung province; and if the two facts, viz., that of Ju-kua's having been a member of the Sung family, and that of his having occupied the post referred to, can be proved, there is room for the suspicion that he may have maintained his position after the fall of his dynasty by voluntarily submitting to the Mongol enemy.

According to the "Catalogue," the chapters regarding foreign countries in the *Sung-shih* are partly based on the information contained in the *Chu-fan-chih*, as the latter work contained more geographical detail than the court archives.

The great cyclopedia in 5,000 volumes, the *T'u-shu-chi-ch'êng*,[1] in its account of Ta-ts'in and

---

[1] Its complete title is *Ch'in-ting-ku-chin-t'u-shu-chi-ch'êng* (欽定古今圖書集成). Some valuable notes regarding it will be found in Mayers, "Bibliography of the Chinese Imperial Collections of Literature," in *China Review*, Vol. VI, p. 218 seqq. Collectors of Chinese books will be glad to hear that a new edition of this gigantic work, a copy of which was bought for the Chinese library of the British Museum in 1877, is about to be published by the T'ung-wên-shu-chü referred to on p. 8. It will be a facsimile reproduction in the size of 20 characters per column of 5⅝ ins. Engl., *i.e.*, about three quarters the size of the original, and the price fixed for the complete work (Shanghai Taels 360=£90) seems exceedingly low if we consider that as much as Tls. 14,000 or £3,500 sterling has been asked for a complete copy (cf. Mayers, *l. c.*, p. 222). The *T'u-shu-chi-ch'êng* is supposed to embrace all the standard works of Chinese literature of all ages up to the time of its being compiled, *i.e.*, the end of the 17th century.

Fu-lin, quotes about all that may be found with regard to the subject in the standard histories and other works, and, by naming the work from which each quotation is derived, becomes infinitely more useful than Ma Tuan-lin's compilation, whose labours, as well as all the cyclopedias published up to the time of K'ang-hsi, appear to be almost superseded by this work. Next to collecting one's-self the original passages regarding any special subject, the study of this exhaustive digest will probably be found the most useful source of information; and it seems that those who have access to the *T'u-shu-chi-ch'êng* need not trouble much about the minor compilations. If such works as Ma Tuan-lin's, the *Yüan-chien-lei-han*, etc., yet play a conspicuous part in sinological research, it is because the larger work has not been accessible.

I have just been allowed to open the volume containing the chapter that interests me (*Ta-ts'in-pu-hui-k'ao*, 大秦部彙考, in ch. 60 of section XIII in the 12th division of the General Index, which alone consists of 20 volumes), and was agreeably surprised to find nearly all the passages regarding my subject, the collecting of which had claimed a considerable part of my time and attention, placed together in chronological order.

The compiler of the Ta-ts'in account in the *T'u-shu-chi-ch'êng* quotes from Fa Hsien's *Fu-kuo-chi*[1] details regarding a country called Ta-ch'in (達親). In applying this name to our Ta-ts'in,

---
[1] Cf. Giles, *Record of the Buddhistic Kingdoms*, ch. XXXV, p. 86.

he is apparently led by the identity in sound and no other motive, for the information embodied in this chapter of the Buddhistic traveller is as heterogeneous with regard to the general tradition as possible. If we cannot explain the account of "a monastery of the former Buddha Chia-yeh, made by hollowing out a great rock," as a fanciful description of buildings seen in the city of Petra, there will be little hope of connecting Fa Hsien's Ta-ch'in with that of the historical writers.

I have collected from the various historical works above referred to all the accounts of Ta-ts'in and Fu-lin written during the period extending from the Former Han dynasty up to that of the Ming, *i.e.*, between the first and seventeenth centuries A.D., and also a few other texts which seemed necessary in order to understand certain clues as to the route leading to that country at certain periods. I now offer a set of translations of all these accounts, the greater part of which is translate *pour la première fois*, whereas those which hab been previously translated by others have been thoroughly revised, and in some passages, sadly misunderstood by former translators, may pass as independent versions altogether. If these notes were written for linguistic purposes, the explanation of errors committed by others would furnish a useful grammatical chapter, but as grammar is, at present, not the object in view, I shall confine myself to drawing attention to such misunderstandings in the Chinese text which may possibly be used as arguments in the identification of the country. The following example will show the necessity of such a procedure. The description of Ta-ts'in as given by von Richthofen (*China*, Vol. I, p. 473) contains the following words: "Die Hauptstadt hat 100 *li* im Umfang und enthält zehn Paläste, die je 10 *li* von einander entfernt sind, *am Wasser liegen und von Säulen getragen werden.*" Von Richthofen borrows this passage from de Guignes' *Histoire Générale des Huns* [Vol. I, Part II, p. LXXVIII], who translates from the *Hou-han-shu* (cf. the passages E 13 to 15 of my translation): "La capitale a 100 *li* de circonférence. Il y a cinq palais à 10 *li* de distance l'un de l'autre. *Ils sont sur le bord de l'eau et soutenus sur des colonnes.*" The Chinese text reads: 宮室皆以水精爲柱 (Kung-shih chieh i shui-ching wei chu), which means that "in the palaces columns are made with crystal." De Guignes' translation is one out of many mistakes he has committed. The reason why it interests us is not the desire to see errors exposed, but that von Richthofen has been grossly misguided by it. The celebrated traveller conjectures that the authority from which de Guignes translated (the Han Annals) is probably of later origin than we usually assume it to be, because the mention made of palaces borne by columns and bordering on the waterside answers better a description of Constantinople than one of Rome.¹ Such a blunder as the one made by de Guignes in the passage referred to would be unpardonable to anyone who has studied Chinese in the days of Schott, Julien, Zottoli, and von der Gabelentz; but we should not forget that when de Guignes' work appeared (A.D. 1756) even the elementary rules of Chinese composition were a mystery to most of the European scholars, whose translations were often nothing better than a sort of mosaic-work, badly cemented by their imagination; translations of Chinese characters, not of Chinese sentences. I have selected the above example as a warning to writers who, not knowing Chinese themselves, may wish to make use of the translations of others. Most of the translations made previous to Rémusat have to be used with great caution, and what even such of our modern *dilettanti* may bring about who persistently neglect to make use of the grammatical helps furnished by others, could be demonstrated in almost every translation of Pauthier's, whose admirable zeal in all matters connected with oriental research was coupled with a strange incomprehension in linguistic questions. I shall refrain from adding to Julien's criticisms, though a good collection of strange renderings may be made from Pauthier's two works pertaining to our subject,² leaving it

---

¹ "Es liegt vielleicht zum Theil ein Irrthum betreffs des Alters der Quelle vor, der die Stelle entnommen ist; denn die Nachricht von den säulengetragenen, am Wasser liegenden Palästen passt besser auf Constantinopel als auf Rom." *See* l. c., p. 473, note.

² See note 3 on p. 6.

to those interested in the linguistic features of each difficulty to draw comparisons if they care to do so. I may, however, be allowed to say that new translations based on the comparative study of various texts seemed to me an absolute necessity to anyone who wished to arrive at an opinion with regard to Ta-ts'in, and that the existence of certain French versions by de Guignes, Visdelou (by far the best), and Pauthier, though carefully examined, has been of very little use to me as a basis. I have endeavoured to do my best in rendering literally; yet, in many cases I have to claim the indulgence of those who, after me, may find time and inclination to subject the difficult parts of these texts to a more thorough scrutiny than I have been able to do. I have had the courage to work my way through some rather obscure passages of ancient Chinese. I must confess that I did not allow myself to be detained too long by these difficulties; but I possess the boldness, too, not possessed by all translators from the Chinese, to supply my critics with the Chinese text itself. I shall be glad to be corrected if found wrong, as I shall be open to every argument against my own views if it helps to reveal the truth.

TRANSLATIONS

AND

CHINESE TEXT.

TRANSLATIONS.

In order to allow of the information contained in these translations being readily analysed, I have placed above every portion of it, as well as above each of the corresponding portions of the Chinese text following, a Roman capital letter, and have numbered the paragraphs in each section. In quoting, capital letters will have the meaning described hereafter.

Most of the Dynastic Histories are divided into three sections: the *ti-chi* (帝紀) or "annals of the emperors," the *chih* (志) or "statistical essays," and the *chuan* (傳) or *lieh-chuan* (列傳) or "biographical, ethnographical, etc., notices" (cf. Wylie, *Chinese Literature*, p. 12). Each of these sub-divisions has its own series of numbers attached to the various chapters or *chüan* (卷), so that a chüan may be quoted by two numbers, *viz.*, the current number it holds in the complete work, and the series number of the sub-division it belongs to. As anyone who is not aware of this distinction must find it difficult to work his way in these bulky histories, I have, in the following list, inserted both the general number (chüan=ch.) and that of the chuan or lieh-chuan.

A=*Shih-chi* 史記, ch. 123: lieh-chuan, 63.
B=*Ch'ien-han-shu* 前漢書, ch. 96A: chuan, 66A.
C=*Hou-han-shu* 後漢書, ch. 86: chuan, 76.
D=ibid. ch. 88: chuan, 78: T'iao-chih and An-hsi.
E=ibid. ch. 88: chuan, 78: Ta-ts'in.
F=*Chin-shu* 晉書, ch. 97: lieh-chuan, 67.
G=*Sung-shu* 宋書, ch. 97: lieh-chuan, 57.
H=*Liang-shu* 梁書, ch. 54: lieh-chuan, 48.
I=*Wei-shu* 魏書, ch. 102: lieh-chuan, 90.
K=*Chiu-t'ang-shu* 舊唐書, ch. 198: lieh-chuan, 148.
L=*Hsin-t'ang-shu* 新唐書, ch. 221: lieh-chuan, 146B.
M=Extract from the Nestorian inscription.
N=*Sung-shih* 宋史, ch. 490: lieh-chuan, 249.
O=*Ming-shih* 明史, ch. 326: lieh-chuan: 214.
P=*Wei-lio* 魏畧, quoted in *San-kuo-chih* 三國志, ch. 30.
Q=Ma Tuan-lin's *Wên-hsien-t'ung-k'ao* 文獻通考, ch. 339.
R=*Chu-fan-chih*, 諸審志, Art. Ta-ts'in:

A.

(*Shih-chi*, written about B.C. 91; ch. 123: Ta-wan.)

[1] When the first embassy was sent from China to An-hsi [Parthia], the king of An-hsi [Parthia] ordered twenty thousand cavalry to meet them on the eastern frontier. [2] The eastern frontier was several thousand li distant from the king's capital. [3] Proceeding to the north one came[1] across several tens of cities, with very many inhabitants, allied to that country. [4] After the Chinese embassy had returned they sent forth an embassy to follow the Chinese embassy to come and see the extent and greatness of the Chinese Empire. [5] They offered to the Chinese court large birds'-eggs, and jugglers from Li-kan.

B.

(*Ch'ien-han-shu*, written about A.D. 90, and embracing facts coming within the period B.C. 206 to A.D. 25; ch. 96A, Hsi-yü-chuan: An-hsi-kuo.[2])

---

[1] 行北至 (Hsing-pei-chih). Julien, *Histoire de la vie de Hiouen-thsang*, Préface, p. XXXVII, seq., makes an artificial distinction in the translation of the two words 行 *hsing* and 至 *chih*, on the ground of a note found in an epilogue appended to the text of the *Ta-t'ang-hsi-yü-chi* (ch. 12, p. 29), by which the former (hsing) is used in the sense of "to arrive at," if the traveller has visited the place referred to in person, whereas the latter (chih) insinuates that the traveller, in his account, speaks of localities he knows merely from hearsay. This rule is certainly of the greatest importance in the interpretations of Hsüan-chuang's Journeys, but it would be useless to make the distinction in these translations.

[2] Cf. Wylie's translation in "Notes on the Western Regions," *Journ. Anthropol. Inst.*, Aug. 1880.

[1] When the emperor Wu-ti [B.C. 140–86] first sent an embassy to An-hsi [Parthia], the king ordered a general to meet him on the eastern frontier with twenty thousand cavalry. [2] The eastern frontier was several thousand li distant from the king's capital. [3] Proceeding to the north one came across several tens of cities, the inhabitants of which were allied with that country. [4] As they sent forth an embassy to follow the Chinese embassy, ·they came to see the country of China. [5] They offered to the Chinese court large birds'-eggs, and jugglers from Li-kan, at which His Majesty was highly pleased.

C.

(*Hou-han-shu*, partly written during the 5th century A.D., and embracing the period A.D. 25 to 220, ch. 86 : Nan-man-hsi-nan-i.)

[1] During the 9th year [of Yung-yüan, A.D. 97] the barbarian tribes [man] outside the frontier and the king of the country of Shan,[1] named Yung-yu-tiao, sent twofold interpreters, and was endowed with state jewels. Ho-ti [the emperor, A.D. 89 to 106] conferred a golden seal with a purple ribbon, and the small chiefs were granted seals, ribbons, and money. - - -
[2] During the 1st year of Yung-ning [=A.D. 120]

---

[1] So pronounced and not Tan ; *see* scholion in the Chinese text and *Ma Tuan-lin*, ch. 330, p. 11. The *Tung-kuan-chi* (東 觀 記), speaking of the same country, calls it Shan (撣); the old *Yün-nan-t'ung-chih* prints 揮 Tan like the *Hou-han-shu*, but Ma Tuan-lin's text (l. c.) has 樿 Chan with the gloss referred to.

the king of the country of Shan, named Yung-yu-tiao, again sent an embassy who, being received to His Majesty's presence, offered musicians and jugglers. The latter could conjure, spit fire, bind and release their limbs without assistance [? cf. P 21], change the heads of cows and horses, and were clever at dancing with up to a thousand balls. [3] They said themselves: "We are men from the west of the sea; the west of the sea is the same as Ta-ts'in. In the south-west of the country of Shan one passes through to Ta-ts'in."[1] [4] At the beginning of the following year they played music at court with [or "before"] An-ti [the emperor, A.D. 107 to 126], when Yung-yu-tiao was invested as a Ta-tu-wei [tributary prince?] of the Han empire by being granted a seal and a ribbon with gold and silver silk embroidered emblems, every one of which had its own meaning.

D.

(*Hou-han-shu*, ch. 88: Hsi-yü-chuan, account of the countries of T'iao-chih and An-hsi.[2])

[1] The city of the country of T'iao-chih is situated on a hill [island, or peninsula, *shan*]; [2] its circumference is over forty li [3] and it

---

[1] This passage has probably led to the mistaken opinion of later Chinese writers that Shan was a country in the north-east of Ta-ts'in. See Porter Smith, *Vocabulary of Chinese Proper Names*, p. 53, s. v. Tan-kwoh.

[2] For translations of 1 to 9, considerably deviating from the present version, see Neumann, *Asiat. Studien*, p. 157, and Rémusat, *Nouv. Mél. Asiat.*, I, p. 215.

borders on the western sea. [4] The waters of the sea crookedly surround it. [5] In the south, [east], and north-east, the road is cut off; only in the north-west there is access to it by means of a land-road. [6] The country is hot and low.¹ [7] It produces lions, rhinoceros, fêng-niu [Zebu, Bos indicus²], peacocks, and large birds [ostriches?] whose eggs are like urns. [8] If you turn to the north and then towards the east again go on horseback some sixty days, you come to An-hsi [Parthia], [9] to which afterwards it became subject as a vassal state under a military governor who had control of all the small cities.

[10] The country of An-hsi [Parthia] has its residence at the city of Ho-tu, [11] it is 25,000 li distant from Lo-yang. [12] In the north it bounds on K'ang-chü, and in the south, on Wu-i-shan-li. [13] The size of the country is several thousand li. [14] There are several hundred small cities with a vast number of inhabitants and soldiers. [15] On its eastern frontier is the city of Mu-lu, which is called Little An-hsi [Parthia Minor]. [16] It is

---

¹ 溼 (shih). This character is usually translated by "damp," but in this instance I am inclined to be guided by the *Êrh-ya*, where it is explained by 陂下者曰溼, pei-hsia-chê-yüeh-shih: "a bank, being low, is called shih," to which a scholiast adds: 下平曰隰, hsia-p'ing yüeh hsi, "low and flat it is called hsi;" see *Êrh-ya*, 釋地 ch. 9. Of a country 3,000 li south-east of T'ien-chu, the *Wei-lio* account, appended to ch. 30 of the *San-kuo-chih*, says that, 其地卑溼暑熱 ch'i-ti-pei-shih-shu-jê, "this country is low and hot." This is the parallel phrase for shih-shu in the above sentence, and shows clearly that its translation should be in accordance with the explanation of the *Êrh-ya*.

² *See* Bretschneider in *Notes and Queries*, Vol. IV., p. 60.

20,000 li distant from Lo-yang. [17] In the first year of Chang-ho, of the Emperor Chang-ti [=A.D. 87], they sent an embassy offering lions and fu-pa. [18] The fu-pa has the shape of a lin (unicorn), but has no horn. [19] In the 9th year of Yung-yüan of Ho-ti [=A.D. 97] the tu-hu (general) Pan Ch'ao sent Kan-ying as an ambassador to Ta-ts'in, who arrived in T'iao-chih, on the coast of the great sea. [20] When about to take his passage across the sea, the sailors of the western frontier of An-hsi [Parthia] told Kan-ying: "The sea is vast and great; with favourable winds it is possible to cross within three months; but if you meet slow winds, it may also take you two years. It is for this reason that those who go to sea take on board a supply of three years' provisions. There is something in the sea which is apt to make man home-sick, and several have thus lost their lives." When Kan-ying heard this, he stopped. [21] In the 13th year [A.D. 101] the king of An-hsi [Parthia], Man-k'ü, again offered as tribute lions and large birds from T'iao-chih [ostriches], which henceforth were named An-hsi-chiao [Parthian birds]. [22] From An-hsi [Parthia] you go west 3,400 li to the country of A-man; from A-man you go west 3,600 li to the country of Ssŭ-pin; from Ssŭ-pin you go south, crossing a river [or by river], and again south-west to the country of Yü-lo, 960 li, the extreme west frontier of An-hsi; from here you travel south by sea, and so reach Ta-ts'in.

[23] In this country there are many of the precious and rare things of the western sea.

E.

(*Hou-hân-shu*, ch. 88: Hsi-yü-chuan,—the first principal account of Ta-t'sin.[1])

[1] The country of Ta-ts'in is also called Li-chien (Li-kin) and, as being situated on the western part of the sea, Hai-hsi-kuo [*i.e*, "country of the western part of the sea"]. [2] Its territory amounts to several thousand li; [3] it contains over four hundred cities, [4] and of dependent states there are several times ten. [5] The defences of cities are made of stone. [6] The postal stations and mile-stones on the roads are covered with plaster. [7] There are pine and cypress trees and all kinds of other trees and plants. [8] The people are much bent on agriculture, and practice the planting of trees and the rearing of silk-worms. [9] They cut the hair of their heads, [10] wear embroidered clothing, [11] and drive in small carriages covered with white canopies; [12] when going in or out they beat drums, and hoist flags, banners, and pennants. [13] The precincts of the walled city in which they live measure over a hundred li in circumference. [14] In the city there are five palaces, ten li distant from each other. [15] In the palace buildings they use crystal to make pillars; vessels

---

[1] Cf. translations by Visdelou in d'Herbelot's *Bibl. Orient.*, IV, p. 390, seqq.; and de Guignes, *Hist. des Huns*, Vol. II, p. LXVIII, seqq.

used in taking meals are also so made. [16] The king goes to one palace a day to hear cases. After five days he has completed his round. [17] As a rule, they let a man with a bag follow the king's carriage. Those who have some matter to submit, throw a petition into the bag. When the king arrives at the palace, he examines into the rights and wrongs of the matter. [18] The official documents are under the control of thirty-six chiang (generals?) who conjointly discuss government affairs. [19] Their kings are not permanent rulers, but they appoint men of merit. [20] When a severe calamity visits the country, or untimely rain-storms, the king is deposed and replaced by another. The one relieved from his duties submits to his degradation without a murmur. [21] The inhabitants of that country are tall and well-proportioned, somewhat like the Chinese, whence they are called Ta-ts'in. [22] The country contains much gold, silver, and rare precious stones, especially the "jewel that shines at night," "the moonshine pearl," the hsieh-chi-hsi,[1] corals, amber, glass, lang-kan [a kind of coral], chu-tan [cinnabar?], green jadestone [ching-pi], gold-embroidered rugs and thin silk-cloth of various colours. [23] They make gold-coloured cloth[1] and asbestos cloth. [24] They further have "fine cloth," also called Shui-yang-ts'ui [*i.e.*, down of the water-sheep]; it is made from the cocoons of wild silk-worms. [25] They collect all kinds of fragrant substances, the juice

---

Cf. Q 19, note.   [2] Cf. P 49^{00}: Chin-t'u-pu.

of which they boil into su-ho (storax). [26] All the rare gems of other foreign countries come from there. [27] They make coins of gold and silver. Ten units of silver are worth one of gold. [28] They traffic by sea with An-hsi [Parthia] and T'ien-chu [India], the profit of which trade is ten-fold. [29] They are honest in their transactions, and there are no double prices. [30] Cereals are always cheap. The budget is based on a wellfilled treasury. [31] When the embassies of neighbouring countries come to their frontier, they are driven by post to the capital, and, on arrival, are presented with golden money. [32] Their kings always desired to send embassies to China, but the An-hsi [Parthians] wished to carry on trade with them in Chinese silks, and it is for this reason that they were cut off from communication. [33] This lasted till the ninth year of the Yen-hsi period during the emperor Huan-ti's reign [=A.D. 166] when the king of Ta-ts'in, An-tun, sent an embassy who, from the frontier of Jih-nan [Annam] offered ivory, rhinoceros horns, and tortoise shell.[1] From that time dates the [direct] intercourse with this country. The list of their tribute contained no jewels whatever, which fact throws doubt on the tradition. [34] It is said by some that in the west of this country there is the

---

[1] In the chronological part of the *Hou-han-shu* [the Ti-hou-chi 帝后紀, ch. 7, p. 4], the fact is recorded under the 9th month of that year (October A.D. 166). It appears that the journey from Ta-ts'in to Annam was performed during the summer months, when south-western winds prevail in those parts.

Jo-shui ["weak water"] and the Liu-sha ["flying sands, desert"] near the residence of the Hsi-wang-mu ["mother of the western king"], where the sun sets. [35] The [Ch'ien]-han-shu says: "From T'iao-chih west, going over 200 days, one is near the place where the sun sets"; this does not agree with the present book. [36] Former embassies from China all returned from Wu-i; there were none who came as far as T'iao-chih. [37] It is further said that, coming from the land-road of An-hsi [Parthia], you make a round at sea and, taking a northern turn, come out from the western part of the sea, whence you proceed to Ta-ts'in. [38] The country is densely populated; every ten li [of a road] are marked by a t'ing; thirty li by a chih [resting-place]. [39] One is not alarmed by robbers, but the road becomes unsafe by fierce tigers and lions who will attack passengers, and unless these be travelling in caravans of a hundred men or more, or be protected by military equipment, they may be devoured by those beasts. [40] They also say there is a flying bridge [fei-chiao] of several hundred li, by which one may cross to the countries north of the sea. [41] The articles made of rare precious stones produced in this country are sham curiosities and mostly not genuine, whence they are not [here] mentioned.

F.

(*Chin-shu*, written before the middle of the 7th century, and embracing the period

A.D. 265-419, ch. 97.[1] This account is mainly a repetition of that in the *Hou-han-shu.*)

[1] Ta-ts'in, also called Li-chien [Li-kin], [2] is in the western part of the western sea. [3] In this country several thousand li in all directions of the compass are covered with cities and other inhabited places. [4] Its capital is over a hundred li in circumference. [5] The inhabitants use coral in making the kingposts of their dwellings; [6] they use opaque glass in making walls, and crystal in making the pedestals of pillars. [7] Their king has five palaces. [8] The palaces are ten li distant from each other. [9] Every morning the king hears cases in one palace; when he has finished he begins anew. [10] When the country is visited by an extraordinary calamity, a wiser man is elected; the old king is relieved from his duties, and the king so dismissed does not dare to consider himself ill-treated. [11] They have keepers of official records and foreigners [interpreters] who are acquainted with their style of writing.[2] [12] They have also small carriages with white canopies, flags, and banners, and postal arrangements, just as we have them in China. [13] The inhabitants are tall, and their faces resemble those of the Chinese, but they wear foreign dress. [14] Their country exports much gold and precious stones, shining pearls, and large conches; they

---

[1] Cf. translation of an identical account, quoted from the *T'ung-tien* (通 典), by Pauthier, *De l'authenticité*, etc., p. 36.

[2] Interpreters were appointed to receive the ambassadors of the barbarians under Constantine. Gibbon, ch. XVII.

have the "jewel that shines at night," the hsieh-chi-hsi, and asbestos cloth; they know how to embroider cloth with gold thread and weave gold-embroidered rugs. [15] They make gold and silver coins; ten silver coins are worth one gold coin. [16] The inhabitants of An-hsi [Parthia] and T'ien-chu [India] have trade with them by sea; its profit is hundred-fold. [17] When the envoys of neighbouring countries arrive there, they are provided with golden money. [18] The water of the great sea which is crossed on the road thither is salt and bitter, and unfit for drinking purposes; the merchants travelling to and fro are provided with three years' provisions; hence, there are not many going. [19] At the time of the Han dynasty, the tu-hu Pan Ch'ao sent his subordinate officer Kan-ying as an envoy to that country; but the sailors who were going out to sea said, "that there was something about the sea which caused one to long for home; those who went out could not help being seized by melancholy feelings; if the Chinese envoy did not care for his parents, his wife, and his children, he might go." Ying could not take his passage. [20] During the T'ai-k'ang period of the emperor Wu-ti [=A.D. 280–290] their king sent an envoy to offer tribute.

G.

[*Sung-shu*, written about A.D. 500, and embracing the period A.D. 420–478, ch. 97].

[1] As regards Ta-ts'in and T'ien-chu [India], far out on the western ocean, we have to say that, although the envoys of the two Han dynasties[1] have experienced the special difficulties of this road, yet traffic in merchandise has been effected, and goods have been sent out to the foreign tribes, the force of winds driving them far away across the waves of the sea. [2] There are lofty [ranges of] hills quite different [from those we know] and a great variety of populous tribes having different names and bearing uncommon designations, they being of a class quite different [from our own]. [3] All the precious things of land and water come from there, as well as the gems made of rhinoceros' [horns] and king-fishers' stones,[2] she-chu [serpent pearls] and asbestos cloth, there being innumerable varieties of these curiosities; and also [the doctrine of] the abstraction of mind [in devotion to] the lord of the world [shih-chu=Buddah];—all this having caused navigation and trade to be extended to those parts.

H.

[*Liang-shu*, written about A.D. 629, and comprising the period A.D. 502–556, ch. 54: account of Chung T'ien-chu.]

---

[1] Chang Ch'ien and Pan Ch'ao.
[2] Ts'ui yü [翠 羽] lit. "King-fishers' wings," which, I presume stands for fei-ts'ui [翡翠] or fei-ts'ui-yü, [翡翠玉], a precious stone called chrysoprase in Bridgman's *Chrestomathy* (p. 430). Cf. Georts, *Les Produits de la Nature Japonaise et Chinoise*, Vol. II., p. 465: "Jadeite; Jade vert aluminaté; Jade fusible." The corresponding terms in the passages K 32, L 35 and P 49° may be similarly explained.

[1] In the west of it [viz., Chung T'ien-chu, or India] they carry on much trade by sea to Ta-ts'in and An-hsi [Parthia], [2] especially in articles of Ta-ts'in, such as all kinds of precious things, coral, amber, chin-pi [gold jadestone], chu-chi [a kind of pearls], lang-kan, Yü-chin [turmeric?] and storax. [3] Storax is made by mixing and boiling the juice of various fragrant trees; it is not a natural product. It is further said that the inhabitants of Ta-ts'in gather the storax [plant, or parts of it], squeeze its juice out, and thus make a balsam [hsiang-kao]; they then sell its dregs to the traders of other countries; it thus goes through many hands before reaching China, and, when arriving here, is not so very fragrant. [4] Yü-chin [turmeric?] only comes from the country of Chi-pin [=a country near the Persian gulf], etc., etc. [5] In the 9th year of the Yen-hsi period of Huan-ti of the Han dynasty [=A.D. 166] the King of Ta-ts'in, An-tun, sent an embassy with tribute from the frontier of Jih-nan [Annam]; during the Han period they have only cnce communicated [with China]. [6] The merchants of this country frequently visit Fu-nan [Siam, Cambodja?[1]] Jih-nan [Annam] and Chiao-chih Tung-king]; [7] but few of the inhabitants of these southern frontier states have come to Ta-ts'in. [8] During the 5th year of the Huang-wu period

---

[1] The *Liang-shu*, quoted in *Hai-kuo-t'u-chih*, ch. 5, p. 15, says: "The country of Fu-nan lies on the great gulf in the west of the sea south of the principality of Jih-nan [Annam]."

of the reign of Sun-ch'üan [=A.D. 226] a merchant of Ta-ts'in, whose name was Ts'in-lun, came to Chiao-chih [Tung-king]; the prefect [t'ai-shou] of Chiao-chih, Wu Miao, sent him to Sun-ch'üan [the Wu emperor], who asked him for a report on his native country and its people. [9] Ts'in-lun prepared a statement, and replied. [10] At the time Chu-ko K'o[1] chastised Tan-yang[2] and they had caught blackish coloured dwarfs. When Ts'in-lun saw them he said that in Ta-ts'in these men are rarely seen. Sun-ch'üan then sent male and female dwarfs, ten of each, in charge of an officer, Liu Hsien of Hui-chi [a district in Chêkiang], to accompany Ts'in-lun. Liu Hsien died on the road, whereupon Ts'in-lun returned direct to his native country.

I.

(*Wei-shu*, written previous to A.D. 572, and embracing the period A.D. 386-556, ch. 102: Hsi-yü-chuan. With one exception, this account is identical with one contained in the *Pei-shih*, a revised history of the same dynasty.[3])

[1] The country of Ta-ts'in is also called Li-kan. [2] Its capital is the city of An-tu. [3] From T'iao-chih west you go by sea, making a bent, ten thousand li. [4] From Tai [=Ta-t'ung fu?] it is

---

[1] Nephew to Chu-ko Liang, *alias* K'ung-ming.

[2] Tan-yang=Kiang-nan.

[3] Cf. translations by Visdelou in d'Herbelot, *Bibl. Orient.*, IV., p. 329, seqq., and Pauthier, *De l'authenticité*, etc., p. 39, seqq.

distant 39,400 li. [5] By the side of its sea one comes out at what is like an arm of the sea,[1] and that the east and the west [of the country] look into that arm of the sea is a natural arrangement. [6] Its territory amounts to six thousand li. [7] It lies between two seas. [8] This country is peacefully governed, and human dwellings are scattered over it like stars. [9] The royal capital is divided into five cities, each five li square; its circuit is 60 li. [10] The king resides in the middle city. [11] In the city ["each city of the four,"—Visdelou] there are established eight high officials [chên] to rule over the four quarters [of the country]; but in the royal city there are also established eight high officials who divide among themselves the government over the four cities. [12] When government matters are deliberated upon, and if in the four quarters [of the country] there are cases not decided, the high officials of the four

---

[1] P'o-hai 渤海. (渤澥海別支名 K'ang-hsi; "a cove or small inlet," also "a large estuary," Williams, s. v. hiai (澥) p. 187). Visdelou translates as follows: "Elle [la Ville Royale] est à 1,000 lieues de distance et à l'Occident du Royaume de *Thiao-chi* (c'est peut-être l'Egipte), un golphe de la Mer entre deux. Elle est éloignée de 3,940 lieues de Tāi (Ville Chinoise). Ce golphe de Mer s'étend au côté du *Taçin* de la même manière que le golphe de Mer qui est entre la Chine et la Corée, et ces deux golphes sont à l'opposite l'un de l'autre, l'un tourné vers l'Orient, l'autre vers l'Occident; ce qui, sans doute, est un effet raisonné de la nature." A careful comparison with the Chinese text will show that Visdelou's translation does not represent what the Chinese author wishes to say. However, even if he were correct in assuming that "*two* gulfs" were spoken of, the one running east and the other west, this could only be interpreted as applying to the gulfs of Suez and of Akabah.

cities hold a council at the king's place. [13] After the king has sanctioned their decision it is put into force. [14] Once in three years the king goes out to convince himself of the morality of the people. [15] If anyone has suffered an injustice he states his complaint to the king who, in minor cases, will censure, but in important cases, will dismiss the country official [responsible for it], appointing a worthier man in his stead. [16] The inhabitants are upright and tall; their mode of dressing, their carriages and flags, resemble those of the Chinese, whence other foreign nations call them Ta-ts'in. [17] The country produces all kinds of grain, the mulberry tree and hemp. The inhabitants busy themselves with silkworms and fields. [18] There is abundance of ch'iu-lin [a kind of jadestone]; lang-kan [a kind of coral]; shên-kuei [a kind of tortoise or its shell]; white horses; chu-lieh [lit. red bristles =a gem?]; ming-chu [shining pearls]; yeh-kuang-pi [the jewel that shines at night]. [19] South-east you go to Chiao-chih [Tung-king]. There is also connection by water with the principalities of Yi-chou [Yünnan] and Yung-ch'ang [near Bhamo]. [20] Many rare objects come from this country. [21] In the west of the water of the sea west of Ta-ts'in there is a river; the river flows south-west; west of the river there are the Nan-pei-shan [north and south hills]; west of the hills there is the Red Water; west [of this] is the Pai-yü-shan [White Jade Hill]; west of the Jade Hill is the

Hsi-wang-mŭ-shan [Hill of the Western King's Mother], where a temple is made of jadestone. [22] It is said that from the western boundary of An-hsi [Parthia], following the crooked shape of the sea [coast], you can also go to Ta-ts'in, over 40,000 li.[1] [23] Although in that country sun and moon, and the constellations, are quite the same as in China, former historians say that going a hundred li west of T'iao-chih you come to the place where the sun sets; this' is far from being true.

K.

[*Chiu-t'ang-shu*, written towards the middle of the 10th century A.D. and embracing the period A.D. 618–906, ch. 198[2]].

[1] The country of Fu-lin, also called Ta-ts'in, lies above the western sea. [2] In the southeast it borders on Po-ssŭ [Persia]. [3] Its territory amounts to over 10,000 li. [4] Of cities there are four hundred. [5] Inhabited places are close together. [6] The eaves, pillars, and window-bars of their palaces are frequently made with crystal and opaque glass. [7] There are twelve honourable ministers who conjointly re-

---

[1] 四萬餘里 ssŭ-wan-yŭ-li. These words appear as 廻萬餘里 hui-wan-yŭ-li, in the text of the *Pei-shih*, meaning "bending around over ten thousand li" [cf. P 14], which is certainly by far the better tradition. Ma-tuan-lin, who has either had both texts, or the authority from which they are both derived, before him, and who apparently copies this passage, also gave the preference to hui. See Q 64.

[2] Cf. translation by Pauthier, *De l'Authenticité*, etc., p. 42, seqq.

gulate government matters. [8] They ordinarily let a man take a bag and follow the king's carriage. When the people have a complaint they throw a written statement into the bag. When the king comes back to the palace he decides between right and wrong. [9] Their kings are not permanent rulers, but they select men of merit. [10] If an extraordinary calamity visits the country, or if wind and rain come at the wrong time, he is deposed and another man is put in his stead. [11] The king's cap is shaped like a bird raising its wings; its trimmings are beset with precious pearls; he wears silk-embroidered clothing, without a lapel in front. [12] He sits on a throne with golden ornaments. [13] He has a bird like a goose; its feathers are green, and it always sits on a cushion by the side of the king.[1] Whenever anything poisonous has been put into the king's meals, the bird will crow. [14] The walls of their capital are built of stone [granite, not brick] and are of enormous height. [15] The city contains in all over 100,000 households.[2] [16] In the south

---

[1] What may have induced Pauthier to translate: "il reste toujours aux côtés du roi, et choisit quelquefois pour siège le sommet de la tête du prince?"

[2] 戶 hu=households, to be distinguished from 口 k'ou, "mouths" or individuals. The number of households may have to be multiplied by 5 or 6 in order to obtain the number of inhabitants, if we may be safe in applying to this case the average number of individuals forming a household in China during the T'ang dynasty. The census taken for fiscal purposes in A.D. 740 fixes the population of China at 8,412,871 households with 48,142,609 individuals. This yields an average of 5·6 members to each household. (*Hsin-t'ang-shu*, ch. 37, Chih 27, p. 2; cf. Sacharoff, *Historische Uebersicht der Bevölkerungs-Verhältnisse China's*, in *Arbeiten der Russ. Gesandtschaft*, German version by Abel, Vol. II, p. 152.)

it faces the great sea. [17] In the east of the city there is a large gate; its height is over twenty chang [=over 235 feet]; it is beset with yellow gold[1] from top to bottom, and shines at a distance of several li. [18] Coming from outside to the royal residence there are three large gates beset with all kinds of rare and precious stones. [19] On the upper floor of the second gate they have suspended a large golden scale, twelve golden balls are suspended from the scale-stick by which the twelve hours of the day are shown. A human figure has been made all of gold of the size of a man standing upright, on whose side, whenever an hour has come, one of the golden balls will drop, the dingling sound of which makes known the divisions of the day without the slightest mistake. [20] In the palaces, pillars are made of sê-sê (瑟瑟),[2] the floors of yellow gold,[3] the leaves of folding doors of ivory, beams of fragrant wood. [21] They have no tiles, but powdered plaster is rammed down into a floor above the house. [22] This floor

---

[1] *See* note to K 20.

[2] In Japanese Shitsu-shitsu. According to the Japanese commentator of the *Pên-ts'ao-kang-mu*, Ono Ranzan, "a bluish variety of Ho-seki (=Pao-shih, 寶石) or precious stones." *See* Geerts, *Les Produits de la Nature Japonaise et Chinoise*, Vol. II, p. 361.

[3] "Yellow gold," huang-chin 黃金, lit. "the yellow metal." This may be real gold, which metal, in opposition to pai-chin 白金, "the white metal"=silver, and 赤金, "the red metal"=copper, is often so called. See *Ko-chih-ching-yüan*, ch. 34, p. 1. But I am inclined to believe that here a kind of bronze is meant, perhaps the yellow bronze called by the Japanese O-to-kin 黃唐金 ("bronze jaune"; Geerts, l.c., Vol. II, p. 486).

is perfectly firm and of glossy appearance like jade-stone. When, during the height of summer, the inhabitants are oppressed by heat, they lead water up and make it flow over the platform, spreading it all over the roof by a secret contrivance so that one sees and knows not how it is done, but simply hears the noise of a well on the roof; suddenly you see streams of water rushing down from the four eaves like a cataract; the draught caused thereby produces a cooling wind, which is due to this skilful contrivance. [23] It is customary for men to have their hair cut and wear robes leaving the right arm bare. [24] Women have no lapels on their dresses, they wear turbans of embroidered cloth. [25] The possession of a great fortune confers superior rank on its owner. [26] There are lambs which grow in the ground; the inhabitants wait till they are about to sprout, and then screen them off by building walls to prevent the beasts which are at large outside from eating them up. The navel of these lambs is connected with the ground; when it is forcibly cut the animal will die, but after the people have fixed the buds themselves, they frighten them by the steps of horses or the beating of drums, when the lambs will yield a sound of alarm, and the navel will be detached, and then the animal may be taken off [separated from ?] the water-plant.[1] [27] The inhabitants are in the

---

[1] An almost identical account regarding the "water-sheep" is quoted from the *Hou-wei-shu* (後魏書) in the *Yüan-chien-lei-han*, ch. 238, p. 20.

habit of cutting their hair and [28] wearing embroidered clothing; [29] they drive in small carriages with white canopies; [30] when going in or out they beat drums and hoist flags, banners, and pennants [31] The country contains much gold, silver, and rare gems. [32] There is the Yeh-kuang-pi [the jewel that shines at night]; the ming-yüeh-chu [the moon-shine pearl]; the hsieh-chi-hsi [the chicken-frightening rhinoceros]; large conches; the chê-ch'ü [mother-o'-pearl?]; cornelian stones; the k'ung-ts'ui[1]; corals; amber; and all the valuable curiosities of the West are exported from this country. [33] The emperor Yang-ti of the Sui dynasty [A.D. 605-617] always wished to open intercourse with Fu-lin, but did not succeed. [34] In the 17th year of the period Chêng-kuan [=A.D. 643], the king of Fu-lin Po-to-li sent an embassy offering red glass, lü-chin-ching [green gold gem, or, gold dust? Visdelou: des pierre lazuli vertes, peut-être des émeraudes], and other articles. T'ai-tsung [the then ruling emperor] favoured them with a message under his imperial seal and graciously granted presents of silk. [35] Since the Ta-shih [Arabs] had conquered these countries they sent their commander-in-chief, Mo-i, to besiege their capital city; by means of an agreement[2] they obtained friendly relations, and asked to be

---

[1] Lit., king-fishers' feathers; probably Jadeïte. *See* note to G. 3.

[2] Regarding Pauthier's and Bretschneider's mistranslation of this passage *see* Phillips, in the *China Review*, Vol. VII., p. 412.

allowed to pay every year tribute of gold and silk; in the sequel they became subject to Ta-shih [Arabia]. [36] In the 2nd year of the period Ch'ien-fêng [=A.D. 667] they sent an embassy offering Ti-yeh-ka. [37] In the first year of the period Ta-tsu [=A.D. 701] they again sent an embassy to our court. [38] In the first month of the 7th year of the period K'ai-yüan [=A.D. 719] their lord sent the ta-shou-ling [an officer of high rank] of T'u-huo-lo [Tokharestan] to offer lions and ling-yang [antelopes], two of each. [39] A few months after, he further sent ta-tê-sêng [priests of great virtue=Nestorian priests?] to our court with tribute.

L.

(*Hsin-t'ang-shu*, written during the middle of the 11th century, its preface being dated A.D. 1060, ch. 221[1].)

[1] Fu-lin is the ancient Ta-ts'in. [2] It lies above the western sea. [3] Some call it Hai-hsi-kuo [*i.e.*, country on the west of the sea]. [4] It is 40,000 li distant from our capital [5] and lies in the west of Chan[2]; north you go straight to the Ko-sa tribe of Tu-ch'üeh. [6] In the west it borders on the sea-coast with the city of Ch'ih-san

---

[1] Cf. translation by Visdelou, l. c., p. 394 seqq.

[2] Chan (苫), old sound Shem or Shim (= 詩廉切, see T'ang-yin 唐音, 24, p. 3.) which, in the account of Ta-shih, is said to be in the west of Ta-shih (*i.e.*, the Khalif empire). I presume that by Chan or Shem, Syria Proper is meant. See Q 41 and R 94.

[7] In the south-east it borders on Po-ssŭ [Persia.] [8] Its territory amounts to 10,000 li; [9] of cities there are four hundred; [10] of soldiers a million. [11] Ten li make one t'ing; three t'ing make one chih. [12] Of subjected small countries there are several times ten. [13] Those which are known by name are called Tsê-san and Lü-fên; Tsê-san is direct north-east, but we cannot obtain the number of li of its road; in the east, by sea 2,000 li, you come to the Lü-fên country. [14] The capital [of Fu-lin] is built of [granite] stone; [15] the city is eighty li broad; [16] the east gate is twenty chang [=235 feet] high and chased with yellow gold.[1] [17] The royal palace has three portals which are beset with precious stones. [18] In the middle portal there is a large golden scale; a man made all of gold, standing. On the yard of that scale there are hanging twelve little balls, one of which will fall down whenever an hour is completed. [19] In making the pillars of palaces they use sê-sê [see K 20], and in making the king-posts of their roofs they use rock crystal and opaque glass; in making floors they use beams of fragrant wood and yellow gold; the leaves of their folding doors are of ivory. [20] Twelve honoured ministers have joint charge of the government. [21] When the king goes out, a man follows him

---

[1] *See* note to K 20. K'ou (釦), chased, according to the Japanese Cyclopedia "ciselures en différents métaux;" *see* Geerts, *l.c.*, Vol. II., p. 487.

with a bag, and whatever complaints there may
be are thrown into the bag; on returning he
examines into right and wrong. [22] When the
country is visited by an extraordinary calamity, the
king is deposed and a worthier man is placed in
his position. [23] The king's official cap is like
the wings of a bird, and pearls are sewn on it; his
garments are of embroidered silk, but there is no
lapel in front. [24] He sits on a couch with
golden ornaments; at his side there is a bird like
a goose, with green feathers; when his majesty
eats anything poisonous it will crow. [25] There
are no roofs made of earthen tiles; but the roofs
are overlaid with white stones, hard and shining
like jadestone. [26] During the height of summer
heat, water is laid up and made to flow down from
the top, the draught [thereby caused] producing
wind. [27] The men there cut their hair; [28] they
wear embroidered clothing in the shape of a gown
that leaves the right arm bare. [29] They ride
in heavy and light carriages and carts covered
with white canopies. [30] When going out or
coming back they hoist flags and beat drums.
[31] Married women wear embroidered tiaras.
[32] The millionaires of the country are the
official aristocracy. The inhabitants enjoy wine
and have a fancy for dry cakes. [33] There
are amongst them many jugglers who can issue
fire from their faces, produce rivers and lakes from
their hands, and banners and tufts of feathers from
their mouths, and who, raising their feet, drop

pearls and jadestones. [34] They have clever physicians who, by opening the brain and extracting worms, can cure mu-shêng [a sort of blindness]. [35] The country contains much gold and silver; the jewel that shines at night and the moon-shine pearl; large conches; chê-ch'ü [mother-o'-pearl?]; cornelian stones; mu-nan;[1] "king-fishers' feathers,"[2] and amber. [36] They weave the hair of the water-sheep [shui-yang] into cloth which is called Hai-hsi-pu [cloth from the west of the sea]. [37] In the sea there are coral islands. The fishers sit in large boats and let iron [wire] nets into the water down to the corals. When the corals first grow from the rocks they are white like mushrooms; after a year they turn yellow; after three years they turn red. Then the branches begin to intertwine, having grown to a height of 3 to 4 chih [up to say 5 feet]. The iron being cast, the coral roots get entangled in the net, when the men on board have to turn round in order to take them

---

[1] A kind of pearl. The *Wên-hsüan-chu* (文選註), a work written about the time when this name must have become known (A.D. 658, see Wylie, p. 192), quoted in the *Yüan-chien-lei-han*, ch. 364, p. 12, identifies it with pi-chu 碧珠 (jade pearl). I do not know on what authority Visdelou (d'Herbelot, IV, p. 400) explains it as "une sorte de parium, qui découle du bec de certains oiseaux où s'amasse." The pearl, it is true, is said to owe its jadelike colour to the saliva of a bird (Q 24), but I can find no allusion to its being a balsam. The Mu-nan is called a pao-shih (寳石) of yellowish colour by the Chinese and Japanese authorities quoted in Geerts, l. c., Vol. II, pp. 359 and 361.

[2] Probably a bluish stone so called from its resemblance in colour to the king-fisher. *See* note to G 3.

out. If they miss their time in fishing for it, the coral will decay. [38] On the western sea there are markets where the traders do not see one another, the price being [deposited] by the side of the merchandise; they are called "spirit markets." [39] There is a quadruped called Ts'ung; it has the size of a dog, is fierce and repulsive, and strong. [40] In a northern district there is a sheep that grows out of the ground; its navel is attached to the ground, and if it is cut the animal will die. The inhabitants will frighten them by the steps of horses or by beating drums. The navel being thus detached, they are taken off the water plants; they don't make flocks. [41] During the 17th year of Chêng-kuan [=A.D. 643] the king Po-to-li sent an embassy offering red glass and lü-chin-ching [green gold gem, green gold dust or sand?], and a cabinet order was issued as an acknowledgment. [42] When the Ta-shih [Arabs] usurped power [over these countries], they sent their general, Mo-i, to reduce them to order. [43] Fu-lin obtained peace by an agreement, but in the sequel became subject to Ta-shih. [44] From the period Ch'ien-fêng [A.D. 666–668] till the period Ta-tsu [A.D. 701] they have repeatedly offered tribute to the Chinese court. [45] In the 7th year of the K'ai-yüan period [=A.D. 719] they offered through the ta-yu [a high official] of T'u-huo-lo [Tokharestan] lions and ling-yang [antelopes]. [46] Crossing the desert in the south-west of Fu-lin, at a distance of 2,000 li, there are two countries called Mo-lin and Lao-p‘o-sa. [47] Their inhabitants are black and of a violent disposition. [48] The country is malarious and has no vegetation. [49] They feed their horses on dried fish, and live themselves on hu-mang; hu-mang is the Persian date [Phœnix dactylifera. according to Bretschneider]. [50] They are not ashamed to have most frequent illicit intercourse with savages; they call this "establishing the relation between lord and subject." [51] On one of seven days they refrain from doing business, and carouse all night.

M.

[Extract from columns 12 and 13 of the Nestorian stone inscription.[1]]

[1] According to the *Hsi-yü-t'u-chi* and the historical records of the Han and Wei dynasties, the country of Ta-ts‘in begins in the south at the Coral Sea, and extends in the north to the Chung-pau-shan [hills of precious stones]; it looks in the west to "the region of the immortals" and "the flowery groves"; in the east it bounds on "the long winds" and "the weak water." [2] This country produces fire-proof cloth; the life-restoring incense; the ming-yüeh-chu [moon-shine pearl];

---

[1] Cf. translations by Boym in Kircher, *Prodromus Coptus* and *China Illustrata* (in Latin; reprinted *Chin. Repos.*, XIV, 202); Visdelou in d'Herbelot, *Bibl. Orient.*, IV, p. 375 (in French); E. C. Bridgman in *Chin. Repos.*, *l. c.* (English); A. Wylie, *J. Am. Or. Soc.*, V, p. 280 (English); Pauthier, *l'Inscription Syro-Chinoise*, etc. (Latin and French); Huc, *le Christianisme en Chine*, Vol. I, p. 52 (French); and others.

and the yeh-kuang-pi [jewel that shines at night. [3] Robberies are unknown there, and the people enjoy peace and happiness. [4] Only the king ["luminous"=Christian] religion is practised; only virtuous rulers occupy the throne. [5] This country is vast in extent; its literature is flourishing.

N.

[*Sung-shih*, written during the 13th or 14th century, and comprising the period A.D. 960–1279, ch. 490.]

[1] The country of Fu-lin. South-east of it you go to Mieh-li-sha; north you go to the sea; both forty days' journey; west you go to the sea, thirty days' journey; in the east, starting from western Ta-shih, you come to Yü-tien [Khoten], Hui-ho and Ch'ing-t'ang, and finally reach China. [2] They have during former dynasties not sent tribute to our court. [3] During the tenth month of the 4th year of the period Yüan-fêng [=November, A.D. 1081], their king, Mieh-li-i-ling-kai-sa,[1] first sent the ta-shou-ling [a high official] Ni-ssŭ-tu-ling-ssŭ-mêng-p'an [Nestouri Ssŭ-mêng-p'an,= Simon P'an?] to offer as tribute saddled horses, sword-blades, and real pearls. [4] He said: the climate of this country is very cold; [5] houses

---

[1] Bretschneider, *Arabs*, etc., p. 25, reads Mieh-li-*sha*-ling-kai-sa. But I have no doubt that the syllables Mieh-li-*sha*, instead of Mieh-li-*i*, have been copied into this name, by an oversight, from the first paragraph in this account, where the former name occurs.

there have no tiles; [6] the products are gold, silver, pearls, western silk cloth, cows, sheep, horses, camels with single humps, pears, almonds, dates, pa-lan,[1] millet, and wheat. [7] They make wine from grapes; [8] their musical instruments are the lute [k'ung-hou: the "flat lute," Dennys, "Notes on Chinese Instruments of Music," *N.-Ch. B. R. Asiat. Soc.*, Vol. VIII., p. 112], the hu-ch'in [the "tea-pot-shaped lute"; Ma Tuanlin, Q 84, has hu-ch'in 胡琴, the "foreign lute," which is apparently a good conjecture]; the hsiao-pi-li [a kind of flageolet, s. Dennys, p. 110], and the p'ien-ku ["side drum"?] [9] The king dresses in red and yellow robes, and wears a turban of silken cloth interwoven with gold thread. [10] In the 3rd month every year he goes to the temple of Fou,[2] to sit on a red couch [palankin?] which he gets the people to lift. [11] His honoured servants [ministers, courtiers, priests?] are dressed like the king, but wear blue, green, purple, white mottled, red, yellow, or brown stuff, wear turbans and ride on horseback. [12] The towns and the country districts are each under the jurisdiction of a shou-ling [chief, sheik?] [13] Twice a

---

[1] A kind of dates, Greek βάλανος (?), Herod. I., 193; or acorns, chestnuts (?); *see* Hehn, *Kulturpflanzen und Hausthiere*, 3te Aufl., p. 342, seqq. (Διὸς βάλανος=chestnut). Chinese dictionaries contain no clue as to the meaning of this term.

[2] 佛寺 Fou-shih, lit. "Temple of Buddha." Fou here clearly means either the Mahommedan Buddha (Mahommed) or the founder of the Christian religion; in other places the Koran is described as 佛經 Fou-ching, the "Mahommedan Canon."

year, during the summer and autumn, they must offer money and cloth [chin-ku-po]. [14] In their criminal decisions they distinguish between great and small offences. Light offences are punished by several tens of blows with the bamboo; heavy offences with up to 200 blows; capital punishment is administered by putting the culprit into a feather bag which is thrown into the sea. [15] They are not bent on making war to neighbouring countries, and in the case of small difficulties try to settle matters by correspondence; but when important interests are at stake they will also send out an army. [16] They cast gold and silver coins, without holes, however; on the pile they cut the words Mi-lê-fou [Melek Fat?] which is a king's name. The people are forbidden to counterfeit the coin. [17] During the 6th year of Yüan-yu [=A.D. 1091] they sent two embassies, and their king was presented, by imperial order, with 200 pieces of cloth, pairs of white gold vases, and clothing with gold bound in a girdle. (?)

O.

(*Ming-shih*, concluded in A.D. 1724, and embracing the period A.D. 1368–1643, ch. 326.[1])

[1] Fu-lin is the same as Ta-ts'in of the Han period. [2] It first communicated with China at the time of the emperor Huan-ti [A.D. 147–168]. [3] During the Chin and Wei dynasties it was also called Ta-ts'in, and tribute was sent to China.

---

[1] Cf. translation by Bretschneider, *China Review*, IV., p. 390.

[4] During the T'ang dynasty it was called Fu-lin. [5] During the Sung it was still so called, and they sent also tribute several times; yet the Sung-shih says that during former dynasties they have sent no tribute to our court [See N, 2], which throws doubt on its identity with Ta-ts'in. [6] At the close of the Yüan dynasty [A.D. 1278–1368] a native of this country, named Nieh-ku-lun,[1] came to China for trading purposes. [7] When, after the fall of the Yüan, he was not able to return, the emperor T'ai-tsu, who had heard of this, commanded him to his presence in the eighth month of the 4th year of Hung-wu [=September 1371] and gave orders that an official letter be placed into his hands for transmission to his king, [8] which read as follows: "Since the Sung dynasty had lost the throne and Heaven had cut off their sacrifice, the Yüan [Mongol] dynasty had risen from the desert to enter and rule over China for more than a hundred years, when Heaven, wearied of their

---

[1] "Pope John XXII appointed Nicolaus de Bentra to succeed John de Monte Corvino as Archbishop of Cambalu, that is, Peking, in the year 1333; and also sent letters to the emperor of the Tartars, who was then the sovereign of China." Mosheim, *Ecclesiastical History*, translated by James Murdock, Vol. II, p. 359; cf. Rémusat, *Nouv. Mél. Asiat.*, Vol. II, p. 198. Bretschneider, *Arabs*, etc., p. 25, says: "It is possible that the Nie-ku-lun of the Chinese Annals is identical with the Monk Nicolas. The statement of the Chinese that Nicolas carried on commerce does not contradict this view. Perhaps he trafficked in fact, or he considered it necessary to introduce himself under the name of a merchant." I fully concur with this view.

misgovernment and debauchery, thought also fit to turn their fate to ruin, and the affairs of China were in a state of disorder for eighteen years. But when the nation began to arouse itself, We, as a simple peasant of Huai-yu, conceived the patriotic idea to save the people, and it pleased the Creator to grant that Our civil and military officers effected their passage across eastward to the left side of the River. We have then been engaged in war for fourteen years; We have, in the west, subdued the king of Han, Ch'ên Yu-liang; We have, in the east, bound the king of Wu, Chang Shih-ch'êng; We have, in the south, subdued Min and Yüeh [=Fukien and Kuang-tung], and conquered Pa and Shu [=Ssŭ-ch'üan]; We have, in the north, established order in Yu and Yen [=Chih-li]; We have established peace in the Empire, and restored the old boundaries of Our Middle Land. We were selected by Our people to occupy the Imperial throne of China under the dynastic title of 'the Great Ming,' commencing with Our reign styled Hung-wu, of which we now are in the fourth year. We have sent officers to all the foreign kingdoms with this Manifesto except to you, Fu-lin, who, being separated from us by the western sea, have not as yet received the announcement. We now send a native of your country, Nieh-ku-lun, to hand you this Manifesto. Although We are not equal in wisdom to our ancient rulers whose virtue was recognised all over the universe, We cannot but let the world know

Our intention to maintain peace within the four seas. It is on this ground alone that We have issued this Manifesto." [9] And he again ordered the ambassador Pu-la and others to be provided with credentials and presents of silk for transmission to that country, who thereafter sent an embassy with tribute. [10] But this embassy was, in the sequel, not repeated until during the Wan-li period [A.D. 1573–1620] a native from the great western ocean came to the capital who said that the Lord of Heaven, Ye-su, was born in Ju-tê-a [Judæa] which is identical with the old country of Ta-ts'in;[1] that this country is known in the historical books to have existed since the creation of the world for the last 6,000 years; that it is beyond dispute the sacred ground of history and the origin of all wordly affairs; that it should be considered as the country where the Lord of Heaven created the human race. [11] This account looks somewhat exaggerated and should not be trusted. [12] As regards the abundance of produce and other precious articles found in this country, accounts will be found in former annals.

P.

(*Wei-lio*, quoted at the end of ch. 30 of the

---

[1] Bretschneider (*China Review*, IV, p. 391) adds: "evidently the view of Ricci." I quite agree to this conjecture which I would slightly modify by adding that Ricci's view seems to have been very near the truth. Ricci's Chinese name, Li Ma-tou (利瑪竇), *i.e.*, Li=Ricci, Matthaeus, is mentioned in a subsequent account of Italy as that of the foreigner who arrived during the period referred to. *See* Bretschneider, l, c,

San-kuo-chih, based on various records referring to the period of the three kingdoms,=A.D. 220--264, and compiled prior to A.D. 429.)

[1] Formerly T'iao-chih was wrongly believed to be in the west of Ta-ts'in; now its real position is [known to be] east. [2] Formerly it was also wrongly believed to be stronger than An-hsi [Parthia]; now it is changed into a vassal state said to make the western frontier of An-hsi [Parthia]. [3] Formerly it was, further, wrongly believed that the Jo-shui [weak water] was in the west of T'iao-chih; now the Jo-shui is [believed to be] in the west of Ta-ts'in. [4] Formerly it was wrongly believed that, going over two hundred days west of T'iao-chih, one came near the place where the sun sets; now, one comes near the place where the sun sets by going west of Ta-ts'in.

[5] The country of Ta-ts'in, also called Li-kan, is on the west of the great sea west of An-hsi [Parthia] and T'iao-chih. [6] From the city of An-ku, on the boundary of An-hsi [Parthia] one takes passage in a ship and, traversing the west of the sea, with favourable winds arrives in two months; with slow winds, the passage may last a year, and with no wind at all, perhaps three years. [7] This country is on the west of the sea whence it is commonly called Hai-hsi. [8] There is a river coming out from the west of this country, and there is another great sea. [9] In the west of the sea there is the city of Ch'ih-san. [10] From below

the country one goes straight north to the city of Wu-tan. [11] In the south-west one further travels by a river which on board ship one crosses in one day; and again south-west one travels by a river which is crossed in one day.¹ [12] There are three great divisions of the country [perhaps: three great cities]. [13] From the city of An-ku one goes by land due north to the north of the sea; and again one goes due west to the west of the sea; and again you go due south to arrive there. [14] At the city of Wu-ch'ih-san, you travel by river on board ship one day, then make a round at sea, and after six days' passage on the great sea, arrive in this country.

[15] There are in the country in all over four hundred smaller cities; its size is several thousand li in all directions of the compass. [16] The residence of their king lies on the banks of a river estuary [*lit.* a river-sea]. [17] They use stone in making city walls. [18] In this country there are the trees sung [pine], po [cypress], huai [sophora?], tzŭ [a kind of euphorbia?]; bamboos, rushes, poplars, willows, the wu-t'ung tree, and all kinds of other plants. [19] The people are given to planting on the fields all kinds of grain. [20] Their domestic animals are: the horse, the donkey, the mule, the camel, and the mulberry silk-worm. [21] There are many jugglers who can issue fire

---

¹ The Chinese text here apparently contains what printers call "a double," and we may perhaps be justified in considering the second part of this paragraph as interpolated.

from their mouths, bind and release themselves, [cf. C 2] and dance on twenty balls. [22] In this country they have no permanent rulers, but when an extraordinary calamity visits the country, they elect as king a worthier man, while discharging the old king, who does not even dare to feel angry at this decision. [23] The people are tall, and upright in their dealings, like the Chinese, but wear foreig [hu¹] dress; they call their country another China. [24] They always wished to send embassies to China, but the An-hsi [Parthians] wanted to make profit out of their trade with us, and would not allow them to pass their country. [25] They can read foreign [hu¹] books. [26] They regulate by law public and private matters. [27] The palace buildings are held sacred. [28] They hoist flags, beat drums, use small carriages with white canopies, and have postal stations like the Chinese. [29] Coming from An-hsi [Parthia] you make a round at sea and, in the north, come to this country. [30] The people live close together. [31] Ten li make one t'ing, thirty li one chih. [32] They have no robbers and thieves; but there are fierce tigers and lions that will attack travellers, and unless these go in caravans, they cannot pass the country. [33] They have several times ten small kings. [34] The residence of their king is over a hundred li in circuit. [35] They have official archives.

---

¹ Hu, foreign, probably applies to the nations of Western Asia. Cf. Neumann, *Asiat. Studien*, p. 198 seqq.

[36] The king has five palaces, ten li apart from each other. The king hears the cases of one palace in the morning till being tired at night; the next morning he goes to another palace; in five days he has completed his round. [37] Thirty-six generals [chiang] always consult upon public matters; if one general does not go [to the meeting] they do not consult. [38] When the king goes out he usually gets one of his suite to follow him with a leather bag, into which petitioners throw a statement of their cases, on arrival at the palace, the king examines into the merits of each case. [39] They use crystal in making the pillars of palaces as well as implements of all kinds. [40] They make bows and arrows.

[41] The following dependent small states are enumerated separately, viz., the kings of Tsê-san, Lü-fên, Ch'ieh-lan, Hsien-tu, Ssŭ-fu, and Yü-lo; and of other small kingdoms there are very many; it is impossible to enumerate them one by one.

[42] The country produces fine ch'ih [hemp or hemp cloth]. [43] They make gold and silver money; one coin of gold is worth ten [of silver] [44] They weave fine cloth, and say they use the down of water-sheep in making it; it is called Hai-hsi-pu [cloth from the west of the sea]. In this country all the domestic animals come out of the water. Some say that they do not only use sheep's wool, but also the bark of trees [vegetable fibre?] and the silk of wild silk-worms in weaving cloth, and the Ch'ü-shu, the T'a-têng, and Chi-chang

class of goods [serge or plush rugs?] of their looms are all good; their colours are of brighter appearance than are the colours of those manufactured in the countries on the east of the sea.[1] [45] Further, they were always anxious to get Chinese silk for severing it in order to make hu-ling [foreign damask, gauze?], for which reason they frequently trade by sea with the countries of An-hsi [Parthia]. [46] The sea-water being bitter and unfit for drinking is the cause that but few travellers come to this country. [47] The hills in this country produce inferior jade-stones [tz'ŭ-yü-shih=half-precious stones?] of nine colours, viz., blue, carnation, yellow, white, black, green, crimson, red, and purple. The Chiu-se-shih [nine-coloured stones] which are now found in the I-wu-shan belong to this category. [48] During the third year of Yang-chia [=A.D. 134] the king and minister of Su-le [Kashgar?] presented to the court each a golden girdle beset with blue stones[2] from Hai-hsi, and the *Chin-hsi-yü-chiu-t'u* says: the rare stones coming from the countries of Chi-pin [=Afghanistan?] and T'iao-chih are inferior jadestones.

[49] The following products are frequently found in Ta-ts'in.

---

[1] Probably the countries on the Persian Gulf (East of the Sea) as opposed to Ta-ts'in, the country on the Red Sea (West of the Sea).

[2] Ch'ing-shih (青石). This name is now a synonym of hei-shih (黑石) and is applied to smaltine or binarseniet of cobalt. (Geerts, l. c., Vol. II, p. 568.) It appears, however, from the context that a more precious mineral is meant, perhaps 'lapis lazuli' (Williams).

[49]
- *a*. Gold.
- *b*. Silver.
- *c*. Copper.
- *d*. Iron.
- *e*. Lead.
- *f*. Tin.
- *g*. Turtoises.
- *h*. White horses.
- *i*. Red hair.[1]
- *j*. Hsieh-chi-hsi.
- *k*. Turtoise shell.
- *l*. Black[2] bears.
- *m*. Ch'ih-ch'ih.
- *n*. P'i-tu-shu.
- *o*. Large conches.
- *p*. Ch'ê-ch'ü.
- *q*. Cornelian stones.
- *r*. Southern gold.
- *s*. King-fishers' gems.
- *t*. Ivory.
- *u*. Fu-ts'ai-yü.
- *w*. Ming-yüeh-chu.
- *x*. Yeh-kuang-chu.
- *y*. Real white pearls.
- *z*. Amber.
- *aa*. Corals.
- *bb*. Ten colours of opaque glass, viz., carnation, white, black, green, yellow, blue, purple, azure, red, and red-brown.
- *cc*. Ch'iu-lin
- *dd*. Lang-kan
- *ee*. Rock crystal
- *ff*. Mei-kuei [garnets?]
- *gg*. Realgar and orpiment.
- *hh*. Five colours of Pi.
- *ii*. Ten kinds of Jade, viz., yellow, white, black, green, a brownish red, crimson, purple, gold, yellow, azure, and a reddish yellow.[3]
- *jj*. Five colours of Ch'ü-shu [rugs?]

---

[1] Cf. I 18 and Q 21; in these passages the expression "red hair" or "red bristles" is also preceded by the mention of white horses. It may be that the two terms belong together.

[2] hsüan (玄): black, dark grey, or brown. Cf. von Strauss und Torney, "Bezeichnung der Farben Blau und Grün im chinesischen Alterthum," in *Z. D. M. G.*, XXXIII, p. 502, seqq.

[3] The translation of these as of all colours is very doubtful.

[49]
- *kk.* Five colours of T'a-têng [rugs?]
- *ll.* Nine colours of Shou-hsia t'a-têng.
- *mm.* Gold embroideries.
- *nn.* Damasks of various colours.
- *oo.* Chin-t'u-pu [Gold-coloured cloth?]
- *pp.* Fei-ch'ih-pu.[1]
- *qq.* Fa-lu-pu.[2]
- *rr.* Fei-ch'ih-ch'ü-pu.
- *ss.* Asbestos cloth.
- *tt.* O-lo-tê-pu.
- *uu.* Pa-tsê-pu.
- *ww.* To-tai-pu.[3]
- *xx.* Wên-sê-pu.[4]
- *yy.* Five colours T'ao-pu.[5]
- *zz.* Chiang-ti.
- *aaa.* Curtains interwoven with gold.
- *bbb.* Five colours of Tou-chang.
- *ccc.* I-wei-mu-êrh (?)
- *ddd.* Storax.
- *eee.* Ti-ti-mi-mi-tou-na.
- *fff.* Pai-fu-tzŭ [a plant].
- *ggg.* Hsün-lu.
- *hhh.* Yü-chin [a kind of Turmeric].
- *iii.* Yün-chiao-hsün, in all 12 kinds of vegetable fragrant substances [?].

[50] After the road from Ta-ts'in had been performed from the north of the sea by land, another road was tried which followed the sea to the south and connected with the north of the outer barbarians at the seven principalities of Chiao-chih [Tung-king]; and there was also a water-road leading through to Yi-chou and Yung-ch'ang [in

---

[1] Called Fei-ch'ih-chu-pu (棑持竹布) in a quotation of the corresponding passage in the *Yüan-chien-lei-han*, ch. 366, p. 7.

[2] Fa-lung-pu (發隆), *ibid.*

[3] Lu-tai-pu (鹿代), *ibid.*

[4] Wên-su-pu (溫宿), *ibid.*

[5] Five colours Chên-pu (枕布), *ibid.*

the present Yün-nan]. It is for this reason that curiosities come from Yung-ch'ang.

[51] Formerly only the water-road was spoken of; they did not know there was an overland route. [53] Now the accounts of the country are as follows. [54] The number of inhabitants cannot be stated. [55] This country is the largest in the west of the Ts'ung-ling. [56] The number of small rulers established [under its supremacy] is very large. [57] We, therefore, record only the larger ones.

[58] The king of Tsê-san is subject to Ta-ts'in. [59] His residence lies right in the middle of the sea. [60] North you go to Lü-fên [see below paragr. 62 seqq.] by water half a year, with quick winds a month; it is nearest to the city of An-ku in An-hsi [Parthia; see above paragr. 6 and 13]. [61] South-west you go to the capital of Ta-ts'in; we do not know the number of li.

[62] The king of Lü-fên is subject to Ta-ts'in. [63] His residence is 2,000 li distant from the capital of Ta-ts'in. [64] The flying bridge across the sea [river?] in Ta-ts'in west of the city of Lü-fên is 230 li in length. [64] The road, if you cross the sea [river?], goes to the south-west; if you make a round at sea [or, on the river?], you go due west.

[65] The king of Ch'ieh-lan is subject to Ta-ts'in. [66] Coming from the country of Ssŭ-t'ao you go due south, cross a river, and then go due west to Ch'ieh-lan 3,000 li; when the road comes

out in the south of the river, you go west. [67] Coming from Ch'ieh-lan you go again straight to the country of Ssŭ-fu [*see below* paragr. 72] on the western river 600 li; where the southern road joins [the]˙ Ssŭ-fu [road] there is the country of Hsien-tu [*see below* paragr. 70] in the south-west. [68] Going due south from Ch'ieh-lan and Ssŭ-fu there is the "Stony Land" [*lit.* accumulated stones]; in the south of the Stony Land there is the great sea which produces corals and real pearls. [69] In the north of Ch'ieh-lan, Ssŭ-fu, Ssŭ-pin and A-man there is a range of hills extending from east to west; in the east of Ta-ts'in [i. q. Hai-hsi, so called from its sea, the red sea, as the western arm of the Great Sea] as well as of Hai-tung [the country on the eastern arm of the Great Sea, *i.e.*, on the Persian Gulf] there are ranges of hills extending from north to south.

[70] The king of Hsien-tu is subject to Ta-ts'in. [71] From his residence you go 600 li north-east to Ssŭ-fu.

[72] The king of Ssŭ-fu is subject to Ta-ts'in. [73] From his residence you go to Yü-lo [*see below* paragr. 74 and 75] north-east 340 li, across the sea.[1]

[74] Yü-lo is subject to Ta-ts'in. [75] Its residence is in the north-east of Ssŭ-fu across the river. From Yü-lo north-east you again cross a

---

[1] It appears that "sea" (hai, 海) here frequently means "river." The "sea" and the "river" in paragraphs 73 and 75 are apparently the same water.

river to Ssŭ-lo; and north-east of this you again cross a river.

[76] The country of Ssŭ-lo is subject to An-hsi [Parthia] and is on the boundary of Ta-ts'in.

[77] In the west of Ta-ts'in there is the water of the sea; west of this is the water of a river; west of the river there is a large range of hills extending from north to south; west of this there is the Ch'ih-shui [Red River]; west of the Ch'ih-shui there is the White Jade Hill; on the White Jade Hill there is the Hsi-wang-mu; west of the Hsi-wang-mu there is the rectified Liu-sha [the "Flying Sands"]; west of the Liu-sha there are the four countries of Ta-hsia, Chien-sha, Shu-yu and Yüeh-chih. West of these there is the Hei-shui [Black or Dark River] which is reported to be the western terminus of the world.

Q.

(Ma Tuan-lin: *Wên-hsien-t'ung-k'ao*, ch. 330.)

[1] Ta-ts'in, also called Li-kan,[1] has been first communicated with during the later Han dynasty. [2] This country, as being in the west of the western sea, is also called Hai-hsi-kuo [*i.e.*, western sea country.] [3] Its king resides at the city of An-tu. [4] In the palaces they use crystal in making

---

[1] A seholion inserted after this name says that its second part 靬 was pronounced with the initial 居 chū, old sound: gu or ku, and the final 言 yen, thus describing the probable ancient sound of the name as Liken. In the same note Ma Tuan-lin insinuates that the country is identical with Li-ken of the *Ch'ien-han-shu* (see B 5; cf. *Shih-chi* A 5).

pillars. [5] From T'iao-chih west, crossing the sea, you make a crooked journey, ten thousand li. [6] Its distance from Ch'ang-an [=Hsi-an-fu] is 40,000 li. [7] This country is even and upright; human dwellings are scattered [over it] like stars. [8] Its territory amounts to a thousand li from east to west and from north to south. [9] It contains over 400 cities and several tens of small tributary states. [10] In the west there is the Great Sea. [11] On the west of the sea there is the royal city of Ch'ih-san. [12] They have keepers of official records and foreigners trained in reading their writings [perhaps: and, as regards writing, they can read hu,=the writing of certain western or central Asiatic nations.] [13] They cut their hair and wear embroidered clothing. [14] They also have small carriages with white canopies, and hoist flags, etc. [15] Every ten li make one t'ing; thirty li make one hou, the same as in China. [16] The country contains many lions who are a great scourge to travellers; for unless going in caravans of over a hundred men and being protected by military equipment, they will be hurt by them. [17] Their king is not a permanent one, but they want to be led by a man of merit. Whenever an extraordinary calamity or an untimely storm and rain occurs, the king is deposed and a new one elected, the deposed king resigning cheerfully. [18] The inhabitants are tall, and upright in their dealings, like the Chinese, whence they are called Ta-ts'in, or Chinese. [19] Amongst precious stones they have the hsieh-chi-hsi [the chicken-frightening rhinoceros.][1] [20] They mix several fragrant substances and fry their juice in order to make Su-ho [Storax]. [21] The country produces gold, silver, and rare precious things; the jewel that shines at night, the moon-shine pearl, amber, opaque glass, turtoises [shên-kuei], white horses, red bristles (?), turtoise-shell, black bears, red glass, the p'i-tu-shu [a kind of rat], large conches, ch'ê-ch'ü,[2] cornelian. [22] The Ts'ung [a quadruped] comes from the western sea; some are domesticated like dogs, but they are mostly fierce and nasty. [23] In the northern possessions of this country there is a kind of sheep which grow naturally out of the ground. They wait till the germs are about to sprout, and then protect them by raising walls lest the beasts at large should eat them. Their navels are connected with the ground; if the navel is cut by force, the animal will die; but if by the sound of striking some

---

[1] The *Pao-p'o-tzŭ* says: The T'ung-t'ien-hsi (Rhinoceros communicating with Heaven) has got a white gem, [suspended] as if on a tassel, which will frighten away the chickens when placed in a heap of rice in the middle of a flock of these animals, whence southern people call it hsieh-chi, *i.e.*, chicken-frightening. [Cf. Visdelou's note in d'Herbelot, *Bibl. Orient.*, Vol. IV, p. 398].

[2] The *Kuang-ya* says: Ch'ê-ch'ü is a stone like jade. [Cf. *Ko chih-ching-yüan*, Ch. 33, p. 16; also Pfizmaier, *Beiträge zur Geschichte der Edelsteine und des Goldes*, Wien 1868, p. 202: "Das Wagennetz." Chinese Ch'ê-ch'ü, or Ch'ê-k'ü, may be identical with Uigur *tscheku*, described by Klaproth as "eine sehr grosse gewundene Seemuschelschale, die für eine Kostbarkeit gehalten wird." *See* "Abhandlung üb. d. Sprache u. Schrift der Uiguren," p. 22, in Appendix to *Verzeichniss*, etc., Paris, 1822.

object they are frightened, this will cause them to disconnect their navels, and they may be taken off the water-plants; they will not form flocks. [24] There is further the Mu-nan, a pearl of jade colour, originating in the coagulation of saliva in the mouth of a flying bird; the natives consider it a precious substance.¹ [25] There are jugglers who can let fires burn on their foreheads; make rivers and lakes in their hands; raise their feet and let pearls and precious stones drop from them; and, in opening their mouths produce banners and tufts of feathers in abundance.² [26] With regard to the hsi-pu [fine cloth] manufactured on their looms, they say they use the wool of water-sheep in making it; it is called hai-chung-pu. [27] They make all kinds of rugs [Ch'ü-sou, T'a-têng, Chi-chang, etc.]; their colours are still more brilliant than are those manufactured in the countries on the east of the sea. [28] They always made profit by obtaining the thick plain silk stuffs of China, which they split in order to make foreign ling kan wên [foreign damask–ling-and purple dyed–kan–mustered goods–wên–?], and they entertained a lively trade with the foreign states

---

¹ [According to] Ts'ao Tzŭ-chien [*see* Mayers, *Manual*, I, No. 759] coral matches, may be mixed with [? *chien* 間] the mu-nan. [Ma Tuan-lin's note. Cf. note i to L 35.]

² When the Emperor Wu-ti of the Former Han dynasty sent an embassy to An-hsi [Parthia], this country offered two jugglers from Li-ken with deformed eyebrows, steep noses, ruffled hair and strong side-curls, and four feet and five inches in length [Ma Tuan-lin's note].

of An-hsi [Parthia] by sea. [29] About 700 or 800 li south-west in the Chang-hai,[1] you come to the Coral Islands. At the bottom of the water there are rocks and the corals grow on them. The inhabitants of Ta-ts'in use large sea-going ships having on board nets of iron. They get a diver first to go down and look for corals; if the nets can be let down, they drop them. When the corals first appear they are white, and by degrees they resemble sprouts, and break through. After a year and some time has elapsed they grow through the meshes of the net and change their colour into yellow; they will then throw out branches and intertwine, having grown to a height of three or four ch'ih [=4 to 5 feet, Engl.], and the larger ones measuring over a ch'ih [say 15 inches, Engl.] in circuit. After three years, their colour has turned into a beautiful carnation red. They are then again looked after to ascertain whether they can be gathered. The fishers thereupon get at the roots with iron pinchers and fasten the net with ropes; they let the men on board turn the vessel round, raise the net and take it out, and return to their country, where the corals are polished and cut according to fancy. If not fished for at the proper time they are liable to be worm-bitten. [30] In this country they make gold and silver coins; ten

---

[1] Chang-hai="Gulf," *i.e.*, the Red Sea, the same name being applied to the Gulf of Tung-king; cf. 勃海 p'o-hai, which, in China, is applied to the Gulf of Pei-chih-li; both terms probably mean "arm of the sea, gr'f;" cf. note to I 5.

silver coins are worth one gold coin. [31] The inhabitants are just in their dealings, and in the trade there are not two prices. [32] Cereals are always cheap, and the budget is well supplied. [33] When the envoys of neighbouring countries arrive at their furthest frontier they are driven by post to the royal capital and, on arrival, are presented with golden money. [34] Their king always wished to send envoys to China; but the An-hsi [Parthians] wished to carry on trade with them in Chinese silks, and this is the cause of their having been shut off from direct communication. [35] It was, further, hard to cross the great sea, travelling merchants taking three years' provisions on board to make this passage, whence the number of travellers was but small. [36] In the beginning of the Yüan-chia period of the emperor Huan-ti [A.D. 151–153], the king of Ta-ts'in, An-tun, sent envoys who offered ivory, rhinoceros' horns, and turtoise-shell, from the boundary of Jih-nan [Annam]; this was the first time they communicated with us. Their tribute contained no precious stones whatever, which fact makes us suspect that the messengers kept them back. During the Ta-k'ang period of the emperor Wu-ti of the Chin dynasty [Ta-k'ang=T'ai-k'ang, A.D. 280–290] their king sent envoys with tribute. [37] Some say that in the west of this country there is the Jo-shui [weak water] and the Liu-sha [flying sands] near the residence of the Hsi-wang-mu [western king's mother], not far from the place where the sun sets.

(Ma Tuan-lin's text is here interrupted by the following note—38 to 61 incl.):

[38] The *Wai-kuo-t'u* [map of foreign countries] says: [39] From Yung-ch'en north there is a country called Ta-ts'in. [40] These people are of great size; they measure five or six ch'ih in height.[1] [41] The *Kuei-huan-hsing-ching-chi*[2] says: The Fu-lin country is in the west of Chan [old sound: Shạm], separated by hills several thousand li; it is also called Ta-ts'in. [42] Its inhabitants have red and white faces. [43] Men wear plain clothes, but women wear silk stuffs beset with pearls. [44] They have many clever weavers of silk. [45] Prisoners are kept in the frontier states till death without their being brought back to their home. [46] In the manufacture of glass they are not equalled by any nation of the world. [47] The royal city is eighty li square; the country in all directions measures several thousand li. [48] Their army consists of about a million men. [49] They have constantly to provide against the Ta-shih [Arabs]. [50] On the west the country bounds on the western sea; on the south, on the southern sea; in the north it connects with K'o-sa T'u-ch'üeh [the Khozar Turks]. [51] In the western sea there

---

[1] Shên-chang wu liu ch'ih (身丈五六尺). Five or six ch'ih,= 6 to 7 feet, would give a reasonable sense; I have, therefore, ventured to translate as above rather than literally: "their bodies are a chang (丈) and five or six ch'ih [in size]".

[2] See note to R 24.

is a market where a silent agreement exists between buyer and seller that, if the one is coming the other will go, and *vice versâ*; the seller will first spread out his goods, and the purchaser will afterwards produce their equivalents, which have to wait by the side of the articles to be sold till received by the seller, after which the purchase may be taken delivery of. They call this a spirit market. [52] There is also a report that in the west there is the country of women [Amazons] who, being affected by the influence of water, give birth to children [perhaps: who are born out of water[1]]. [53] It is further said: the country of Mo-lin is on the south-west of the country of Yang-sa-lo; crossing the great dessert 2,000 li you come to this country. [54] Its inhabitants are black and of ferocious manners. [55] Cereals are scarce, and there is no vegetation in the way of shrubs and trees; horses are fed on dried fish; men eat hu-mang, that is, the Persian date. [56] The country is very malarious. [57] The hill tribes which one has to pass in pursuing the overland road of these countries, are of the same race. [58] Of religions there are several kinds: there is the Ta-shih, the Ta-ts'in, and the Hsün-hsün religion. [59] The Hsün-hsün have most frequent illicit intercourse with barbarians; while

---

[1] The former seems to be the orthodox rendering. In the New Testament (Hongkong, London Mission, 1869) the words: τὸ γὰρ ἐν αὐτῇ γεννηθέν, ἐκ πνεύματός ἐστιν ἁγίου (Matthew, I, 20) have been rendered by 蓋所孕者感於聖神也.

eating they do not speak. [60] Those who belong to the religion of Ta-shih have a rule by which brothers, children and other relatives may be impeached for crime without implicating their kin, even if the crime be brought home to them. They do not eat the flesh of pigs, dogs, donkeys, and horses; they do not prostrate [or kneel down] before the king, nor before father or mother, to show their veneration; they do not believe in spirits, and sacrifice to heaven alone. Every seventh day is a holiday, when they will refrain from trade, and not go in or out, but drink wine and yield to dissipation till the day is finished. [61] The Ta-ts'in are good physicians in eye-diseases and diarrhœa, whether by looking to matters before the disease has broken out [*i.e.*, whether by the prophylactic method], or whether by extracting worms from the brain [trepanning].

---

[62] In the south-east of this country you go to Chiao-chih [Tung-king]; there is also a water-road communicating with the I-chou and Yung-ch'ang principalities [both in the present Yün-nan]. Many rare things come from there. [63] It is said that in the west of Ta-ts'in there is the water of a sea; west of the [sea] water there is a river; the river flows south-west; west of the river there are hills extending from south to north; west of the hills there is the Red Water;

west of this is the White Jade Hill; west of the Jade Hill is the Hill of the Hsi-wang-mu [western king's mother] who lives in a temple built of jadestone. [64] Coming from the western boundary of An-hsi [Parthia], following the crooked shape of the sea, you also come to Ta-ts'in, bending round over 10,000 li. [65] Although in that country the sun, the moon, and the constellations appear not different from what they are in China, former historians say that in the west of T'iao-chih you go a hundred[1] li to the place where the sun sets; this is far from being true. [66] In the 17th year of Chêng-kuan of the T'ang dynasty [=A.D. 643] the king of Fu-lin, Po-to-li,[2] sent envoys offering red glass and green gold ching [stones, gems, dust?], and a cabinet order was issued as an acknowledgement. [67] The Ta-shih [Arabs] waged war against the country which in the sequel became subject to them. [68] Between the periods Ch'ien-fêng and Ta-tsu [A.D. 666–701] they repeated their court offerings. [69] In the 7th year of K'ai-yüan [A.D. 719] they offered through the ta-yu [a high official] of T'u-huo-lo [Tokharestan] lions and ling-yang [antelopes].

---

[1] My edition of Ma Tuan-lin [d.d. A.D. 1524] has 北 *pei*, north, instead of 百 *pai*, hundred. This is apparently either a misprint or a blunder of the author's, as the Wei-shu, where this passage occurs, has *pai*. See I 23. I have made the correction and translated accordingly.

[2] Our author, in a two-column note added here, quotes the *Hsin-t'ang-shu* to say that Fu-lin is identical with the ancient Ta-ts'in Cf. L 1. The *Chiu-t'ang-shu* (K 1) contains the same remark. This shows that Tuan-lin prefers the former as an authority.

[70] The Dwarfs. These are in the south of Ta-ts'in. They are scarcely three ch'ih [say 4 feet, Engl.] large. When they work in the fields they are afraid of being devoured by cranes. Whenever Ta-ts'in has rendered them any assistance, the Dwarfs give them all they can afford in the way of precious stones to show their gratitude.

[71] The Hsüan-ch'ü. Their country contains many "birds of nine colours," with blue pecks, green necks, red-brown wings, red breasts, purple crests, vermilion feet, jade-coloured bodies, yellowish backs, and blackish tails. Another name of this animal is "bird of nine tails," or chin-fêng [the brocaded phœnix]. Those which have more blue than red on them are called Hsiu-luan [embroidered argus pheasant]. These birds usually come from the west of the Jo-shui [weak water]. Some say that it is the bird of the Hsi-wang-mu [western king's mother]. The coins of the country are the same as those of the country of San-t'ung.

[72] The San-t'ung are a thousand li south-west of Hsüan-ch'ü. The inhabitants have three ching-chu [clear pearls=eyes?], and sometimes four tongues by means of which they may produce one kind of sound and speak one language. They trade in plantains, also in rhinoceros' horns and ivory;[1] they make golden coins on which they imitate the king's, also the queen's face [with the

---

[1] I am not very clear about this and the following passage.

king's together?]; if the husband is changed, they use the king's face; if the king dies, they re-melt the coin.

[73] The above three countries border on Ta-ts'in whence they are here appended.

[74] Tsê-san was heard of during the Wei dynasty. It is subject to Ta-ts'in. Its residence lies right in the middle of a sea [perhaps "of a river."] North you go to Lü-fên by water half a year, with quick winds a month. It is nearest to Ch'êng-ku[1] of An-hsi [Parthia]. South-west you go to the capital of Ta-ts'in; we do not know how many li.

[75] Lü-fên was heard of during the Wei dynasty. It is subject to Ta-ts'in. Its residence is 2,000 li distant from the capital of Ta-ts'in. The flying bridge across the sea [river?] in Ta-ts'in west of the city of Lü-fên is 240 li in length [cf. P 64]. The road, if you cross the sea [river?], goes to the south-west; if you make a round at sea [or, on the river], you go due west.

---

[76] Fu-lin. In the south and east of the country of Fu-lin you go to Mieh-li-sha [old sound Miliksha]; north you go to the sea, forty days' journey; west you go to the sea, thirty days' journey. [77] In the east, starting from western

---

[1] Cf. P 60, which passage I presume contains the correct reading: An-ku-ch'êng.

Ta-shih [the remnants of the Khalif empire] you come to Yü-tien [Khoten], Hui-ho, Ta-ta [Tartary?] and Ch'ing-t'ang, and finally reach China. [78] They have during former dynasties not sent tribute to our court. [79] During the tenth month of the fourth year of the period Yüan-fêng [=November A.D. 1081], their king Mieh-li-i-ling-kai-sa[1] first sent the ta-shou-ling [a high official] Ni-ssŭ-tu-ling-ssŭ-mêng-p'an [Nestouri Ssŭ-mêng-p'an; Simon Pan?] to offer as tribute saddled horses, sword-blades and real pearls. [80] He said: the climate of this country is very cold; [81] houses there have no tiles; [82] the products are gold, silver, pearls, western silk cloth, cows, sheep, horses, camels with single humps, pears, almonds, dates, pa-lan[2] millet, and wheat. [83] They make wine from grapes. [84] Their musical instruments are the lute, the hu-ch'in, the hsiao-pi-li, and the p'ien-ku [see N 8]. [85] The king dresses in red and yellow robes, and wears a turban of silken cloth interwoven with gold thread. [86] In the third month every year he goes to the temple of Fou[3], to sit on a red couch [palankin?] which he gets the people to lift. His honoured servants [ministers, courtiers, priests?] are dressed like the king, but wear blue, green, purple, white mottled, red, yellow, or brown stuff; wear turbans and ride on horseback. [97] The towns and the country districts are each under the jurisdiction of a shou-ling [chief, sheik?].

---

[1] See note to N 3. [2] See note to N 6. [3] See note to N 10.

[88] Twice a year during the summer and autumn they must offer money and cloth [chin-ku-po]. [89] In their criminal decisions they distinguish between great and small offences. Light offences are punished by several hundreds[1] of blows with the bamboo; heavy offences with up to 200 blows; capital punishment is administered by putting the culprit into a feather bag which is thrown into the sea. [90] They are not bent on making war to neighbouring countries, and in the case of small difficulties try to settle matters by correspondence; but when important interests are at stake they will also send out an army. [91] They cast gold and silver coins, without holes, however; on the pile they cut the words Mi-lê-fou [Melek Fat?] which is a king's name; the people are forbidden to counterfeit the coin. [92] During the 6th year of Yüan-yu [=A.D. 1091] they sent two embassies, and their king was presented, by Imperial order, with 200 pieces of cloth, pairs of white gold [=silver?] vases, and clothing with gold bound in a girdle (?).

[93] According to the historians of the T'ang dynasty, the country of Fu-lin was held to be identical with the ancient Ta-ts'in. It should be remarked, however, that, although Ta-ts'in has from the after Han dynasty, when China was first

---

[1] This is clearly an error in my edition of Ma Tuan-lin; it should not read *shu-pai* [several hundred], but *shu-shih* [several tens]. This, at all events, is the wording of the Sung-shu. See N 14.

communicated with, till down to the Chin and T'ang dynasties has offered tribute without interruption, yet the historians of the "four reigns"[1] of the Sung dynasty, in their notices of Fu-lin, hold that this country has not sent tribute to court up to the time of Yüan-feng [A.D 1078–1086] when they sent their first embassy offering local produce. If we, now, hold together the two accounts of Fu-lin as transmitted by the two different historians, we find that, in the account of the T'ang dynasty, this country is said "to border on the great sea in the west;" whereas the Sung account says that "in the west you have still thirty days' journey to the sea;" and the remaining boundaries do also not tally in the two accounts; nor do the products and the customs of the people. I suspect that we have before us merely an accidental similarity of the name, and that the country is indeed not identical with Ta-ts'in. I have, for this reason, appended the Fu-lin account of the T'ang dynasty to my chapter on Ta-ts'in, and represented this Fu-lin [of the Sung dynasty] as a separate country altogether.

---

[1] *Ssŭ-ch'ao-shih*; probably the title of an historical publication, embracing the last four emperors of the Sung dynasty, and anticipating the *Sung-shih*. Ma Tuan-lin (ch. 192, p. 16 seqq.) describes a work, containing historical records of the Sung dynasty, under the title *Ssŭ-ch'ao-kuo-shih* (四朝國史), and in connection therewith says that the term *san-ch'ao* refers to the first two emperors (A.D. 960 to 1022), *liang-ch'ao*, to the next two (A.D. 1023 to 1167), and *ssŭ-ch'ao*, to the last four (A.D. 1068 to 1127). It appears that, in another work, *ssŭ-ch'ao* means the first four emperors of the southern Sung (A.D. 1127 to 1225). I refer to the *Ssŭ-ch'ao-wên-chien-lu*, regarding which *see* Wylie, p. 158.

R.

(*Chu-fan-chih*, by Chao Ju-kua of the Sung dynasty.[1])

[1] The country of Ta-ts'in, also called Li-kan, is the general meeting-ground for the nations of the western heayen,[2] and the place where the foreign merchants of Ta-shih [the Arabs of the Khalif empire] assemble. [2] Their king is styled Ma-lo-fou [cf. N 16]. [3] He rules at the city of An-tu. [4] He wears a turban of silk with gold-embroidered characters, and the throne he sits upon is covered with a silken rug. [5] They have walled cities and markets with streets and lanes. [6] In the king's dwelling they use crystal in making pillars; [7] and they use plaster in lieu of tiles. [8] They frequently erect tabernacles with seven entrances all round, each holding a garrison of thirty men. [9] Tribute-bearers from other countries pay their respects below the platform of the [palace] steps, whence they withdraw on having offered their congratulations. [10] The inhabitants are tall and of bright complexion, somewhat like the Chinese, which has been the cause of their being called Ta-ts'in. [11] They have keepers of official records and foreign interpreters knowing

---

[1] Cf. translations by Huc (?) in *Le Christianisme èn Chine*, Vol. I, p. 74; and Pauthier, *De l'Anthenticité*, etc., p. 51 seqq.

[2] 西天諸國, hsi-t'ien-chu-kuo, which may stand for 西天竺國, "the western part of India," to which Ta-ts'in belonged according to Chinese ideas, just as the Seres were looked at as an eastern appendage to India by the Romans.

their style of writing.¹ [12] They trim their hair and wear embroidered dresses. [13] They also have small carriages with white canopies, and flags, etc.; [14] and at the distance of every ten li there is a t'ing, and at the distance of every thirty li there is a hou. [15] There are in the country many lions who will attack travellers and may devour them unless they go in caravans of a hundred men and be protected by military equipment. [16] Underneath the palace they have cut into the ground a tunnel communicating with the hall of worship at a distance of over a li. [17] The king rarely goes out; but, to chant the liturgy and worship, on every seventh day, he proceeds by way of his tunnel to the hall of worship where, in performing divine service, he is attended by a suite of over fifty men.² But few amongst the people

---

¹ Or: "and as regards writing they know the hu style;" cf. Q 12. The character jên (人), which does not appear before chieh (睹) in E 9 and K 27, would then have to be separated from hu (胡) as belonging to the next sentence. The two sentences (12 and 13) afford a striking illustration of the superiority of the comparative method over the haphazard guesses of translators à la Pauthier. The latter (de l'Authenticité, etc., p. 52) translates: "Il y a plusieurs sortes de magistrats à la tête des lettres et la littérature est très-pratiquée. Tous les étrangers (hóu-jin) conservent leurs cheveux sur la tête," etc. A comparison of the Chinese version of these sentences with the parallel passage in the Chin-shu (F 11) might have prevented M. Pauthier to fall into this error.

² Pauthier, l. c., translates as follows: "Sous les habitations il y a des caves; les routes sont ouvertes à tous, et chacun peut y pratiquer ses rites. Il est permis d'avoir des chapelles à environ un li de distance pour y prier. Le roi sort rarement de son palais. Il n'y fait que lire les livres sacrés et faire ses dévotions à Fo. Quand

know the king's face; if he goes out he sits on horseback, protected by an umbrella; the head of his horse is adorned with gold, jade, pearls and other jewels. [18] Every year the king of the country of Ta-shih [the Arabs of the Khalif empire] who is styled Su-tan [=Sultan] sends tribute-bearers, and if in the country some trouble is apprehended, he gets the Ta-shih to use their military force in restoring order. [19] Their food mainly consists in cooked dishes, cakes and meat; they do not drink wine; but they use vessels made of gold and silver, and help themselves to their contents by means of ladles; after meals they wash hands in a golden bowl filled with water. [20] The products of the country consist in opaque glass, corals, raw gold, brocades, sarcenets, red cornelian stones and real pearls; also the hsieh-chi-hsi, which is the same as the T'ung-t'ien-hsi [21] At the beginning of the Yen-hsi period [A.D. 158–167; cf. E 33, where the 9th year, *i.e.*, nearly the end, of the Yen-hsi period is given as the date] the ruler of this country sent an embassy who, from outside the frontier of Jih-nan, came to offer rhinoceros horns, ivory and turtoise-shell, this

viennent les réunions du septieme jour (le dimanche), de toutes les routes du pays on arrive faire ses dévotions dans les chapelles et adorer Bouddha. Chaque groupe se compose de cinquante personnes environ." I select this example to show that disregard of the grammatical structure of the language does not merely result in little inaccuracies which may be passed over in charity; but that the general sense may also be lost without a trace.

being the first direct communication with China. As their presents contained no other precious matters and curiosities, it may be suspected that the ambassadors kept them back. [22] During the T'ai-k'ang period of the Chin dynasty [A.D. 280–289] further tribute was brought from there. [23] There is a saying that in the west of this country there is the Jo-shui [weak water] and the Liu-sha [flying sands] near the place where the Hsi-wang-mu [western king's mother] resides, and where the sun sets [24] The *Tu-huan-ching-hsing-chi*[1] says: The country of Fu-sang[2] is in the west of the Chan country; it is also called Ta-ts'in. [25] The inhabitants have red and white faces. [26] Men wear plain clothes, but women wear silk stuffs beset with pearls. [27] They are fond of wine and dry cakes. [28] They have many clever weavers of silk. [29] The size of the country is a thousand li. [30] Their army consists of over 10,000 men and has to ward off the Ta-shih [Arabs]. [31] In the western sea there is a market where a silent agreement exists between buyer and seller that, if the one is coming the other will go, and *vice versâ;* the seller will first spread out

---

[1] This may be the correct title of the work quoted by Ma Tuan-lin (Q 41), and there (perhaps owing to a misprint,—桂 kuei for 杜 tu) called *Kuei-huan-hsing-ching-chi*. Ma Tuan-lin himself has tu (杜) in several other places where he apparently quotes from the same work.

[2] *Sic*. I presume that *sang* 桑 is a mistake for *lin* 林, cf. Q 41. As Ma Tuan-lin's version contains more details than the above, and has not this mistake, I presume that he has had the text quoted before him, and does not borrow from Chao Ju-kua.

his goods, and the purchaser will afterwards produce their equivalents, which have to wait by the side of the articles to be sold till received by the seller, after which the purchase may be taken delivery of. They call this a spirit market.

CHINESE TEXT.

大秦國全錄 係德國人 夏德編纂

〔A〕第一采史記第一百二十三卷大宛列傳第六十三

初¹漢使至安息安息王令將二萬騎迎於東界東界去王都數千里行³比至過數十城人民相屬甚多漢使還而後發使隨漢使來觀漢廣大以⁵大鳥卵及黎軒善眩人獻于漢

〔B〕第二采前漢書第九十六卷上西域傳第六十六上

武¹帝始遣使至安息王令將二萬騎迎於東界東界去王都數千里行³比至過數十城人民相屬師古曰屬聯也音之欲反因⁴發使隨漢使者來觀漢地以⁵大鳥卵及犁軒眩人獻於漢天子大說師古曰說讀曰悅

〔C〕第三采後漢書第八十六卷南蠻西南夷列傳第七十六

永¹元九年徼外蠻及撣國王雍由調揮音擅東觀記作擅字遣重譯奉國珍寶和

帝賜金印紫綬小君長皆加印綬錢帛○○○永寧元年撣國王雍由調復遣使者詣闕
朝賀獻樂及幻人能變化吐火自支解易牛馬頭又善跳丸數乃至千自言我海西人海
西卽大秦也撣國西南通大秦明年元會安帝作樂於庭封雍由調爲漢大都尉賜印綬
金銀綵繒各有差也

〔D〕 第四采後漢書第八十八卷西域傳第七十八

條[1]支國城在山上周回四十餘里臨西海海水曲環其南及東北三面路絕唯西北隅通
陸道土地暑溼出師子犀牛封牛孔雀大雀大雀其卵如甕轉北而東復馬行六十餘口
至安息後役屬條支爲置大將監領諸小城焉安息國居和櫝城去洛陽二萬五千里北
與康居接南與烏弋山離接地方數千里小城數百戶口勝兵最爲殷盛其東界木鹿城
號爲小安息去洛陽二萬里章帝章和元年遣使獻獅子符拔符拔形似麟而無角和帝
永元九年都護班超遣甘英使大秦抵條支臨大海欲度而安息西界船人謂英曰海水

廣大往來者逢善風三月乃得度若遇遲風亦有二歲者故入海人皆齎三歲糧海中善
使人思土戀慕數有死亡者英聞之乃止十三年安息王滿屈復獻獅子及條支大鳥時
謂之安息雀自安息西行三千四百里至阿蠻國從阿蠻西行三千六百里至斯賓國從
斯賓南行度河又西南至于羅國九百六十里安息西界極矣自此南乘海乃通大秦其
土多海西珍奇異物焉

〔E〕第五采後漢書第八十八卷西域傳第七十八

大秦國一名犂鞬以在海西亦云海西國地方數千里有四百餘城小國役屬者數十以
石為城郭列置郵亭皆堊之[6]有松柏諸木百草人俗力田作多種
樹蠶桑皆髡頭而衣文繡乘輜軿白蓋小車出入擊鼓建旌旗幡幟所居城邑周圜百餘
里城中有五宮相去各十里宮室皆以水精為柱食器亦然其王日游一宮聽事五日而
後徧常使一人持囊隨王車人有言事者即以書投囊中王至宮發省理其枉直各有官

曹文書置三十六將皆會議國事其王無有常人皆簡立賢者國中災異及風雨不時輒[19]
廢而更立受放者甘黜不怨其人民皆長大平正有類中國故謂之大秦土多金銀奇寶[20][21][22]
有夜光璧明月珠駭雞犀 抱朴子曰通天犀有曰理如綖者以盛米置羣雞中雞欲啄米至輒驚卻故南人名爲駭雞 珊瑚琥珀琉璃琅玕朱丹[24]
青碧刺金縷繡識成金縷罽雜色綾作黃金塗火浣布又有細布或言水羊毳野蠶繭所
作也合會諸香煎其汁以爲蘇合凡外國諸珍異皆出焉以金銀爲錢銀錢十當金錢一[25][26][27]
與安息天竺交市於海中利有十倍其人質直市無二價穀食常賤國用富饒隣國使到[28][29][30][31]
其界首者乘驛詣王都至則給以金錢其王常欲通使於漢而安息欲以漢繒綵與之交[32]
市故遮閡不得自達 代反閡五 至桓帝延熹九年大秦王安敦遣使自日南徼外獻象牙犀角[33]
瑇瑁始乃一通焉其所表貢並無珍異疑傳者過焉或云其國西有弱水流沙近西王母[34]
所居處幾於日所入也漢書云從條支西行二百餘日近日所入則與今書異矣前世漢[35][36]
使皆自烏弋以還莫有至條支者又云從安息陸道繞海北行出海西至大秦人庶連屬[37][38]

十里一亭三十里一置〔置驛也〕終無盜賊寇警而道多猛虎獅子遮害行旅不百餘人齎兵器輒為所食又言有飛橋數百里可度海北諸國所生奇異玉石諸物譎怪多不經故不記云〔魚豢魏略曰大秦國俗多奇幻口中出火自縛自解跳十二九巧妙異常〕

〔F〕第六采晉書第九十七卷列傳第六十七

大秦國一名犁鞬在西海之西其地東西南北各數千里有城邑其城周迴百餘里屋宇皆以珊瑚為梲栭琉璃為牆壁水精為柱礎其王有五宮其宮相去各十里每旦於一宮聽事終而復始若國有災異輒更立賢人放其舊王被放者亦不敢怨有官曹簿領而文字習胡亦有白蓋小車旌旗之屬及郵驛制置一如中州其人長大貌類中國人而胡服其土多出金玉寶物明珠大貝有夜光璧駭雞犀及火浣布又能刺金縷繡及織錦縷罽以金銀為錢銀錢十當金錢之一安息天竺人與之交市於海中其利百倍鄰國使到者輒稟以金錢途經大海海水鹹苦不可食商客往來皆齎三歲糧是以至者稀少漢時都

護班超遣掾甘英使其國入海船人曰海中有思慕之物往者莫不悲懷若漢使不戀父母妻子者可入英不能渡武帝太康中其王遣使貢獻[20]

〔G〕第七采宋書第九十七卷列傳第五十七

若[1]夫大秦天竺迥出西溟二漢銜役特艱斯路而商貨所資或出交部汎海陵波因風遠至又[2]重峻參差氏眾非一殊名詭號種別類殊[3]山深水寶由茲自出通犀翠羽之珍蛇珠火布之異千名萬品竝世主之所虛心故舟舶繼路商使交屬

〔H〕第八采梁書第五十四卷列傳第四十八

其[1]西與大秦安息交市海中[2]多大秦珍物珊瑚琥珀金碧珠璣琅玕鬱金蘇合是合諸香汁煎之非自然一物也又云大秦人采蘇合先笮其汁以為香膏乃賣其滓與諸國[3]賈人是以展轉來達中國不大香也鬱金獨出罽賓國[4]○○○[5]漢桓帝延熹九年大秦王安敦遣使自日南徼外來獻漢世唯一通焉其國[6]人行賈往往至扶南日南交趾其南徼[7]

〔1〕 第九采魏書第一百二卷列傳第九十

諸國人少有到大秦者孫權黃武五年有大秦賈人字秦論來到交趾交趾太守吳邈遣送詣權權問方土謠俗論具以事對時諸葛恪討丹陽獲黝歙短人論見之曰大秦希見此人權以男女各十人差吏會稽劉咸送論於道物故論乃徑還本國

大秦國一名黎軒都[2]安都城從[3]條支西渡海曲一萬里去代[4]三萬九千四百里其海傍出[5]猶渤海也而東西與渤海相望蓋自然之理地方[6]六千里居兩海之間其地平正人居星[7][8]布其[9]王都城分為五城各方五里周六十里王居[10]中城城置八臣以主四方而王城亦置八臣分主四城若[12]謀國事及四方有不決者則四城之臣集議王所王自聽之然後施行王[14]三年一出觀風化人有寃枉詣王訴訟者當方之臣小則讓責大則黜退令其舉賢人以代之其人端正長大衣服車旗擬儀中國故外域謂之大秦其土宜[17]五穀桑麻人務蠶[18]田多珍琳琅玕神龜白馬朱鬣明珠夜光璧[19]東南通交趾又水道通益州永昌郡多出異[20]

物大秦西海水之西有河河西南流河西有赤水西有白玉山玉山西有[21]
西王母山玉爲堂云從安息西界循海曲亦至大秦四萬餘里於彼國觀日月星辰無異[22][23]
中國而前史云條支西行百里日入處失之遠矣

〔K〕第十朵舊唐書第一百九十八卷列傳第一百四十八

拂菻國一名大秦在西海之上東南與波斯接地方萬餘里列城四百邑居連屬其宮宁[1][2][3][4][5][6]
柱櫳多以水精琉璃爲之有貴臣十二人共治國政常使一人將囊隨王車百姓有事者[7][8]
卽以書投囊中王還宮省發理其枉直其王無常人簡賢者而立之國中災異及風雨不[9][10]
時輒廢而更立其王冠形如鳥舉翼冠及瓔珞皆綴以珠寶著錦繡衣前不開襟坐金花[11][12]
牀有一鳥似鵝其毛綠色常在王邊倚枕上坐每進食有毒其鳥輒鳴其都城疊石爲之[13][14]
尤絕高峻凡有十萬餘戶南臨大海城東面有大門其高二十餘丈自上及下飾以黃金[15][16][17]
光煇燦爛連曜數里自外至王室凡有大門三重列異寶雕飾第二門之樓中懸一大金[18][19]

秤以金九十二枚屬於衡端以候日之十二時焉爲一金人其大如人立於側每至一時

其金丸輒落鏗然發聲引唱以紀日時毫釐無失其殿[20]以瑟瑟爲柱黃金爲地象牙爲門

扇香木爲棟梁其俗[21]無瓦擣白石爲末羅之塗屋上其堅密光潤還如玉石至於盛暑之

節人厭囂熱乃引水潛流上徧於屋宇機制巧密人莫之知觀者惟聞屋上泉鳴俄見四

簷飛溜懸波如瀑激氣成涼風其巧妙如此風俗男子剪髮披帔而右袒婦人不開襟錦

爲頭巾家資滿億封以上位[26]有羊羔生於土中其國人候其萌乃築牆以院之防外獸

所食也然其臍與地連割之則死唯人著甲走馬及擊鼓以駭之其羔驚鳴而臍絕便逐

水草俗皆髡[28]而衣繡乘輜軿白蓋小車出入擊鼓建旌旗幟[31]土多金銀奇寶有夜光璧

明月珠駭雞犀大貝車渠瑪瑙孔翠珊瑚琥珀凡西域諸珍異多出其國隋[33]煬帝常將通

拂菻竟不能致貞觀[34]十七年拂菻王波多力遣使獻赤玻瓈綠金精等物太宗降璽書答

慰賜以綾綺焉自大食強盛漸陵諸國乃遣大將軍摩栧伐其都城因約爲和好請每歲

翰之金帛遂臣屬大食焉[36]乾封二年遣使獻底也伽大足元年復遣使來朝[37]開元七年正月其主遣吐火羅大首領獻獅子羚羊各二不數月又遣大德僧來朝貢[38][39]

〔L〕第十一采唐書第二百二十一卷下列傳第一百四十六下

拂菻[1]古大秦也居西海上[2]一曰海西國去京師四萬里在苫西北直突厥可薩部西瀕海[3][4][5][6]有遲散城東南接波斯地方萬里城四百勝兵百萬十里一亭三亭一置臣役小國數十[7][8][9][10][11][12]以名通者曰澤散曰驢分澤散直東北不得其道里東度海二千里至驢分國重石爲都城廣八十里東門高二十丈釦以黃金王宮有三襲門皆飾異寶中門中有金巨稱一作[13][14][15][16][17]金人立其端屬十二丸奉時改一丸落以瑟瑟爲殿柱水精琉璃爲梲香木梁黃金爲地[18][19]象牙闔有貴臣十二共治國王出一人挈囊以從有訟書投囊中還省柱直國有大災異[20][21][22]輒廢王更立賢者王冠如鳥翼綴珠衣錦繡前無襟坐金蘤榻側有鳥如鵝綠毛上食有[23][24]毒輒鳴無陶瓦屋白石甃屋堅潤如玉盛暑引水上流氣爲風男子翦髮衣繡右袒而帔[25][26][27][28]

乘輜耕白蓋小車出入建旌旗擊鼓婦人錦巾家貲億萬者爲上官俗喜酒嗜乾餅多幻[29][30][31][32][33]
人能發火于顏手爲江湖口幡眭舉足墮珠玉有善醫能開腦出蟲以愈目眚土多金銀[34][35]
夜光璧明月珠大貝車磲碼碯木難孔翠虎魄織水羊毛爲布曰海西布海中有珊瑚洲[36][37]
海人乘大舶墮鐵網水底珊瑚初生磐石上白如菌一歲而黃三歲赤枝格交錯高三四
尺鐵發其根繫網舶上絞而出之失時不取卽腐西海有市貿易不相見置物旁名鬼[38]
市有獸名饕大如狗獷惡而力北邑有羊生土中臍屬地割必死俗介馬而走擊鼓以驚[39][40]
之羔臍絕卽逐水草不能羣貞觀十七年王波多力遣使獻赤玻璨綠金精苔薆大[41][42]
食稍疆遣大將軍摩拽伐之拂菻約和遂臣屬乾封至大足再朝獻開元七年因吐火羅[43][44][45]
大酋獻師子羚羊自拂菻西南度磧二千里有國曰磨鄰老勃薩其人黑而性悍地瘴[46][47][48]
癘無草木五穀飼馬以槁魚人食鶻莽鶻莽波斯棗也不耻烝報於夷狄最甚號曰尋其[49][50]
君臣七日一休不出納交易飲以窮夜[51]

〔M〕 第十二采大秦景敎流行中國碑

案¹西域圖記及漢魏史策大秦國南統珊瑚之海北極衆寶之山西望仙境花林東接長風弱水其土出火綄布返魂香明月珠夜光璧俗無寇盜人有樂康法非景不行主非德²不立土宇廣闊文物昌明³

〔N〕 第十三宋史第四百九十卷列傳第二百四十九

拂菻國¹東南至滅力沙北至海皆四十程西至海三十程東自西大食及于闐回紇靑唐乃抵中國歷代未嘗朝貢元豐四年十月其王滅力伊靈改撒始遣大首領你廝都令廝孟判來獻鞍馬刀劍真珠言²其國地甚寒土屋無瓦產金銀珠³西錦牛羊馬獨蜂駝梨杏千年棗巴欖粟麥以蒲萄釀酒樂有箜篌壺琴箏篥偏鼓⁴王服紅黃衣以金線織絲布纏⁵頭歲三月則詣佛寺坐紅牀使人舁之貴臣如王之服或青綠緋白粉紅黃紫竝纏頭跨⁶馬城市田野皆有首領主之每歲惟夏秋兩得奉給金錢錦穀帛以治事大小為差刑罰⁷

皋輕者杖數十重者至二百大皋則盛以毛囊投諸海不尙鬭戰鄰國小有爭但以文字來往相詰問事大亦出兵鑄金銀爲錢無穿孔面鏨彌勒佛皆爲王名禁民私造元祐六年其使兩至詔別賜其王帛二百四白金瓶襲衣金束帶

〔O〕第十四采明史第三百二十六卷列傳第二百十四

拂菻卽漢大秦桓帝時始通中國晉及魏皆曰大秦嘗入貢唐曰拂菻宋仍之亦數入貢而宋史謂歷代未嘗朝貢疑其非大秦也元末其國人捏古倫入市中國元亡不能歸太祖聞之以洪武四年八月召見命齎詔書還諭其王曰自有宋失馭天絶其祀元興沙漠入主中國百有餘年天厭其昏淫亦用隕絶其命中原擾亂十有八年當羣雄初起朕爲淮右布衣起義救民荷天之靈授以文武諸臣東渡江左練兵養士十有四年西平漢王陳友諒東縛吳王張士誠南平閩粵戡定巴蜀北定幽燕奠安方夏復我中國之舊疆朕爲臣民推戴卽皇帝位定有天下之號曰大明建元洪武於今四年矣凡四夷諸邦皆

遣官告諭惟爾拂菻隔越西海未及報知今遣爾國之民捏古倫齎詔往諭朕雖未及古
先哲王俾萬方懷德然不可不使天下知朕平定四海之意故茲詔告已而復命使臣普
刺等齎敕書綵幣招諭其國乃遣使入貢後不復至萬曆時大西洋人至京師言天主耶
蘇生於如德亞即古大秦國也其國自開闢以來六千年史書所載世代相嬗及萬事萬
物原始無不詳悉謂為天主肇生人類之邦言頗誕漫不可信其物產珍寶之盛具見前
史

〔P〕

第十五采三國志第三十卷註內所引魏略

前世謬以為條支在大秦西今其實在東前世又謬以為強於安息今更役屬之號為安
息西界前世又謬以為弱水在條支西今弱水在大秦西前世又謬以為從條支西行二
百餘日近日所入今從大秦西近日所入大秦國一號犁靬在安息條支西大海之西從
安息界安谷城乘船直截海西遇風利二月到風遲或一歲無風或三歲其國在海西故

俗謂之海西有[8]河出其國西又有大海海[9]西有遲散城從國下直北至烏丹城西南又渡[10][11]
一河乘船一日乃過西南又渡一河一日乃過凡[12]有大都三都從安谷城陸道直北行之[13]
海北復直西行之海西復直南行經之烏遲散城渡一河乘船一日乃過周迴繞海凡當[14][16][17]
渡大海六日乃到其國國[15]有小城邑合四百餘東西南北數千里其王治濱側河海以石
爲城郭其土地有松柏槐梓竹葦楊柳梧桐百草民俗田種五穀畜有馬驢騾駱駝桑蠶[18][19][20]
俗多奇幻口中出火自縛自解跳十二丸巧妙其國無常主國中有災異輒更立賢人以[21][22]
爲王而生放其故王王亦不敢怨其俗人長大平正似中國人而胡服自云本中國一別[23]
也常[24]欲通使於中國而安息圖其利不能得過其俗能胡書其制度公私宮室爲重屋旌[25][26][27][28]
旗擊鼓白蓋小車郵驛亭置如中國從安息繞海北到其國人民相屬十里一亭三十里[29][30][31]
一置終無盜賊但有猛虎獅子爲害行道不羣則不得過其國置小王數十其王所治城[32][33][34]
周回百餘里有官曹文書王有五宮一宮間相去十里其王平旦之一宮聽事至日暮一[35][36]

宿明日復至一宮五日一周置三十六將每議事一將不至則不議也王出行常使從人持一韋囊自隨有白言者受其辭投囊中還宮乃省爲決理以水晶作宮柱及器物作弓矢其別枝封小國曰澤散王曰驢分王曰且蘭王曰賢督王曰汜復王曰于羅王其餘小王國甚多不能一一詳之也國出細絺作金銀錢金錢一當銀錢十有織成細布言用水羊毳名曰海西布此國六畜皆出水或云非獨用羊毛也亦用木皮或野繭絲作織成氍毹毾㲪罽帳之屬皆好其色又鮮於海東諸國所作也又常利得中國絲解以爲胡綾故數與安息諸國交市於海中海水苦不可食故往來者希到其國中山出九色次玉石一曰青二曰赤三曰黃四曰白五曰黑六曰綠七曰紫八曰紅九曰紺今伊吾山中有九色石即其類陽嘉三年時疏勒王臣槃獻海西青石金帶各一又今西域舊圖云罽賓條支諸國出琦石即次玉石也大秦多金銀銅鐵鉛錫神龜白馬朱髦駭雞犀瑇瑁玄熊赤螭辟毒鼠大貝車渠瑪瑙南金翠爵羽翮象牙符采玉明月珠夜光珠真白珠琥珀珊瑚赤

白黑綠黃青紺縹紅紫十種流離琳琅玕水精玫瑰雄黃碧五色玉黃白黑綠紫
紅絳紺金黃縹留黃十種氍㲣五色毾㲪五色九色首下氍㲪金縷繡雜色綾金塗布緋
持布發陸布緋持渠布火浣布阿羅得布巴則布度代布溫色布五色桃布絳地金織帳
五色斗帳一微木二蘇合狄提迷迭㮲納白附子薰陸鬱金芸膠薰草木十二種香大秦
道既從海北陸通又循海而南與交阯七郡外夷北又有水道通益州永昌故永昌出異
物前世但論有水道不知有陸道今其略如此其民人戶數不能備詳也自蔥領西此國
最大置諸小王甚多故錄其屬大者矣澤散王屬大秦其治在海中央北至驢分水行半
歲風疾時一月到最與安谷城相近西南詣大秦都不知里數驢分王屬大秦其治
去大秦都二千里從驢分城西之大秦渡海飛橋長二百三十里渡海道西南行繞海直
西行且蘭從思陶國直南渡河乃直西行之且蘭三千里道出河南乃西行從
且蘭復直西河之汜復國六百里南道會汜復乃西南之賢督國且蘭汜復直南乃有積

石積石南乃有大海出珊瑚眞珠且蘭氾復斯賓阿蠻北有一山東西行大秦海東各[69]
有一山皆南北行賢督王屬大秦其治東北去氾復王屬大秦其治東北[70]
于羅三百四十里渡海也于羅屬大秦其治在氾復東北渡河從于羅東北又渡河斯羅[74]
東北又渡河斯羅國屬安息與大秦接也大秦西有海水海水西有河水河水西南北行[76]
有大山西有赤水赤水西有白玉山白玉山西有西王母西王母西有修流沙流沙西有大[77]
夏國堅沙國屬縓國月氏國四國西有黑水所傳聞西之極矣

〔Q〕 第十六采文獻通考第三百三十九卷

大秦一名犁軒 犁軒居言反一云前後漢時始通焉其國在西海之西亦云海西國其王治[1][2][3]
安都城宮室皆以水精爲柱從條支西度海曲萬里去長安蓋四萬里其國平正人居星[4][5]
布其地東西南北各數千里有四百餘城小國役屬者數十西有大海海西有遲散城干[6][7][8][9][10][11]
城有官曹簿領而文字習胡人皆髠頭而衣文繡亦有白蓋小車旌旗之屬又十里一亭[12][13][14][15]

三十里一堠一如中州地多師子遮害行旅不百餘人持兵器輒為所傷其王無常人皆[16]
循立賢者有災異及風雨不時輒廢而更立受放者無怨其人長大平正有類中國故謂[17]
之大秦或曰本中國人也玉有駭雞犀[18]抱朴子云通天犀有一白理如綖者以盛米置[19]
羣雞中欲啄米至輒驚去故南人名為駭雞也合會[20]
諸香煎其汁以為蘇合[21]土為金銀奇寶夜光璧明月珠琥珀琉璃神龜自馬朱髦璣玄[22]贊截
熊赤璃璧毒鼠大貝車渠渠石廣雅云車渠石似玉瑪瑙玉似贊出西海有養者似狗多方力獷惡宗反
北附庸小邑有羊羔自然生於土中候其欲萌築墻護之恐獸所食也其臍與地連割之絕[23]
則死擊物驚之遂絕逐水草無羣又有木難出趙鳥口中結沫所成碧色珠也土人珍之[24]
曹子建冊有幻人能額上為炎爐手中作江湖舉足而珠玉自墮開口則旛旄亂出前漢武帝遣使
瑚間木難[25]有織成細布言用水羊毛名曰海中布作氍毹䄛罽帳[26][27]
至安息安息獻犂靬幻人二皆戚眉峭鼻亂髮拳鬢長四尺五寸眕人志反[28]
之屬其色又鮮於海東諸國所作也又常利得中國縑素解以為胡綾紺紋數與安息諸
胡交市於海中西南漲海中可七八百里行到珊瑚洲水底有盤石珊瑚生其上大秦人[29]

常乘大舶載鐵網令水工沒先入視之可下網乃下初生白而漸漸似苗拆甲歷一歲許
出網目間變作黃色支格交錯高極三四尺大者圍尺餘三年色乃赤好復視之知可採
便以鐵鈔發其根乃以索繫網使人於舶上絞車舉出還國理截恣意所作若失時不舉
便蠧敗其國以金銀爲錢銀錢十當金錢一其人質直市無二價穀食常賤國用富饒鄰
國使到其界首者乘驛詣王都至則給以金錢其王常欲通使於漢而安息欲以漢繒綵
與之交市故遮閡不得自達又塗經大海商客往來皆齎三歲糧是以至者稀桓帝元嘉
初大秦王安敦遣使自日南徼外獻象牙犀角瑇瑁始乃一通馬其所表貢並無珍異疑
傳者隱之至晉武帝大康中其王遣使貢獻或云其國西有弱水流沙近西王母所處幾
於日所入也 外國圖云從嘂北有國名大秦其種長大身丈五六尺桓環行經記云拂菻國有苫國西隔山
數千里亦曰大秦其人顏色紅白男子悉著素衣婦人皆服珠錦多工巧善織絡或有俘在諸國
守死不改鄕風琉璃妙者天下莫比王城方八十里四面境土各數千里勝兵約有百萬常與大食相禦西枕西

海南枕南海北接可薩突厥西海中有市客主同和我往則彼去彼往則我歸賣者陳之於前買者酬之於後皆[51]
以其直置諸物傍待領直然後收物名曰鬼市又聞西有女國感水而生又云麼鄰國在秧薩羅國西南渡大磧[52][53]
行二千里至其國其人黑其俗獷少米麥無草木馬食乾魚人食鶻莽鶻莽即波斯棗也瘴癘特甚諸國陸行之[54][55][56]
所經山胡則一種法有數般有大食法有大秦法有尋尋法其尋尋蒸報於諸夷狄中最甚食不語其大食法[57]
者以弟子親戚而作刑典縱有徵過不至相累不食豬狗驢馬等肉不拜國王父母之尊不信鬼神祀天而已其[58][59][60]
俗每七日一假不買賣不出納唯飲酒放浪終日其大秦善醫眼及痢或未病先見或開腦出蟲[61]
其國東南通交趾又水道通益州永昌郡多出異物大秦西海水水西有河河西南流河[62][63]
西有南北山山西有赤水西有白玉山玉山西有西王母山玉爲堂室云從安息西界循[64]
海曲亦至大秦迴萬餘里於彼國觀日月星辰無異中國而前史云條支西行北里日入[65]
處失之遠矣唐貞觀十七年拂菻王波多力 新唐書云拂菻即古大秦也 遣使獻赤玻璃綠金精下詔答[66][68][69]
賚大食強而伐之遂臣屬焉乾封至大足再朝獻開元七年因吐火羅大酋獻師子羚羊[67]

70. 小人

小人在大秦之南軀纔三尺其耕種之時懼鶴所食大秦每衞助之小人竭其珍以酬報

71. 軒渠

軒渠其國多九色鳥青口綠頸紫翼紅膺紺頂丹足碧身緗背玄尾亦名九尾鳥亦名錦鳳其青多紅少謂之繡鸞常從弱水西來或云是西王母之禽也其國幣貨同三童國

72. 三童

三童在軒渠國西南千里人皆服有三精珠或有四舌者能爲一種聲亦能俱語貨常多用蕉葧犀象作金幣率效國王之面亦效王后之面若丈夫交易則用國王之面王死則更鑄[73]已上三國與大秦隣接故附之

74. 澤散

澤散魏時聞焉屬大秦其治在海中央北至驢分水行半歲風疾時一月到最與安息城谷相近西南詣大秦都不知里數

75. 驢分

驢分魏時聞焉屬大秦其治去大秦都二千里從驢分城西之大秦度海飛橋長二百四十里發海道西南繞海道直西行至焉

76. 拂菻

拂菻國南東至滅力沙北至海皆四十程西至海三十程東自西大食及于闐回紇達靼青唐乃抵中國歷代未嘗朝貢宋元豐四年十月其王滅力伊靈改撒始遣大首領你廝都令厮孟判來獻鞍馬刀劍真珠言其國地甚寒土屋無瓦產金銀珠胡錦牛羊馬獨峰駝梨杏千年棗巴攬粟麥以蒲萄釀酒樂有箜篌胡琴小篳篥偏鼓王服紅黃衣以金線織絲布纏頭歲三月則詣佛寺坐紅床使人昇之貴人如王之服或青綠緋白粉紅褐紫並纏頭跨馬城市田野皆有首領主之每歲唯夏秋兩得俸給金錢錦穀帛以治事大小為差刑罰罪輕者杖數百重者至二百大罪則盛以毛囊投諸海不尚鬪戰鄰國小有爭

但以文字往來相詰問事大亦出兵鑄金銀為錢無穿孔面鏨彌勒佛皆為王名禁民私造元祐六年其使兩至詔別賜其王帛二百疋白金餅對衣金束帶

按唐史有拂菻國以為即古大秦自後漢始通中國歷晉唐貢獻不廢而宋四朝史拂菻傳則以為其國歷代未嘗朝貢至元豐時始遣使入獻方物今以二史兩拂菻傳參之唐傳言其國西瀕大海宋傳則言西至海尚三十程而餘界亦齟齬不合土產風俗亦不同恐是其名偶同而非大秦也今故以唐之拂菻附入大秦而此拂菻自為一國云

〔R〕第十七采諸番志

大秦國 一名犁靬 西天諸國之都會大食番商所萃之地也其王號麻囉弗理安都城以帛織出金字纏頭所坐之物則織以絲罽有城市里巷王所居舍以水精為柱以石灰代瓦多

設簾幃四圍開七門置守者各三十人有他國進貢者拜於階陛之下祝壽而退其人長[10]大美晳頗類中國故謂之大秦有官曹簿領而文字習胡人皆髡頭而衣文繡亦有白蓋[13]小車旌旗之屬及十里一亭三十里一堠地多獅子遮害行旅不百人持兵器偕行易為[15]所食宮室[16]下鑿地道通禮拜堂一里許王少出惟誦經禮佛遇七日即由地道往禮拜堂拜佛從者五十餘人國人罕識王面若出遊則騎馬用傘馬之頭頂皆飾以金玉珠寶遞[18]年大食國王有號素丹者遣人進貢國內有警即令大食措置兵甲撫定所食之物多[19]飯餅肉不飲酒用金銀器以匙挑之食已即以金盤貯水濯手土產琉璃珊瑚生金花錦[20]縵布紅瑪瑙真珠又出駿雞犀駿雞犀即通天犀也漢延熹初其國主遣使自日南徼外[22]來獻犀象瑇瑁始通中國所供無他珍異或疑使人隱之晋太康中又來貢或云其國西[23]有弱水流沙近西王母所處幾於日所入也按杜還經行記云拂桑國在苫國西亦名大[25]秦其人顏色紅白男子[26]悉著素衣婦人皆服珠錦好飲酒尚乾餅多工巧善織絡地方千

VARIANTS.

In the following list of readings only such discrepancies have been included which may possibly involve a change in the meaning or a difference in the sound of a name. The portions A to Q of the text have been compared with palace editions of the present dynasty; I have had no opportunity of comparing the extract R with another edition.

In A 3 and B 2 I have read with Ma Tuan-lin who, in his description of Au-hsi, copies this passage, and translated with Wylie, 北 *pei*, north, for *pi* 比. My attention was drawn by Mr. E. H. Parker to the latter character being quite in order, it being explained by 及 *chi* in native Dictionaries. The translation would thus read: "The eastern frontier was several thousand li distant from the king's capital, and on the way thither one came across several cities, etc." Palace editions have 比 *pi*, I have therefore retained this character in the Chinese text.

F 11. The *Yüan-chien-lei-han*, quoting this passage, has 異習 *i-hsi* ("uncommonly well versed in—") for 習胡 *hsi-hu*.

N 16. A Kien-lung P. Ed. has 背 *pei*, "back," for 皆 *chieh*, "all"; accordingly the Mi-lê-fou appears on the pile, and the king's name on the back of the coin. I read 皆 *chieh* in both the editions of Ma Tuan-lin I had before me, in the passage Q 91.

N 17. 玉 *yü* for 王 *wang*, in P. Ed.

P 41, and *passim*. 汜復 *fan-fu* for 汜復 *ssŭ-fu*, in P. Ed.

P 49ˣˣ 宿 *su* for 色 *sê*, in P. Ed. See also notes 1 to 5 on p. 74.

P 49eee. 迷迭 *mi-tieh* for 迷迷 *mi-mi*, in P. Ed.

P 67. 西行之 *hsi-hsing-chih* for 西河之 *hsi-ho-chih*, in P. Ed.

P 41, 73 seqq. 於羅 for 于羅 (*yü-lo*), in P. Ed.

Q 22. 寶 *pao* for 賫 *ts'ung*, in both editions.

Q 41. 苦 *k'u* for 苫 *chan*, in both editions.

Q 46. 璃琉 *li-liu*. Sic in both editions.

Q 51. 幾 *chi* for 我 *wo*, in P. Ed.

Q 79. 沙 *sha* for 伊 *i*, in P. Ed.; mine (d. d. A. D. 1524) has 伊 *i*.

前買者酬於之後皆以其直置諸物旁待領直然後收物名曰鬼市

里勝兵萬餘與大食相禦西海中有市客主同和我往則彼去彼來則我歸賣者陳之於

INDEX TO TRANSLATIONS
OR
CHINESE TEXT.

A.

ACBATANA; see A-MAN.

AGRICULTURE, E 8; I 17; P 19.

ALEXANDRIA; see CH'IH-SAN; WU-CH'IH-SAN.

ALMONDS, N 6; Q 82.

A-MAN (Acbatana), D 22; P 69.

AMAZONS, Q 52.

AMBER, E 22; H 2; K 32; L 35; P 49 *z*; Q 21.

AN-HSI (Parthia), accounts of, A 1-5; B 1-5; D 10-22; E 37; Q 74.

—— boundary of, eastern, A 1-3; B 1-3; D 15, 16.

—— boundary of, western, D 20, 22; I 22; P 2, 76. *See also* AN-KU; T'IAO-CHIH; YÜ-LO.

—— capital of (=Hekatompylos) D 10, 22; distance from eastern frontier, A 2; B 2; distance from Lo-yang, D 11; from Acbatana (A-man), D 22.

—— first embassy from China to, A 1; B 1.

—— land road of; D 8, 22; E 37.

—— sends embassies to China, A 4-5; B 4-5; D 17.

—— trade with, E 28, 32; F 16; H 1; P 24, 45; Q 28, 34.

AN-KU (city on the western boundary of An-hsi), P 6, 13, 60; (=*Ch'êng-ku*, Q 74).

ANNAM, E 33; H 5-8; I 19; P 50; Q 36, 62; R 21.

ANTELOPES (*ling-yang*), K 38; L 45; Q 69.

ANTIOCH; see AN-TU,

ANTIOCHIA MARGIANA; see MU-LU.

AN-TU, city of (capital of Ta-ts'in), besieged by Arabs, K 45.

—— breadth, L 15,

—— circumference, E 13; F 4; I 9; P 34; Q 47.

—— city walls, E 5; K 14; L 14, 15; P 17.

—— clepsydra, K 19; L 18.

—— described, I 9 seqq.

—— east gate K 17; L 16.

—— four quarters (tetrapolis) governed by eight magistrates, I 11.

——magistrates residing at, I 10-12.

——name (An-tu) I 2; Q 3; R 3.

——public buildings (palaces), E 14 seq.; F 7-8; K 17-18; L 17.

——situation K 16; P 16, 61, 63 seqq.; Q 74, 75.

AN-TUN, king of Ta-ts'in (=M. Aurelius Antoninus); see EMBASSIES, etc., A.D. 166.

ARABS; see TA-SHIH.

ARCHITECTURE OF PALACES, etc., eaves, pillars and window-bars ornamented with crystal and glass, K 6.
floor-beams of fragrant wood, K 20; L 19.
floors of yellow gold, K 20; L 19.
kingposts ornamented with coral, F 5; with crystal and glass, L 19.
leaves of folding doors of ivory, K 20; L 19.
pillars ornamented with crystal, E 15; F 6; P 39; Q 4; R 6.
——with Sê-sê, K 20; L 19.
roofs have no tiles, but are plastered, K 21, 22; L 25; N 5; Q 81; R 7.
walls ornamented with glass, F 6.
water led on roofs of houses to produce coolness, K 22; L 26.
ARCHIVES; see DOCUMENTS.
ARISTOCRACY, K 25; L 31.
ARMY, L 10; N 15; Q 48, 90; R 30.
——garrisoned in tents, R 8.
ASBESTOS; see CLOTH.

B.

BARK, trees', used in weaving cloth, P 44.
BARTER (in Ceylon); see SPIRIT MARKETS.
BEARS, BLACK, P 49 ^{l}; Q 21.
BIRD of NINE COLOURS, Q 71.
BIRD, the KING'S, K 13; L 24.
BIRDS, LARGE; see OSTRICHES.
BOUNDARIES; see SITUATION.
BOWS and ARROWS, P 40.
BRIDGE, E 40; P 64; Q 75.
BRISTLES; see HAIR.

BUDDHISM encouraging trade between India and China, G 3.
BUDGET, E 30; Q 32.

C.

CAKES, people enjoy, L 32; R 19, 27.
CAMELS, N 6; P 20; Q 82.
CAPITAL; see AN-TU.
CARAVANS, E 39; P 32; Q 16; R 15.
CARRIAGES, E 11; F 12; I 16; K 29; L 29; P 28; Q 14; R 13.
CEREALS; see GRAIN.
CHAN (=Sham, Syria), L 5; Q 41; R 24.
CHANG CH'IEN, his mission to the West, A 1; B 1.
CH'Ê-CH'Ü, K 32; L 35; P 49^p; Q 21 (see Note).
CHI-PIN (country), H 4; P 48.
CHI-SHIH (the Stony Land=Arabia Petraea?), P 68.
CHIANG (generals?) thirty-six, in charge of official documents, E 18; P 37.
CHIAO-CHIH; see AN-NAM.
CH'IEH-LAN (dependent state) P 41, 65 seqq.; 69.
CHIEN-SHA (country), P 77.
CH'IH-SAN (Alexandria?) L 6; P 9 (cf. P 14); Q 11; cf. WU-CH'IH-SAN.
CH'IH-CH'IH (red dragon,-product), P 49^m.
CH'IH-SHUI (red water) I 21; P 77; Q 63.
CH'ING-T'ANG, country on the road to China, N 1; Q 77.
CHU-KO K'O, H 10.
CHU-LIEH (product), I 18; cf. Q 21; P 49^i (see Note).

CINNABAR (*chu-tan*), E 22.

CITIES and MARKETS, R 5.

CITIES, Number of, E 3; F 3; K 4; L 9; P 15; Q 9.

CITY WALLS; *see* AN-TU.

CITY WALLS of Stone, E 5; K 14; P 17.

CLEPSYDRA, K 19; L 18.

CLIMATE cold, N 4; Q 80.

CLOTH, Asbestos, E 23; F 14; G 3; M 2; P 49[ss]

——*Chi-chang*, P 44; Q 27.

——*Chiang-ti* (cloth?) P 49[tt].

——*Chin-t'u-pu* (gold-coloured cloth), P 49[oo], cf. E 23.

——*Ch'ü·shu* (*Ch'ü-sou*) five colours of, P 49[jj], cf. P 44; Q 27.

——*Ch'ü - shu - t'a - têng - chi - chang* (serge and plush rugs?), P 44; Q 27.

——Curtains interwoven with gold, P 49[aaa].

——Damasks of various colours, P 49[nn].

——embroidered with gold thread, E 22; F 14; P49[mm]; Q 85.

——*Fa-lu-pu*, P 49[qq].

——*Fei-ch'ih-ch'ü-pu*, P 49[rr].

——*Fei-ch'ih-pu*, P 49[pp].

——Fine (*Hsi-pu*), E 24; P 44; Q 26; cf. *Hai-hsi-pu*.

——gold-coloured, E 23.

——*Hai-hsi-pu, i. q., Hsi-pu* or Fine cloth *q. v.*; E 24; L 36; P 44; Q 82.

——made of bark (fibre?) of trees, P 44.

——made of silk; *see* SILK CLOTH.

CLOTH, made of silk from wild silkworms, P 44.

——*O-lo-tê-pu*, P 49[u].

——*Pa-tsê-pu*, P 49[uu].

——Rugs interwoven with gold, E 22; F 14; P 49[aaa].

——*Shou-hsia-t'a-têng*, P 49[ll].

——Silk; *see* SILK CLOTH.

——*T'a-têng*, five colours of, 49[kk]; cf. P 44, 49[u]; Q 27.

——*T'ao-pu*, five colours, P 49[vv].

——*Tou-chang* (rugs), of five colours, P 49[bbb].

——*To-tai-pu*, P 49[ww].

——*Wên-sê-pu*, P 49[xx].

——yellow gold-coloured cloth, E 23 (cf. *Chin-t'u-pu*).

——*see also* RUGS.

COINS, E 27; F 15, ·17; N 16; P 43; Q 30, 72, 91; *cf.* GOLD COINS and SILVER COINS.

——in the Hsüan-ch'ü country, Q 71.

——in the San-t'ung country, Q 72.

CONCHES (*pei*), F 14; K 32; L 35; P 49[o]; Q 21.

COPPER, P 49[c].

CORAL-FISHING described, L 37; Q 29.

CORALS, E 22; H 2; K 32; L 37; P 49[aa], 68; R 20.

CORAL SEA; *see* SEA, RED.

CORALS used as Ornaments on Kingpost, F 5.

CORNELIAN STONES, K 32; L 35; P 49[q]; Q 21; R 20.

Cows, N 6; Q 82.

CRYSTAL (product), P 49[a].

——used as an ornament to pillars, E 15; K 6; P 39; Q 4; R 6.

CRYSTAL, used as an ornament to pedestals of pillars, F 6.
———used as an ornament to eaves, pillars and window-bars, K 6.
———implements and vessels made of, E 15; P 39.
CYPRESS (*po*) trees, E 7; P 18.

D.

DATES, L 49; N 6; Q 55, 82.
DEPENDENT STATES, how many, E 4; L 12; P 33, 41, 56 seqq.; Q 9.
DESERT S. W. of Fu-lin, L 46; Q 53.
DINING, Etiquette in, R 19.
DISTANCE of Ta-ts'in from China, I 4, 22; L 4; Q 6.
DOCUMENTS, Official, E 18; F 11; P 35; Q 12; R 11.
DOMESTIC ANIMALS, P 20; said to come out of water (?) P 44.
DONKEYS, P 20.
DRESS worn by the People [cf. KING: his dress].
 embroidered clothing, E 10; K 28; L 28; Q 13; R 12.
 embroidered turban worn by women (calautica?), K 24; L 31.
 foreign (*hu*) dress worn, F 13; P 23.
 men's dress leaving right arm bare (toga), K 23; L 28.
 no lapels worn in front of women's dresses, K 24.
 pearls on women's dresses, Q 43; R 26.
 plain clothes worn by men, Q 43; R 26.
 resembling Chinese dress, I 16.
 silk worn by women, Q 43; R 26.

DRUMS, E 12; K 26, 30; L 30, 40; N 8; P 28; Q 84.
DWARFS (*tuan-jên*) in China, H 10.
———or Pygmies (*hsiao-jên*), country of, Q 27.

E.

EMBASSIES and other Missions to China:
 A.D. 120 (jugglers and musicians), C 2-4.
 A.D. 166 (An-tun)=E 33; H 5; O 2; Q 36; R 21.
 A.D. 226 (Ts'in-lun)=H 8 seqq.
 A.D. 280-290=F 20; Q 36; R 22.
 A.D. 643 (Po-to-li)=K 34; L 41; Q 66.
 A.D. 667=K 36.
 A.D. 701=K 37.
 A.D. 666 to 701=L 44; Q 68.
 A.D. 719=K 38, 39; L 45; Q 69.
 A.D. 1081=N 3; Q 79.
 A.D. 1091=N 17; Q 92.
 A.D. 1368 (about)=O 6 seqq.; cf. O 9.
 A.D. 1583 (Matthaeus Ricci) =O 10.
——— how received in Ta-ts'in, E 31; F 17; Q 33; R 9.
EMBASSY from China to An-hsi (Parthia), A 1 seqq.; B 1 seqq.
EMBROIDERIES; *see* CLOTH; DRESS.

F.

FEATHER BAG (hair or woollen bag?): a mode of inflicting capital punishment, N 14; Q 89.
FÊNG-NIU (Zebu?), D 7.

FESTIVALS, L 51; Q 60; R 17.
FLAGS and BANNERS, E 12; F 12; I 16; K 30; L 30; P 28; Q 14; R 13.
FLYING SANDS; see LIU-SHA.
FOOD OF THE PEOPLE, R 19.
FU-LIN *i.q.* Ta-ts'in, K 1; L 1; O 1, 4, 5; Q 41, 93.
FU-NAN (country), H 6.
FU-PA (an animal), D 17, 18.
FU-SANG, wrongly used for Fu-lin, R 24.

G.

GEMS; see PRECIOUS STONES.
GLASS, E 22; F 6; K 6, 34; P 49^{bb} (ten colours), Q 21; R 20.
—— red, sent to China as tribute (A.D. 643), K 34; L 41; Q 66.
—— the best manufactured in Ta-ts'in, Q 46.
—— used as an ornament to walls, F 6; to eaves, pillars and window-bars, K 6.
GOLD, E 22; F 14; K 31; L 35; N 6; P 49^a; Q 21, 82; R 19-20.
GOLD COINS, E 27, 31; F 15, 17; N 16; P 43; Q 30, 33, 72, 91.
GOLD, SOUTHERN (*nan-chin*) P 49'.
GOLD, YELLOW, K 17; L 16, 20.
GOVERNMENT; see KING.
GOVERNMENT OFFICIALS: Thirty-six chiang (generals?) in charge of official documents, discussing government matters, E 18; P 37; cf. F 11; Q 12; R 11.
eight officials ruling over the four quarters of the country, I 11.
eight officials ruling over the four quarters of the city (tetrapolis), who advise the king

GOVERNMENT OFFICIALS—*Cont.*
in matters not decided by the country officials, I 11-13.
twelve ministers (*kuei-ch'ên*, bishops?) in charge of government during the T'ang dynasty, K 7; L 20.
ministers (*kuei-ch'ên*, bishops?) during the Sung dynasty; their mode of dressing, N 10; Q 86.
shou-ling, or chiefs of towns and districts, during the Sung dynasty, N 12; Q 87.
GOVERNMENT, PEACEFUL, I 8; N 15; Q 90.
—— well regulated, P 26; see also BUDGET, POSTAL ARRANGEMENTS, etc.
GRAIN, E 30; I 17; N 6; P 19; Q 32.

H.

HAI-HSI and HAI-TUNG, the terms, used in opposition, P 44, 69; Q 27.
HAI-HSI-KUO *i.q.* Ta-ts'in, C 3; E 1; F 2; L 3; P 7, 48; Q 2.
HAI-PEI-CHU-KUO (the countries on the north of the sea), E 40; cf. P 13, 50.
HAI-TUNG-CHU-KUO (the countries on the east of the sea), P 44; cf. P 69; Q 27.
HAIR, custom of cutting, E 9; K 23, 27; L 27; Q 13; R 12.
HAIR, red (?), I 18; P 49^c; Q 21.
HEI-SHUI ("Black water," the western terminus of the world,—Okeanos?), P 77.
HEKATOMPYLOS; see AN-HSI (capital of).
HEMP (*ma*), I 17; (*ch'ih*) P 42.
HILLS, ranges of, I 21; P 69, 77; Q 63.

HIRA (=Yü-lo), see YÜ-LO; cf. T'IAO-CHIH.
HORSES, I 18; K 26; L 40; N 6; P 20; P 49ʰ; Q 82.
—— fed on fish, L 49; Q 55.
—— saddled, sent as tribute, N 3; Q 79.
HO-TI, emperor, C 1-4.
HO-TU (capital of An-hsi=Hekatompylos), D 10.
HSI-NÜ-KUO; see AMAZONS.
HSI-WANG-MU, E 34; I 21; P 77; Q 37, 63, 71; R 23.
HSIAO-JÊN; see DWARFS.
HSIEH-CHI-HSI, E 22; F 14; K 32; P 49ʲ; Q 19; R 20.
HSIEN-TU (dependent state), P 41, 67, 70.
HSÜAN-CHʲÜ (country), Q 71.
HSÜN-HSÜN, religion, Q 58-59.
HSÜN-LU (incense, gum olibanum?) P 49 *ggg*;
HU-LING (foreign damask), made of silk imported from China, P 45; Q 28.
HU-MANG; see DATES.
HUI-HO, country on the road to China, N 1; Q 77.

I.

I-CHOU; see YUNG-CHʻANG.
IMITATIONS and SHAM CURIOSITIES, E 41.
INCENSE and FRAGRANT DRUGS, (names being mostly doubtful), P 49*ccc* seqq.
INDIA; see Tʻien-CHU.
INHABITANTS described, E 21; F 13; I 16; P 23; Q 18, 40, 42; R 10, 25.
—— honest in trade, E 29; Q 31.

INHABITANTS, licentiousness amongst, L 50; Q 59 (Hsün-hsün).
INTERPRETERS, F 11; P 25; Q 12; R 11.
—————— twofold, sent to China by the king of Shan, C 1.
IRON, P 49ᵈ.
IVORY, E 33; P 49ᵗ; Q 36, 72; R 21.
I-WEI-MU-ÊRH (product) P 49 *ccc*

J.

JADE and other PRECIOUS STONES.
Chin-pi, H 2.
Ching-pi, E 22.
Ching-shih (blue stone), P 48.
Chʻiu-lin, I 18; P 49*cc*.
Chiu-sê-shih, P 47.
Fu-tsai-yü, P 49ᵘ.
Mei-kuei (garnets?), P 49*ff*,
Pi (serpentine?), P 49*hh*.
Sê-sê, K 20; L 19.
Tzŭ-yü, P 47.
Yü, ten colours of, P 49ⁿ; see also the articles CHʻÊ-CHʻÜ; CORNELIAN STONES; CRYSTAL; HSIEH-CHI-HSI, KINGFISHERS' GEM; YEH-KUANG-PI; and LÜ-CHIN-CHING.
JEWEL THAT SHINES AT NIGHT; see YEH-KUANG-PI.
JIH-NAN; see ANNAM.
JO-SHUI (weak water), E 34; P 3; Q 37, 71; R 23.
JUDAEA, Ta-tsʻin identified with, by Ricci, O 10 (see Note).
JUGGLERS frequent, L 33; P 21; Q 25.
—— from Li-kan sent to China by embassy from An-hsi (Parthia), A 5; B 5.
—— from Ta-tsʻin sent to China by the king of Shan, C 2-3.

K.

KAN-YING sent in search of Ta-ts'in, D 19, seq.; F 19.

K'ANG-CHÜ, a country in the north of An-hsi, D 12.

KHOTEN, on the road to China, N 1; Q 77.

KING, having to sanction the decisions of his councillors, I 13.
his bird, K 13; L 24.
his cap, K 11; L 23.
his clerical functions, N 10; Q 86; R 17.
his dress, L 23; N 9; Q 85; R 4, 17.
his horse, R 17.
his religion, M 4.
his residence, I 10.
his title or name, N 16; Q 91; R 2.
his throne, K 12; L 24; R 4.
may be deposed if a calamity visits the country, E 20; F 10; K 10; L 22; P 22; Q 17.
meting out justice, E 16–17; F 9; I 14 seq; K 8; L 21; P 36, 38.
seldom seen by the people, R 17.

KINGDOM not hereditary, E 19; K 9; P 22; Q 17.

KINGFISHERS' GEM, G 3; K 32; L 35; P 49ʳ.

K'O-SA-PU (the Khozar Turks), L 5; Q 50.

KTESIPHON; see SSŪ-PIN.

L.

LAMBS; see WATERSHEEP.

LANG-KAN (a kind of coral?), E 22; H 2; I 18; P 49ᵈᵈ.

LAO-PO-SA (a country inhabited by black tribes), L 46 seqq.

LAW, criminal, and capital punishment, N 14; Q 89; banishment Q 45; forbidding the counterfeiting of coins, N 16; Q 91.

LAW; see KING meting out justice.

LEAD, P 49ᵉ.

LI ($=\frac{1}{30}$ chih or hou, i.e., parasang), E 38; L 11; P 31; Q 15; R 14.

LI-KAN (or Li-kin) i. q. Ta-ts'in, E 1; F 1; I 1; P 5; Q 1; R 1.

LI-KAN, jugglers from, sent to China by Parthia, A 5; B 5.

LIONS, in T'iao-chih, D 7; in Ta-ts'in, E 39; K 38; L 45; P 32; Q 16, 69; R 15.

LIONS offered by An-hsi (Parthia), D 17, 21.

LITERATURE flourishing, M 5.

LIU-LI; see GLASS.

LIU-SHA or Flying Sands, E 34; P 77; Q 37; R 23.

LO-YANG, capital of China, D 10, 16.

LÜ-CHIN-CHING (green gold gem or powder?), K 34; L 41; Q 66.

LÜ-FÊN (dependent state), L 13; P 41, 60, 62 seqq.; Q 74, 75.

M.

MA-LO-FOU, the king's title, R 2. (cf. MI-LÊ-FOU).

MAN-K'Ü, king of An-hsi (A.D. 102), D 21.

MEDICINE; see PHYSICIANS; THERIAC.

MIEH-LI-I-LING KAI-SA sending embassy in A.D. 1081, N 3; Q 79.

MIEH-LI-SHA (country or ruler)– S.W. of Fu-lin, N 1; Q 76.

MI-LÊ-FOU, the king's name, cast on coins, N 16; Q 91.

MILESTONES, E 6.

MILLET, N 6; Q 82.

MILLIARY SYSTEM; see POSTAL ARRANGEMENTS.

MO-I (=Moavia), a general of the Ta-shih (Arabs), K 35; L 42.

MO-LIN (a country inhabited by black tribes), L 46 seqq.; Q 53 seqq.

MONEY; see COINS.

MOONSHINE PEARL; see PEARLS.

MÔURU; see MU-LU.

MULBERRY TREE, E 8; I 17.

MULES, P 20.

MU-LU (city in An-hsi,=Antiochia Margiana. Môuru), D 15.

MU-NAN; see PEARLS.

MUSICAL INSTRUMENTS, N 8; Q 84. See also DRUMS.

MUSICIANS from Ta-ts'in sent to China by king of Shan, C 2-4.

N.

NEGRO (?) tribes, L 47; Q 54, 57; cf. MO-LIN and LAO-PO-SA.

NESTORIANS; see PRIESTS.

NIEH-KU-LUN (=Nicolaus de Bentra), his journey to China, O 6.

NI-SSŪ-TU-LING SSŪ-MÊNG-P'AN, his mission to China, N 3; Q 79.

O.

ORPIMENT, P 49*w*

OSTRICHES (large birds), D 7, 21.

———eggs sent from An-hsi to China, A 5; B 5; D 7.

P.

PALACES, E 14 seqq.; P 27, 36. See also ARCHITECTURE; and AN-TU, city of: public buildings.

PA-LAN (dates? chestnuts?), N 6 (see Note); Q 82.

PAI-FU-TZŪ (a plant), P 49*u*.

PAN CH'AO's expedition (A.D. 97), D 19; F 19.

PARTHIA; see AN-HSI.

PEACOCKS, D 7 cf. BIRD OF NINE COLOURS.

PEARLS, generally, N 6; P 68; Q 82.

———*Chu-chi*, H 2.

———*Ming-chu* (shining pearl), F 14; I 18.

———Moonshine, or *Ming-yüeh-chu*, E 22; K 32; L 35; M 2; P 49*w*; Q 21.

———*Mu-nan*, L 35 (see Note); Q 24 (see Note).

———Real, N 3; P 68; Q 79; R 20.

———Real White, P 49*y*.

———*Shé-chu*, G 3.

———Worn by women, Q 44; R 26.

PEARS, N 6; Q 82.

PERSIA; see PO-SSŪ.

PETITIONS, how received by the King; see KING meting out justice.

PHYSICIANS, L 34; Q 61.

PINE (*sung*) trees, E 7; P 18.

P'I-TU-SHU (poisonous rat?) P 49*x*; Q 21.

PLANTAINS, Q 72.

PLANTS, E 17; P 18.

PLASTER used in covering postal stations and milestones, E 6.

———used in covering roofs, K 21; L 25 (?); R 7.

PO-LI; see GLASS.

POPULATION, E 38; F 3; I 8; K 5, 15; P 30, 54; Q 7.

PO-SSŪ (Persia), bounding on Fu-lin, K 2; L 7.

POSTAL ARRANGEMENTS, E 6, 31, 38; F 12; L 11; P 28, 31, 32; Q 15, 33; R 14.

Po-to-li, his Mission to China, K 34; L 41; Q 66.

Precious Stones, generally, D 23; E 22, 26, 41; F 14; G 3; H 1; I 20; K 31; Q 21, 63.
Ta-ts'in a depository of produce from other countries, E 26; K 32.
for various kinds; see Jade, &c.

Priests (Ta-tê-sêng=Nestorians?) offering tribute at the Chinese Court in A.D. 719; K 39.
clerical (?=tê, virtuous) rulers; M 4.

Prisoners, how dealt with, Q 45.

Products, passim; for long list of, see P 49.

Pu-la, sent to Fu-lin, O 9.

Punishments; see Law.

Pygmies, see Dwarfs.

R.

Rank conferred on the rich, K 85; L 31.

Rats, see P'i-tu-shu.

Realgar, P 49ff.

Red Water, see Ch'ih-shui.

Rekem (Petra) see Li-kan.

Religion, Q 58; Christian, M 4.

Rhinoceros, D 7.

Rhinoceros' Horns, E 33; G 3; Q 36, 72; R 21.

Ricci, Matthaeus, his arrival at the Chinese court alluded to, O 10.

River of Ta-ts'in (the Nile?), P 8.

Roads, E 39; P 32.

Robberies unknown, E 39; M 3; P 32.

Roofs of Houses, how constructed, K 21, seq.; L 25; N 5; Q 81; R 7.
—— how watered, K 21 seq.; L 26.

Routes between China and Ta-ts'in.

1. from Hekatompylos (capital of An-hsi) to Yü-lo on the western boundary of An-hsi, D 8, 22.

2. from T'iao-chih, An-ku, or Yü-lo (Hira), the terminus of the Parthian land-road, by sea to Ta-ts'in (gulf of Akabah), D 20, 22; E 37 (?); F 18, 19; I 3; I 22; P 6, 29 (?); Q 5, 64.

3. overland (from An-ku on the Euphrates?) to Ta-ts'in, P 13, 50, 51; cf. the accounts of countries near the Parthian frontier, P 58–76; perhaps also E 37 to 40; P 29.

4. by sea direct from Ta-ts'in to Annam, E 33; H 5–7; I 19; P 50; Q 36, 62; R 21.

5. by sea direct from Ta-ts'in to Birmah into Yün-nan, I 19; P 50; Q 62.

6. from Wu-ch'ih-san (Alexandria?) to Ta-ts'in (Antioch?), P 14.

7. overland through Central Asia during the Sung dynasty, N 1.

Rugs, gold-embroidered, E 22; F 14; P 49aaa.

Rushes (?), P 18.

S.

San-t'ung (country), Q 71–72.

Sea, countries north, east and west of the western—; see Hai-hsi, Hai-pei, Hai-tung.

Sea, Mediterranean, L 6; P 8–9, 14; Q 10, 50, 63.

Sea, Red (=Hai-hsi, Coral Sea, Chang-hai), I 5; M 1; P 68; Q 29, 50.

SEA, WESTERN, described, D 19; F 18, 19; P 5, 46; Q 35.
―――― the city of T'iao-chih on its coast, D 3, 19.
―――― Ta-ts'in or Fu-lin on its coast, F 2; K 1, 16; L 1.
SHAN (country in the S.W. of China), C 1–4.
SHAN-LI; see WU-I-SHAN-LI.
SHEEP, N 4; Q 82. cf. WATER-SHEEP.
SHUI-YANG; see WATER-SHEEP.
SHUI-YANG-TS'UI; see CLOTH, FINE.
SHU-YU (country), P 77.
SILK, Chinese, imported for re-manufacture, P 45; Q 28.
―――― cloth, E 22, 32; N 6; P 44, 45, 49^{nn}; Q 82; R 20.
―――― cultivation of, E 8, 24; I 17; P 20.
―――― *ling-kan-wên*, Q 28.
―――― trade, Parthians monopolizing, E 32; P 24, 45; Q 28, 34.
―――― weavers, Q 44; R 26.
―――― worms, E 8, 24; P 20, 44.
―――― worn by women, Q 43.
SILVER, E 22; K 31; L 35; N 6; P 49^b; Q 21, 82; R 19.
―――― coins, E 27; F 15; N 16; P 43; Q 30, 91.
SITUATION of TA-TS'IN and FU-LIN, I 5, 7; K 1-2; L 2, 6; M 1; N.1; P 5; Q 76.
SIZE of the Country; see TERRITORY.
SPIRIT MARKET, L 38; Q 51; R 31.
SSŬ-FU (dependent state), P 41, 67-69, 71, 72 seqq.
SSŬ-LO (Seleucia), P 74 seq.
SSŬ-PIN (Ktesiphon), D 22; P 69.
SSŬ-T'AO (country), P 66.

STONY LAND, the; see CHI-SHIH.
STORAX (*Su-ho*), E 25; H 2-3; M 2 (? life-restoring incense); P 49^{ddd}; Q 20.
SU-LÊ (Kashgar?), P 48.
SUN-CH'ÜAN, emperor of China (Wu), H 8–10.
SUN, place where it sets, E 34, 35; I 23; P 4; Q 37, 65; R 23.
SWORD-BLADES sent to China as Tribute, N 3; Q 79.
SU-TAN (Sultan) of the Ta-shih, R 18.

T.

TABERNACLES, R 8.
TA-HSIA (country in the west of Ta-ts'in), P 77.
TA-SHIH (the Arabs of the Khalif empire) making war to, besieging the capital of, and conquering Fu-lin, K 35; L 42-43; Q 49, 67; R 30.
―――― assemble in Ta-ts'in for trade, R 1.
―――― assist Fu-lin with their army R 18.
―――― in the east of Fu-lin, N 1; Q 77.
―――― religion, Q 58, 60.
TA-TA, country on the road to China, Q 77.
TA-TÊ-SÊNG; see PRIESTS.
TA-TS'IN identified with Judaea by Ricci, O 10.
―――― name explained, E 21; I 16 P 23; Q 18; R 10.
―――― religion, Q 58, 61.
―――― so called during Han, Chin and Wei dynasties, O 1, 3.
TAI (capital of China during the Wei dynasty), I 4.

T'AI-TSU, emperor of the Ming, O 7 seqq.

T'AI-TSUNG, emperor of the T'ang, K 34.

TAURUS, range of hills, alluded to, P 69.

TAXES, N 13; Q 88.

TENTS for soldiers, R 8.

TERRITORY, E 2; F 3; I 6; K 3; L 8; M 5; P 15, 55; Q 8, 47; R 29.

THERIAC; see TI-YEH-KA.

T'IAO-CHIH (Chaldaea, the country of Yü-lo, Hira) D 1-9; E 35-36; I 3, 23; P 1-4; Q 5.

——— Kan-ying arrives in, D 19 seqq.

——— Precious stones from, P 48.

T'IEN-CHU (India), traffic with, by sea, E 28; F 16; G 1; H 1.

TIGERS, E 39; P 32.

TIGRIS RIVER (?), D 22; P 75.

TIN, P 49*f*.

TI-YEH-KA, K 36.

TOKHARESTAN; see TU-HUO-LO.

TORTOISES and TORTOISE SHELL, E 33; P 49*k*; Q 36; R 21. *Shên-kuei*, I 18; P 49*g*; Q 21.

TOU-NA (a fragrant substance?), P 49*eee*.

TRADE, inhabitants honest in, E 29; Q 31.

——— Parthians monopolizing, in silk, between China and Ta-ts'in, E 32; P 24, 45; Q 28, 34.

——— profit derived from maritime, E 28; F 16.

——— Ta-ts'in centre of Western, R 1; especially in precious stones, E 26.

TRADE, with Parthia and India, E 28; F 16; H 1; P 24, 45; Q 28, 34.

TREES, all kinds of, E 7-8.

——— Bamboos, P 18.

——— *Huai* (Sophora?), P 18.

——— *Po*; see CYPRESS TREES.

——— Poplars, P 18.

——— *Sung*; see PINE TREES.

——— *Tzŭ* (Euphorbia?), P 18.

——— Willows, P 18.

——— *Wu-t'ung* (Eleococca Verrucosa?), P 18.

TREPANNING, L 34; Q 61.

TSE-SAN (dependent State), L 13; P 41, 58 seqq.; Q 74.

TS'IN-LUN (a traveller from Ta-ts'in), H 8-10.

TS'UNG (a quadruped), L 39; Q 22.

T'U-CH'ÜEH (Turks), L 5; Q 50.

TU-HUO-LO (Tokharestan), K 38; L 45; Q 69.

TUNG-KING; see ANNAM.

TUNNEL leading from the king's palace to the hall of worship, R 16.

V.

VASES, gold, pairs, received from China, N 17; Q 92.

W.

WATER led over roofs to produce coolness, K 21 seqq; L 26.

WATER-SHEEP, cloth made from wool of, E 24; L 36; P 44; Q 26

——— described, K 26; L 40; Q 23.

WEAK WATER; *see* JO-SHUI.

WEEK of seven days alluded to, L 51; Q 60; R 17.

WESTERN KING'S MOTHER; *see* HSI-WANG-MU.

WHEAT, N 6; Q 82.

WINE, Fu-lin people make and enjoy, L 32; N 7; Q 83; R 27; the people do not drink wine, R 19.

WU-CH'IH-SAN (city=Alexandria?) P 14; cf. CH'IH-SAN.

WU-I (country), E 36.

WU-I-SHAN-LI (country or countries), D 12; cf. WU-I.

WU-TAN (city), P 10.

WU-TI, the emperor, sends an embassy to An-hsi (Parthia), A 1; B 1.

Y.

YANG-SA-LO (country near the desert in the S. W. of Fu-lin,=Jerusalem?), Q 53.

YANG-TI, emperor of the Sui dynasty, wishing for traffic with Ta-ts'in, K 33.

YEH-KUANG-PI or "Jewel that shines at night," E 22; F 14; I 18; K 32; L 35; M 2; P 49* (*yeh-kuang-chu*); Q 21.

YI-CHOU; *see* YUNG-CH'ANG.

YUNG-CH'ANG (district in Yün-nan), I 19; P 50; Q 62.

—————at one time a market for Ta-ts'in produce, P 50.

YUNG-CH'ÊN (country in the south of Ta-ts'in), Q 38.

YUNG-YU-TIAO, King of Shan, C 1-4.

YÜ-CHIN (a kind of turmeric) H 2, 4; P 49^{hhh}.

YÜEH-CHIH (Bactria), P 77.

YÜ-LO (Hira), D 22; P 41, 73 seqq.

YÜN-CHIAO-HSÜN (a kind of incense?) P 49^{iii}.

YÜN-NAN; *see* YUNG-CH'ANG.

YÜ-TIEN (Khoten), during the Sung a station on the road to China, N 1; Q 77.

Z.

ZEBU; *see* FÊNG-NIU.

IDENTIFICATIONS.

IDENTIFICATIONS.

In attempting to trace the ancient route from Central Asia to the country of Ta-ts'in, it is of the greatest importance to determine the situation of another country which, in the oldest Chinese records, has always been mentioned together with Ta-ts'in, or with Li-kan, as it was then called. In the chapter regarding Ta-wan by Ssŭ-ma Ch'ien (*Shih-chi*, ch. 123, lieh-chuan, 63), it is said that "Li-kan and T'iao-chih are several thousand li west of An-hsi." This must be information brought to China by Chang Ch'ien, the first explorer of western countries, about B.C. 120, and we are probably safe in assuming that the country of Ta-ts'in, under its old name Li-kan, was not known to the Chinese previous to that period. Even then, the Chinese did not probably know much more than that Li-kan was the name of a country in the far west, whence, in all probability, certain products reached China through the hands of intermediary nations, especially the Parthians, in exchange for large quantities of silk bought up by the merchants of Li-kan. The Chinese were probably aware of the importance of both these countries; why, otherwise, should the Chinese general Pan Ch'ao, two centuries later, have sent his lieutenant Kan-ying on an exploring expedition to them (D 19 seqq.)? The Chinese then did not even know much about the relative position of the two countries. So great was their ignorance in this respect before Kan-ying's discovery, that Li-kan, *i.e.*, Ta-ts'in, was believed to be the nearer country and T'iao-chih the more distant one (P 1).

At the close of the first century A.D., the general Pan Ch'ao, a brother of Pan Ku, the author of the *Ch'ien-han-shu*, proceeded to the west with apparently peaceful intentions.[1] He then came to the borders of the kingdom of An-hsi which his subordinate Kan-ying traversed from east to west. Kan-ying, we learn from the *Hou-han-shu* (D 19–20), arrived in T'iao-chih and was there persuaded not to undertake the passage to Ta-ts'in. We learn from the same passage that T'iao-chih was so situated that ships could start from its city and sail to Ta-ts'in, and that it was on the western frontier of An-hsi (cf. P 2). In order to find the site of T'iao-chih, therefore, the question first to be settled is the identity of the country of An-hsi.

The *Ch'ien-han-shu* (ch. 96A, chuan, 66A)

---

[1] Klaproth and Rémusat, and with them Humboldt and others, entertained the idea, quite unsupported by Chinese authorities, of Pan Ch'ao's military designs against Ta-ts'in. Messrs. E. C. Taintor and A. Wylie, in reply to a question regarding the subject, have shown the fallacy of this assumption in *Notes and Queries on China and Japan*, Vol II (1868) pp 60 and 153.

says with regard to An-hsi: "The king of the country of An-hsi rules at the city of P'an-tou (番兜)¹; its distance from Ch'ang-an is 11,600 li. The country is not subject to a tu-hu [a Chinese governor in Central-Asiatic possessions]. It bounds north on K'ang-chü, east on Wu-i-shan-li, west on T'iao-chih. The soil, climate, products, and popular customs are the same as those of Wu-i and Chi-pin. They also make coins of silver, which have the king's face on the obverse, and the face of his consort on the reverse. When the king dies, they cast new coins. They have the ta-ma-ch'üo [a bird, the description of which by the Chinese commentator answers to an ostrich]. Several hundred small and large cities are subject to it, and the country is several thousand li in extent, that is, a very large country. It lies on the banks of the Kuei-shui [Oxus]. The carts and ships of their merchants

---

¹ Several examples suggest to me, as they did to others, the probability of an affinity of some kind between a final *r* in western Asiatic names and a Chinese final *n*. *An* = *ar* in An-hsi, *i.e.* Arsak, the name for Parthia; and perhaps in An-ku = Orchoë (P 6, 13 and 60); also possibly in Yen-ts'ai or An-ts'ai (奄蔡), the name of a country in the north of Parthia, which, during the After Han, was changed into A-lan-na (阿蘭那), and which I identify with the Aorsi of Strabo, and the Alani of other writers ("Sarmatie Asiatique," de Guignes, *Histoire des Huns*, Vol. II, p. XCI). I do not hesitate, therefore, to identify the name P'an-tou with old Persian *Parthuva*, the origin of Herodotus' Πάρθοι, if not the city of Παρθαύνισα of Isidorus Characenus, held to have been the same as Hekatompylos by Mannert (*see* Karl Müller ad Isid. Mansiones Parthicae, 12, in *Geographi Graeci Minores*, Vol. 2, p. 252). Cf. Kiepert, *Lehrbuch der alten Geographie*, p. 65 seq.

go to the neighbouring countries. They write on leather [parchment], and draw up documents in rows running sideways. [Here follows the passage B 1 to 5]. In the east of An-hsi are the Ta-yüeh-chih."[1]

The above account, as describing matters known from records of the former Han dynasty, refers to the first and second centuries B.C. The country best answering its details at that period is the Parthian kingdom.[2] It extended to the banks of the Oxus; the Parthians were the middle-men in trade between Central and Western Asia. Some of their coins have been shown to contain the face of a king on the obverse and that of a woman on the reverse[3]; they used, like other nations of western Asia, the horizontal way of writing, though Rawlinson[4] says that, in the earlier times, the writing material commonly used was linen, and shortly before the time of Pliny, papyrus. Finally, linguistic grounds, which, as a matter of principle, I

---

[1] Cf. translation by Wylie in "Notes on the Western Regions," *Journ. Anthrop. Inst.*, Aug. 1880.

[2] The identity was apparently first recognised, though not proved in detail, by de Guignes (*Hist. des Huns*, Vol II, p. 51). Visdelou, whose work ("Monument de la Religion Chrétienne, etc., en Chine" in d'Herbelot's *Bibliothèque Orientale*, Vol. IV, p. 369 seqq.) appeared after de Guignes', but was written before its publication, translated An-hsi by Assyria; so did Neumann (*Asiat. Studien*, p. 157).

[3] Wylie, l. c., quotes Rawlinson's description of a Parthian coin: "The coins of Phraataces have on one side his head, which is being crowned by two Victories; on the other the head of Musa [his mother], etc." [*The Sixth Great Oriental Monarchy*, p. 220.]

[4] *The Sixth Great Orient. Mon.*, p.p. 424-425, quoted by Wylie, *l. c.*

do not wish to consider except when strongly supported by the identification of other facts, point to Parthia in the two names P'an-tou (=Parthuva) and An-hsi (=Arsak).

The description of An-hsi appearing in the *Hou-han-shu* quite corresponds with what we know through Pliny of Parthia during the corresponding period. At that time the country had considerably gained in extent, and its boundaries had been moved farther west. The capital was then, as before, at the city called by Greek writers Hekatompylos. This name, meaning "the city of a hundred gates," is not the original Parthian name, but a Greek word intended to express the central position of the city, which, through its many gates was considered the terminus of all the land-roads of the country. The Parthian name has not been preserved in western authors, but we may safely accept the clue contained in the Chinese histories, as there can be no doubt that the Hekatompylos of Greek and Roman writers, being the chief capital of the empire, is identical with the city of P'an-tou (Parthuva?) mentioned in the *Ch'ien-han-shu* and with the city of Ho-tu (old sound Wodok?[1]) mentioned in the *Hou-han-shu* (D 10).

The same account says: "On its eastern frontier is the city of Mu-lu, which is called little An-hsi [Parthia Minor]; it is 20,000 li distant

---

[1] Possibly Vologesia, as at Pan Ch'ao's time Vologeses I (A.D. 90 to 107) was king of Parthia, who may have re-named his capital. Vologesia was also the name of a city in Babylonia.

from Lo-yang" (D 15–16.) As the distance, from Lo-yang, of the capital city of Ho-tu is stated to have been 25,000 li, the distance between Ho-tu and Mu-lu must have been 5,000 li. I propose to show hereafter my reasons for assuming that the li of Chinese records are, in these countries where the Greek mode of measuring distances was combined with the Persian method (stadia, schoeni, parasangae), corresponds to the stadium of western itineraries. This will furnish the key to quite a number of puzzles, of which the relative sites of the cities of Ho-tu and Mu-lu would be one, but for the knowledge preserved of both the capital and the eastern frontier district in Pliny, Strabo, and other authorities.[1] This eastern out-station of Parthia, which lay on the road to China, is there called Margiana; its city was the city of Antiochia, the old Bactrian name of which is mentioned in the Vendidad section of the Zend-Avesta, as Môuru, the mediaeval Merw.[2]

---

[1] Plin., *Nat. Hist.*, rec. Detlefsen, VI, 15 (17), 44: ipsum vero Parthiae caput Hecatompylos - - -; and *ibid.* 16 (18), 46: where the isolated Parthian dependency Margiana is described; Strab., c. 510 (Meineke), cf. Bunbury, *Hist. of Ancient Geogr.*, Vol. II, p. 412.

[2] "The Zend-Avesta," translated by J. Darmesteter, in Max Müller's *The Sacred Books of the East*, Vol. IV, pp. 2-6, and Vol. XXIII, p. 123. Cf. Kiepert, *Lehrbuch der alten Geographie*, p. 58. Mr. Parker draws my attention to Bretschneider's identification of the mediaeval Merw with the names Ma-lu (馬魯) and Ma-li-wu (麻里兀) in Yüan records (*see* Bretschneider, *Notes on Chinese Mediaeval Travellers to the West*, pp. 8 and 77, or *Chinese Recorder*, Vol. V, pp. 120 and 325). The former name occurs in the *Yüan-shih*, the latter on the Chinese map of Western Asia called *Yüan-ching-shih-ta-tien-ti-li-t'u* (元經世大典地理圖), of the Yüan period,

IDENTIFICATIONS. 143

The identity of this name (Môuru) with Chinese Mu-lu is too suggestive to be passed over as an accidental similarity; for the distance of 5,000 stadia laid thence across the Hyrcanian hills in a westerly direction takes us just to the neighbourhood of the probable site of Hecatompylos, the capital.[1]

From all we may conclude from the traditions handed down in the Han records, T'iao-chih was first a powerful kingdom, more powerful even than An-hsi (Parthia), as we may read between the lines in a passage of the *Wei-lio* (P 2): this I presume

---

though the copy before me, a re-print in the *Hai-kuo-t'u-chih*, has, probably by mistake, *chiu* (九) for *wu* (元). Both these names (Ma-lu and Ma-li-wu) are clearly meant to be identical in sound with Mu-lu.

[1] See Bunbury, l. c., Vol. I, p. 479. As the site of Hecatompylos is, in ancient geography, still one of the many points in dispute, the distances east (to Môuru, D 10-16) and west (to A-man, = Acbatana, D 22) as stated in the *Hou-han-shu*, deserve some consideration. The 5,000 li (stadia) west of Môuru take us to the neighbourhood of modern Damghan, and not to the neighbourhood of Djadjerm, which site is merely about 3,500 stadia west of Môuru. On the other hand the country of A-man, which I am going to identify with the region of Acbatana, is stated to be 3,400 li (stadia) west of An-hsi (here= "capital of Parthia"). This is just about the distance in stadia from Acbatana to the neighbourhood of Damghan; the Djadjerm site would have been about 4,800 stadia east of Acbatana. This seems to me a palpable proof that, whatever confusion may have prevailed in the minds of the most enlightened geographers of antiquity with regard to China, Chinese historians were sufficiently well informed with regard to western geography not only to confirm the testimony of ancient western authors, but even in some instances to furnish supplementary information where our own classical literature fails.

refers to the period when Parthia was confined to its original territory in the east. In the first and second centuries A.D. Parthia had extended its boundaries to the west of the Euphrates. It is scarcely necessary to dwell on the classical sources of ancient geography in order to show that the western boundary ran along the upper course of the Euphrates from Samosata down to the Babylonian territory: here it began to branch off to the west towards the Syrian desert, embracing the cultivated tracts outside the Chaldaean Lake and the Pallacopas Canal, which connected a rich and densely-populated province by means of a navigable[1] channel with the coast of the Persian Gulf. The following reasons have determined me to identify this region, the country of Babylonia or Chaldaea, with the T'iao-chih of Chinese records.

Its political relations with Parthia correspond to those represented in the Chinese records as existing between T'iao-chih and An-hsi. The earliest mention of the country appears in the *Ch'ien-han-shu*, which embraces the period B.C. 206 to

---

[1] It is doubtful whether the Pallacopas was used as a channel for navigation, or the Euphrates itself. (*See* Bunbury, *l. c.*, Vol. I, p. 524.) However, so much seems certain, that maritime trade extended to the ports in the Chaldaean Lake. According to Masudi, sea-going ships entered from the Persian Gulf during the fifth century (Yule, *Cathay*, Vol. I, p. LXXVII), and, whether in the original sea-going barges or in river-boats, the Euphrates could be used as a channel between the Gulf and Babylon. (Euphrate navigari Babylonem e Persico mari CCCCXII p. tradunt Nearchus et Onesicritus. Plin., VI, 26 (30), 124).

23 A.D.[1], and the *Shih-chi*, covering, in its geographical portion, about the same period. It was during this period that Babylonia which, under Seleucid rule, had been a Syrian province, fell into the hands of Parthian rulers (about B.C. 140). This fact is apparently alluded to in the *Ch'ien-han-shu*. It continued to be a satrapy on the western frontier of Parthia during the later Han dynasty (D 9; P 2). Since the time of Trajan, the Roman empire had repeatedly extended its frontiers to the banks of the Tigris, so that T'iao-chih (or, as it was apparently called during the period of the

---

[1] *Ch'ien-han-shu*, ch. 96 A, Hsi-yü-chuan 66 A, in the description of Wu-i-shan-li (烏弋山離). This country "is in the west, conterminous with Li-kan and T'iao-chih [the two names perhaps denoting at that period the western and eastern parts of the Seleucid empire respectively, whence they are found together here and in other passages]. Going somewhat over a hundred days, you come to the country of T'iao-chih, bordering on the Western Sea, hot and low, but growing rice in fields. There are large birds'-eggs, resembling jars (or urns). The country is densely populated; it used to be governed by petty rulers, but An-hsi (Parthia), reducing them to vassalage, made it into an outer state [*i.e.*, one of its foreign possessions]. They have clever jugglers. The elders of An-hsi [Parthia] have the tradition that in T'iao-chih there is the Jo-shui [weak water] and the Hsi-wang-mu [western king's mother], but they have not been seen. From T'iao-chih by water you may go west over a hundred days to come near the place where the sun sets, they say." Wylie (in "Notes on the Western Regions," *l.c.*, p. 19) translates: "The people are very numerous, and are often under petty chieftains, subject to the Parthians, who consider foreigners clever at jugglery." The corresponding Chinese words are 人衆甚多往往有小君長安息役屬之以爲外國善眩, and Shih-ku says 安息以條支爲外國如言番國, "An-hsi considered T'iao-chih as an outer country, meaning as it were a foreign country." I think there can be little doubt that, in dividing the text into sentences, I am right here to follow the scholiast. Cf. *Shih-chi*, ch. 123.

Three Kingdoms, Yü-lo) may be found mentioned as a dependency of Ta-ts'in (the Roman Orient) in the *Wei-lio* (P 41, 74). The tradition according to which T'iao-chih was, previous to its annexation, more powerful than An-hsi (Parthia) may refer to either the times of the Babylonian empire from Nebuchadnezzar down to the Persian conquest, or the period when it was joined with Syria to the Seleucid empire (second century B.C.) allusion to which seems to be contained in the joined expression "Li-kan T'iao-chih" (*i.e.*, Syria and Babylonia) of the *Ch'ien-han-shu* or *Shih-chi*.

Chaldaea was the only district of the Parthian empire which combined the two conditions, set forth in the Chinese records in connection with T'iao-chih, of being at the same time situated on the extreme west frontier of An-hsi (Parthia), and on the coast of the "western sea." It is true that both the Caspian Sea and the Indian Ocean may be called western sea (*hsi-hai* 西 海),[1] but the Caspian cannot possibly be meant as that "western sea"

---

[1] The passage D 3 says that the city of T'iao-chih lies on the "western sea," which, in other passages is called "the great sea," (*ta-hai*, 大 海, D 19; F 18). I have not the slightest doubt that in both cases the Indian Ocean with its gulfs, and not the Caspian, is meant. The latter is called Hsiao-hai (小 海), "the small sea," in an unmistakable description of Taberistan found in the *Hsin-t'ang-shu* (*see* Neumann, *Asiatische Studien*, p. 177; *cf.* Rémusat *Nouv. Mélanges Asiatiques*, Vol. I, p. 254). On the other hand, the Indian Ocean is frequently called "western sea," *e.g.*, in the *Hou-han-shu*, on the page following the description of Ta-ts'in (ch. 88), where the Hsi-hai (western sea) is said to be in the south-west of the countries of Yüeh-chih and Kao-fu (從月氏高附國以西南至西海).

on which T'iao-chih was situated: for, at Pan Ch'ao's time, the western boundary of Parthia extended far beyond the Caspian, and navigation on that sea cannot possibly have extended to a distance of 40,000 or even 10,000 li (I 22), or allowed of passages lasting two months (P 6), three months, or up to three years (D 20; F 18; P 6). The Mediterranean Sea is quite out of the question in A.D. 97. The only sea, therefore, on which a trip of the described length could have been made from a port on the western boundary of Parthia, is the Persian Gulf.

The description given of the city of T'iao-chih (D 1-5), which was situated on a *shan* (山, here, "peninsula)," surrounded by water on three sides, so that access to it by land was only possible in the north-west, answers in every respect to the peninsula in the Chaldaean Lake. A glance at the sketch map representing that neighbourhood, which I copied from Kiepert's *Nouvelle Carte Générale des Provinces Asiatiques de l'Empire Ottoman* (Berlin, 1884), embodying the results of the surveys made by Commr. Selby and Lieuts. Bewsher and Collingwood, of the British Navy,[1] shows that the peninsula in the Chaldaean Lake is, up to the

---

[1] For further details *see* Kiepert, "Zur Karte der Ruinenfelder von Babylon," and the map, in *Zeitschrift der Gesellschaft für Erdkunde*, Berlin, Vol. XVIII (1883), p. 1. Cf. the map of Chaldaea, Susiana, etc., in W. Kennett Loftus' "Notes of a Journey from Baghdad to Busrah," in *J. R. G. S.*, Vol. XXVI, (1856), p. 131. A comparison of the two maps will show what progress has been made in the ancient topography of these parts within the past thirty years.

present day, "crookedly surrounded by water;" that access to it is cut off by the lake, swamps or canals from all sides, except from the north-west, which is indeed the only quarter of the compass allowing of a land-road in the direction of Seleucia and Ktesiphon. This land-road leading out to the north-west exists at the present day. According to Kiepert it connects the present city of Nedjef, which stands quite close to the ruins of ancient Hira, with the present Bagdad *viâ* Kerbela. Although I doubt whether ancient records throw much light on the former configuration of the Lake and its connection with either the Euphrates or the Persian Gulf direct, it may be assumed that it presented rather a larger, than a smaller, sheet of water in ancient times when compared with its present shape.[1]

In selecting this peninsula of the Chaldaean Lake as the probable site of the city of T'iao-chih I am chiefly guided by the idea that it is apparently the only place in Chaldaea which answers the Chinese description, that as a terminus of navigation in the Persian Gulf its port must have been a most convenient place for the embarkment of travellers coming from Central Asia *viâ* Ktesiphon: for, the river passage from Hira to the coast of the Gulf is even at the present day about 600 stadia shorter than the passage on the Tigris from

---

[1] "quoniam rigandi modus ibi manu temperatur," Plin., *Nat. Hist.*, XVIII 18 (47), 170 Cf. the descriptions of the lower course of the Euphrates in Plin., VI, 26 (30), 124 seqq.; and Pomponius Mela, III, 76 seqq.

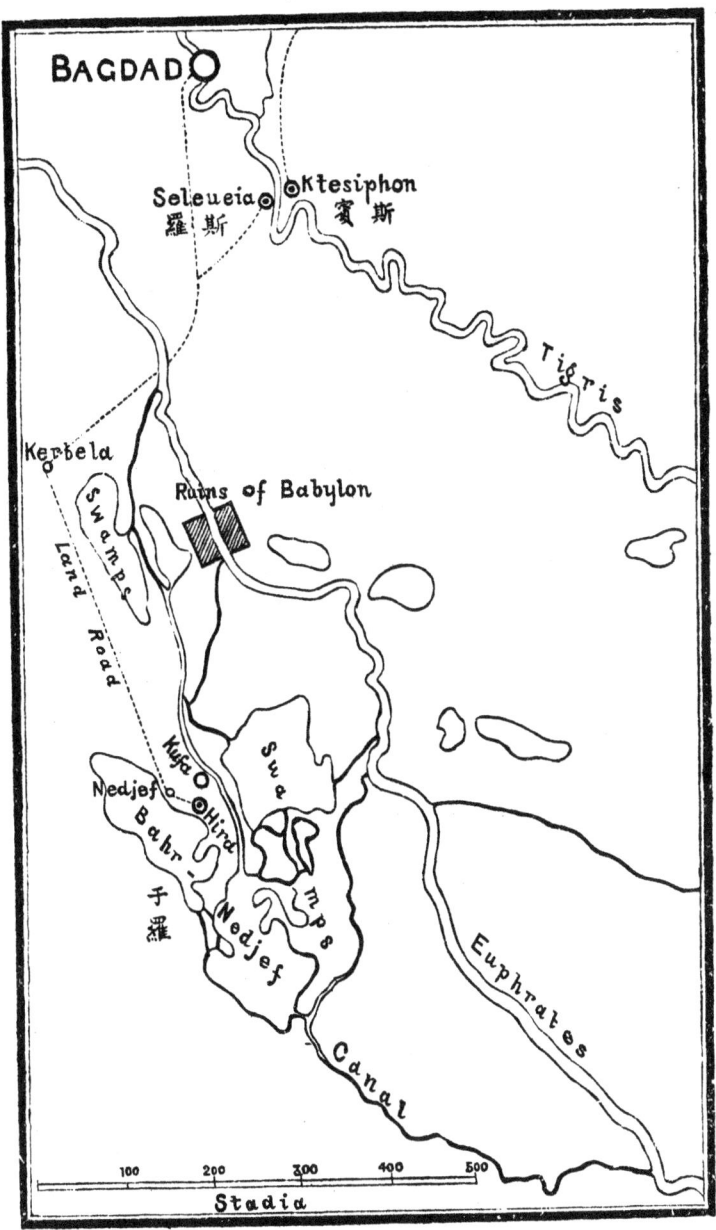

SKETCH MAP OF THE OVERLAND ROUTE FROM KTESIPHON TO HIRA.

IDENTIFICATIONS. 149

Ktesiphon to the mouth of the river; and if, as Strabo seems to have assumed,[1] the Euphrates had its separate outlet, or if, further, the Pallacopas canal furnished a short cut from the Lake direct into the Gulf, the advantage of taking passage in one of the Lake ports becomes still more obvious. For this reason, I consider it quite probable that the place where Kan-ying received his information regarding the terrors of a sea voyage (D 20; F 19), *i.e.*, the city of T'iao-chih, stood somewhere in the neighbourhood of the present Nedjef. Its name is not mentioned in connection with Kan-ying's expedition; but it is very probable that a populous city existed on the peninsula long before the foundation of Hira, the great trading town and chief city of the kingdom of that name, founded about 200 A.D., *i.e.*, towards the close of the Han dynasty.[2]

---

[1] "From the terms in which he [Strabo] speaks of the outflow of the two great rivers into the Persian Gulf, it is clear that each of them in his day had still its separate outlet to the sea, instead of uniting their streams into one as they do at the present day." Bunbury, *History of Ancient Geography*, Vol. II, p. 289.

[2] This kingdom of Hira was founded by tribes of Arab origin who, on having wandered from their original seats in Arabia towards Bahrein, were opposed in their eastward progress by the Persian Gulf, and thus directed their migrations towards the north. "There, attracted by the rich and well-watered vicinity, the strangers took up their abode, and about A.D. 200 laid the foundations of the city. The Arsacide monarchy was then crumbling under revolt and disastrous war; and the young colony, swelled by needy adventurers and desperate refugees from Arabia, grew unmolested into an important state. Another city not far distant from Hira, called Anbâr, was either founded, or having been previously in existence was taken possession of, by the Arabs." "By some the establishment of this town has been referred back to the time of Nebuchadnezzar II, who is

Hira, I assume, was known by name to the Chinese.

said to have left here the captives carried off in his inroad into Arabia. But this is a mere hypothesis of the Arab historians, who are very expert in imagining such causes for the origin of towns and kingdoms, etc." "The question is not one of much importance. The main point is undoubted, viz., that the kingdom of Hira originated in an *Arab* colony." (William Muir, *The Life of Mahomet*, Vol. I, p. CLXVI; of. de Guignes, *Hist. des Huns*, Vol. I, p. 320). As I have already intimated, Hira was about two centuries later known as a shipping port for maritime trade. Yule (*Cathay*, Vol. I, LXXVII), speaking of Arab trade to those parts, says: "The earliest date to which any positive statement of such intercourse appears to refer is the first half of the fifth century of our era. At this time, according to Hamza of Ispahan and Masudi, the Euphrates was navigable as high as Hira, a city lying south-west of ancient Babylon, near Ku-fa (now at a long distance from the actual channel of the river), and the ships of India and China were constantly to be seen moored before the houses of the town. Hira was then abounding in wealth, and the country round, now a howling wilderness, was full of that life and prosperity which water bestows in such a climate." Priaulx, "On the Indian Embassies to Rome, etc.," in *J. R. G. S.*, Vol. XIX, p. 295, speaking of the Indian trade of Palmyra, says: "Arab, and perhaps native, vessels brought the produce of India up the Persian Gulf to the mouth of the Euphrates; and, if they did not themselves ascend the river, at Teredon they discharged their cargoes intended for Vologesia, which was reached either by land on camels, or in vessels of lighter draught by the river." Vologesia, the chief trading town in the neighbourhood of Babylon, must have been somewhere between the site of Hira and the Euphrates. This city flourished at Josephus' time and was founded by king Vologeses who reigned A.D. 51 to 91, but previous to A.D. 73, because Pliny mentions the name (VI 26 (30), 122: nuper Velogeses rex aliud oppidum Velogesocertam in vicino condidit). As long as there is no positive evidence as to its site, we are free to assume that the facilities for trade causing the site of Hira to be a lucky one during the third century A.D., existed also during the first and second centuries, and that the city of Vologesia may have been similarly situated. Another city which may have stood on the peninsula is that of Alexandria, probably founded by Alexander the Great during his stay at Babylon (*see* Spruner-Menke, Atlas Antiquus, map No. VIII).

The city and state of that name flourished early enough to find notice in the *Hou-han-shu;* we, therefore, find the name mentioned as Yü-lo[1] in the itinerary describing the route from the capital of An-hsi (Parthia) west to the port of embarcation for Ta-ts'in (D 22). Yü-lo occupied apparently the the same or at least a similar site as "the city of T'iao-chih," Kan-ying's port; it was on the extreme west frontier of An-hsi (Parthia) and, from there "you travel south by sea to Ta-ts'in." As belonging to the country of T'iao-chih it was, of course, a Parthian possession during the Han dynasty; but as the city had been temporarily under Roman rule, Yü-lo is mentioned as a dependency of Ta-ts'in during the Wei dynasty (P 41, 74). The Roman boundary was then held to run between Yü-lo (Hira) and Ssŭ-lo (Seleucia); for "from Yü-lo north-east you cross a river [the Euphrates] to Ssŭ-lo; and north-east of this you again cross a river [the Tigris]; the country of Ssŭ-lo is subject to An-hsi [Parthia] and is on the boundary of Ta-

---

[1] 于羅, *yü-lo*. The sound of the first character appears to have corresponded to the present 和 *ho*, as ancient 于闐 *yü-tien* was changed into modern 和闐 *ho-tien* (Hoten, now usually spelt Khoten, the city in Central Asia), thus clearly suggesting that the pronunciation of 于 *yü* in ancient times may have been similar to modern 和 *ho*. The same city was called 劀賓 *huo-tien* by the Hu (胡) barbarians (= Ouigurs?), as I gather from a modern commentary of the *Ch'ien-han-shu*. Moreover, the *Ch'êng-yün* (正員), according to K'ang-hsi (s. v. 于) describes the sound of the character 于 by 休居切, *i.e.*, *hü* or *hu*. The old sound may be therefore set down as *ho-lo, hü-lo* or *ho-lat*, *i.e.*, Hîra or Hîrat ("*Hîrat al Nomân*, contracted by the Syrians, Greeks and Romans into *Hîrta*." William Muir, *l. c.*, p. CLXXI).

ts'in" (P 75-76). Finally, the distance from Ktesiphon, which name I consider to be the same as the Chinese Ssŭ pin (D 22; P 69), to Yü-lo, viz., 960 li or stadia, as stated in the *Hou-han-shu* (D 22), if measured by the land-road viâ the present Kerbela, corresponds as nearly with the actual length of that road as we may possibly expect in the most reliable classical author.

These are the reasons which have induced me to give the preference to the Chaldaean peninsula, as the site of both the city of T'iao-chih and of Yü-lo, amongst all other localities which may seem to answer the Chinese description at first sight. However ingenious the suggestions hitherto made with regard to the identification of T'iao-chih may be, I have never seen the attempt made to take more than a one-sided view of the question. I need not say that the method of investigating this subject should not consist in the consideration of one or two points in which the identity of the two countries seems to suggest itself; but that, apart from the principal features being traced in detail, the Chinese account contains no statement which may contradict the assumption arrived at. I shall not attempt to prove the reasons why the various suggestions made with regard to T'iao-chih[1] should be rejected. If the identifications set

---

[1] Identified with Egypt by Visdelou; with Persia by de Guignes who (*Hist. des Huns.*, Vol. II, p. 51) disposes of all difficulties by the few words: "On dit que ce pays est voisin de la mer d'occident; c'est sans doute le Golphe Persique. On y trouve des grains en abondance et un oiseau dont les œufs sont très-gros. Anciennement ces

forth in these notes are wrong, the demonstration of logical errors committed by others could not possibly make them appear in a better light; if they are correct, it will not be necessary to collect evidence of a negative character to support them: for, as Fichte[1] justly remarks, "für Entdeckung der Wahrheit ist die Bestreitung der entgegengesetzten Irrthümer von keinem beträchtlichen Gewinn." I propose, therefore, in the sequel not to take up the polemic point of view, but to leave it to the reader to form his opinion on the rival literature if he chooses to do so.

The route from Hekatompylos to Kan-ying's shipping-port may be clearly traced in the *Hou-han-shu*. That portion of it which led from Hekatompylos to the banks of the Tigris probably partly coincided with the track of Alexander's campaign through Media (B.C. 330). "From An-hsi (=Hekatompylos)," the Annals say (D 22), "you go west 3,400 li to the country of

peuples étaient gouvernés par leurs princes, mais dans la suite les Gan-sié les ont soumis et ont réduit ce royaume en province; c'est ce que les Parthes ont fait de la Perse." De Guignes' opinion appears to have become that of most of the scholars in Europe; but with the identification of Ta-ts'in with Italy, it was not compatible that T'iao-chih should be so far east as the Persian Gulf, which caused some to let Kan-ying arrive on the Mediterranean coast of Syria; while others, misled by a misunderstanding as to the meaning of the term "Western Sea," place the country near the coast of the Caspian (cf. Query and Replies: "Advance of a Chinese General to the Caspian," in *Notes and Queries*, Vol. II); von Richthofen suggests, not very confidently, though, the oasis of Khiva (*China*, Vol. I, p. 452) and Kingsmill (*China Review*, Vol. VIII, p. 164), Sarangia (Drangiana).

[1] *Vorlesungen üb. d. Bestimmung des Gelehrten*, V.

A-man[1]; from A-man you go west 3,600 li to the country of Ssŭ-pin; from Ssŭ-pin you go south, crossing a river and again south-west to the country of Yü-lo, 960 li, the extreme west frontier of An-hsi (Parthia); from here you travel south by sea, and so reach Ta-ts'in." A-man, I presume, is the city of Acbatana (=Assyrian Akmatan, the present Hamadán), the first centre of population on the road west of Hekatompylos. The distance could not have been stated more accurately in the Chinese record, and as the road leads through a plain, it may be expected to agree with reality. The track between the modern Damghan, the probable site of Hekatompylos, and the site of Acbatana, about which no doubt is entertained, measures just about 3,400 stadia.

By continuing the high-road in a westerly direction we have to pass through a broad range of hills, running from the north-west to the south-east, thus offering considerable interruptions in the straight line of travelling; the road probably meandered a good deal and went up and down hill every now and then, until it reached the plain, not too far away from the banks of the Tigris. We need not be astonished, therefore, to find a comparatively longer distance (36,000 li or stadia) assigned to the shorter route, viz., that from Acbatana to Ktesiphon; for, with

---

[1] Old sound Uk-man, if the *Yün-hui-hsiao-pu* (韻會小補), quoted in K'ang-hsi s. v. 阿, is right in giving this character the sound 屋, in Cantonese *ŭk*.

this name belonging to one of the Parthian capitals, I identify the Chinese Ssŭ-pin, which in modern Cantonese is pronounced Sĭ-pan, and the old sound of which may have been similar to this. Sĭ-pan or Ssŭ-pin, though not at first sight reminding one of the name Ktesiphon, will pass as a fair equivalent, if we allow for some mutilation, as all those conversant with the Chinese way of imitating foreign sounds will readily admit.

At Ktesiphon the Tigris had to be crossed, and then the road led south-west to Yü-lo, at a distance of 960 stadia or li. I have shown my reasons for assuming the identity of Yü-lo and Hira on the peninsula in the Chaldaean lake (*see* above, p. 147 seqq.) One of these reasons was, that the journey by boat from Ktesiphon down the Tigris would have been longer than the route *via* Hira. However, it may be that at some time or other the largest of the canals connecting the Tigris with the Euphrates, the present Schatt-el-Amâra, was used as a conductor of traffic, whether in small boats, or as accompanying a land-road (a feature frequently observed in modern China and probably quite as common in ancient western countries), thus offering a short cut to those who did not wish to visit Hira. The chief town near the present junction of this canal with the waters of the Euphrates, was the city of Uruku (Hebr. Erek, Greek 'Ορχόη, the present Warka)[1]; and this I venture to

---

[1] Cf. Kiepert, *Lehrb. d. alten Geogr.*, p. 144.

propose may have been the second shipping-port of Parthia, whence travellers were in the habit of embarking for the journey to Ta-ts'in. It seems to answer well enough to the Chinese An-ku (P 6, 13 and 60; cf. Q 7*), the linguistic value of which name may be set down as Ar-ku (*see* note on p. 139). I must admit that the evidence in favour of this identification is not strong, as it mainly rests on linguistic grounds, a most deceitful class of argument. Mr. Kingsmill, to whom I mentioned the case, thinks of Charax Spasinu, and if we can agree about the identity the first syllable of Greek XAPAK [1] and Chinese *an, ngan* (安), the suggestion deserves being further considered. The question still to be settled is this: which was the port from which, in order to reach Syria, one could either sail south (through the Persian Gulf and the Red Sea), or, proceed due west (by land, through the Syrian desert), or due north (through Mesopotamia to Antioch)? For such, I understand from the passage P 13, was the situation of An-ku. It should also be taken into consideration that An-ku is said to be a Parthian city and must have been situated close to the Roman boundary, since one of the tributary states of Ta-ts'in (Tsê-san) is said to be in its neighbourhood (P 58-60).

---

[1] Χάραξ in Greek, and *Karka* in Syriac (*see* Kiepert, l. c., p. 146) means "town or city." If Chinese *an* becomes *ar* in *Arsak*, it is difficult to justify its becoming *kar* in *karka*.

Whatever the situation of T'iao-chih (Yü-lo and An-ku) may have been, so much is certain, that it contained a shipping-port, where a passage by sea, lasting between two (P 6) or three (D 20) months and two years (D 20), continued the overland route from China, *viâ* the capital of An-hsi (Hekatompylos), A-man (Acbatana) and Ssŭ-pin (Ktesiphon), and led to a port, which was the port of Ta-ts'in. It seems to me that the description given of T'iao-chih in the *Hou-han-shu* (D 1 to 9) does not contradict that supposition [1]).

Which, then, was the port of Ta-ts'in? The *Hou-han-shu* says (E 37): "Coming from the

---

[1] It will be found in this description that the road of Kan-ying's or somebody else's journey from T'iao-chih back to the capital of An-hsi (Parthia) is described again, as from the interpretation of the route stated in the account of An-hsi (D 22) we may expect it to be. "If you turn to the north," the Annals say (D 8), "and then towards the east again go on horseback some sixty days, you come to An-hsi (Parthia)." By An-hsi we have to understand here, according to a usage often met with in these texts, the capital of the country, and not its boundary. From T'iao-chih, wherever it was situated on or near the mouth of the Euphrates, you go north to Ktesiphon, whence an overland route ("on horseback") takes the traveller east, *viâ* Acbatana to Hekatompylos. I cannot help drawing attention here to the mistake into which Neumann fell when *(Asiatische Studien*, p. 157*)* he translated this passage by: "Das Land hat einen Umfang von ungefähr 60 Tagereisen zu Pferde und ward später von den Asi oder Assyriern abhängig." The length of the road performed on horseback (60 days) corresponds to the 7,000 (3,400 + 3,600) li between Ssŭ-pin (Ktesiphon) and the capital of An-hsi (Parthia). If we assume these identifications to be correct, the average rate of travelling on horseback in these parts would have been about 117 li or stadia in a day. Cf. Ma Tuan-lin's T'iao-chih, in Rémusat's translation, *Nouv. Mél. As.*, Vol. I, p. 215.

land-road of An-hsi (Parthia), you make a round at sea and, taking a northern turn, come out from the western part of the sea whence you proceed to Ta-ts'in." Starting at the head of the Persian Gulf, the passage here described takes us round the Arabian peninsula, and then northward into the Red Sea. The coast of this sea contained various outlets of oriental trade, all of which may perhaps claim to have been ports of Ta-ts'in. There was the route from Berenice, probably the southernmost, to Koptos on the banks of the Nile, and another, shorter route from Myos Hormos to the same river-port, goods being carried by camels over-land in caravans; at Koptos they were placed on board river-boats and carried down the Nile to Alexandria.[1] This was probably the commercial route for a considerable part of the traffic between India and Rome. The Chinese trade differed from the Indian trade mainly in that the bulk of its material consisted in silk textures which, before they were thrown on the Roman market, had to undergo the process of dyeing, chiefly purple dyeing, at Tyre or Sidon, or that of being woven (re-woven?) at Berytus or Tyre.[2] The next route from the

---

[1] Plin., VI 23 (26), 102, seqq. Cf. O. de Beauvoir Priaulx, "On the Indian Embassies to Rome from the Reign of Claudius to the Death of Justinian" in *Journ. R. Asiat. Soc.*, Vol. XIX, p. 294.

[2] Priaulx, *l. c.* p. 296, quotes from Procopius, *Hist. Arcana*, 25 c., p. 140: ἱμάτια τὰ ἐκ μετάξης ἐν Βηρυτῷ μὲν καὶ Τύρῳ πόλεσι ταῖς ἐπὶ Φοινίκης ἐργάζεσθαι ἐκ παλαιοῦ εἴωθεν, etc., and from Vopiscus, Carinus XX, *Hist. Aug. Scrip.* "Quid lineas Aegypto petitas loquar?

Red Sea to the manufacturing towns of the Phœnician coast, however, did not lead through Egypt, but through the country of the Nabataeans.[1] The port of Ta-ts'in at which Chinese goods were chiefly landed must have been at the head of the present Gulf of Akabah, the ancient Sinus Aelaniticus. At the Ta-ts'in epoch (say B.C. 140 up to about the sixth century A.D.) the ancient Phœnician glory had passed away, it is true; but the industries of the Phœnician cities and the commercial relations depending on them lasted for centuries after the beginning of our era. The natural advantages of a country like Syria must at any time have commanded a superior position in the oriental trade of Rome, a position which is quite compatible with its inferior position as a political power. The sea-port of Syria in the Red Sea was at the head of the eastern one of the

---

Quid Tyro et Sidone tenuitate perlucidas micantes purpura, plumandi difficultate pernobiles." Priaulx gathers from the difficultate plumandi that the stuffs from Tyre and Sidon were of silk.

[1] Strabo, XVI, p. 781 ed. Casaub. (Meineke), thinks of the distribution of Indian and other oriental goods over the western part of the empire when he says: ἐκ μὲν οὖν τῆς Λευκῆς κώμης εἰς Πέτραν, ἐντεῦθεν δ' εἰς ʿΡινοκόλουρα τῆς πρὸς Αἰγύπτῳ Φοινίκης τὰ φορτία κομίζεται κἀντεῦθεν εἰς τοὺς ἄλλους, νυνὶ δὲ τὸ πλέον εἰς τὴν Ἀλεξάνδρειαν τῷ Νείλῳ· κατάγεται δ' ἐκ τῆς Ἀραβίας καὶ τῆς Ἰνδικῆς εἰς Μυὸς ὅμρον· εἶθ' ὑπέρθεσις εἰς Κοπτὸν τῆς Θηβαΐδος καμήλοις ἐν διώρυγι τοῦ Νείλου κειμένην. [εἶτ'] εἰς Ἀλεξάνδρειαν. The fact that the greater part of oriental (Indian) goods were discharged at Myos Hormos does not exclude the bulk of Chinese silks being taken to the dyeing and re-weaving cities in Phœnicia direct.

two gulfs forming the peninsula of Sinai. Two ports of this neighbourhood are mentioned as the channels of Phœnician trade in remote antiquity, the port of Êlath, the Aïla or Aelana of the Romans, near the present Akabah, and the port of 'Eçeôngeber. It was from these ports that King Solomon sent his fleet to Ophir, and the first-named port, Aelana, was under the Romans an important military station; and a Christian bishop resided there during several centuries at the beginning of our era.

Only about 60 miles north of this port was the city of Petra, so called by Greek conquerors who translated one of its Aramaean names, Sela, *i.e.*, rock, into their language,[1] from the Greek name of which the Romans called the country Arabia Petraea. The principal local name of the city, however, was not Petra, but Rekem or Rekam.[2] During the first two centuries A.D., Petra or Rekem was the seat of an immense commerce—the great emporium of Indian [and, we may add, Chinese] commodities, where merchants from all parts of the world met for the purposes of traffic. The city fell under the Mahommedan empire, and from that time to the beginning of the present century was nearly lost from the memory of man.

---

[1] Cf. Kiepert, *Lehrb. d. alten Geogr.* Berlin, 1878, p. 184.

[2] According to Eusebius and Hieronymus; Rokom, according to Epiphanius, and Arekeme or Arkem, according to Josephus (Antiqq. Jud. IV, 4, 7 and 7, 1), quoted in Riehmer, *Handwörterb. d. bibl. Alterthums*, p. 1284. Cf. Kiepert, *l. c.*

When Burckhardt[1] discovered its forgotten site in the year 1811, he found only a solitary column and one ruinous edifice left standing, of all the sumptuous structures that once crowded this romantic vale [2] "Under the auspices of Rome, Petra rose, along with her dependencies, to an incredible opulence. Unheeded in the desert, and for centuries forgotten, the stately ruins of the hill-encircled city and its chiselled rocks still remain an evidence that may not be gainsayed of the mighty traffic once passing through the marts of Petra, of the princely magnificence of her merchants, of the truth of history, and of the unerring certainty of prophetic denunciation. Pliny and Strabo both describe the city in its unmistakable features. Athenodoras the Stoic visited it, and related with admiration to Strabo, his friend, the excellence of the government under a native prince, and the security with which Romans and other foreigners resided there. It need hardly be added that this prosperity was entirely dependent upon the caravan trade, which at this entrepôt changed carriage, and passed from the hands of the southern to those of the northern merchants. To this cause Diodorus Siculus attributes the superiority of the Nabathaeans over the other Bedouin tribes:—"Their commercial

---

[1] The celebrated Swiss traveller, author of *Travels in Syria and the Holy Land*, London 1822; *Travels in Arabia*, London 1829, etc.

[2] Olin, *Travels in Egypt, Arabia Petraea and the Holy Land*, Vol. II, p. 49.

pursuits," he says, "are the chief cause of their greater prosperity. For many of the tribes follow the business of transporting to the Mediterranean, frankincense, myrrh, and other costly spices, which are transferred to them by the carriers from Arabia Felix?"[1]. Strabo also writes that the merchandise of the Arabian Gulf used to be transported from Leuke Kome on the Red Sea, to Petra; thence to Rhinokolura *(Al Arish)*, a town upon the Mediterranean; and so to other ports.[2] And Pliny notices the double route which bifurcated at Petra."[3] The passage referred to (Pliny VI, 28 (32), 144) reads thus: "huc convenit utrumque bivium, eorum qui Syria Palmyram petiere et eorum qui a Gaza venerunt," and Heeren[4] adds: "From the words of Pliny, one thing at least is certain, that at Petra the commercial road parted in two directions, one leading to the left, towards Gaza and the shores of Syria; the other to the right, towards Palmyra." The Palmyrian road supplied the east of Syria, where the city of Bostra, the capital of Arabia Petraea under the Romans, the present Bosrah, was known as another centre of oriental trade. The road to Gaza connected the Gulf with the west of Syria, or, the Red Sea with the Mediterranean Sea. It looks almost as if the *Wei-shu* (I 5,) referred to these routes

---

[1] See Forster's *Arabia*, Vol. I, p. 224.
[2] Strabo XVI, p. 781, (see note 1 on p. 159.)
[3] William Muir, *Life of Mahomet*, Vol. I, p. CXXXV seq.
[4] *Historical Researches*, Vol. II, Appendix IX.

in saying: "By the side of its sea one comes out at what is like an arm of the sea; that the east and the west [of the country] look into that arm of the sea is a natural arrangement." The "east and west" may be the "bivium" mentioned by Pliny, uniting at Petra or Aelana thus, as it were, "looking into" the Gulf.[1] The *Wei-shu* (I 7), is, further, right in saying that "the country lies between two seas," meaning the Red Sea on the one hand and the Mediterranean on the other; and the *Tu-huan-hsing-ching-chi*, quoted by Ma Tuan-lin (Q 50), is still clearer about the point in saying: "on the west, the country bounds on the western sea, on the south, on the southern sea,"[2] though the terms "western" and "southern" are in this instance to be understood from the Ta-ts'in or Syrian point of view. Apart from this, as I have shown, the term Hsi-hai, *i.e.*, western sea, may be applied to the Indian Ocean with its dependencies (the Persian Gulf and the Red Sea) as well as to the Caspian. The term Hai-hsi, *i.e.*, west of the sea or western arm of the sea, answers to the Red Sea, just as the term Hai-tung, *i.e.*, east of the sea or eastern arm of

---

[1] The passage quoted from the *Wei-shu* may be interpreted in a two-fold manner. Either as above, in which case the Sinus Aelaniticus would correspond to the "arm of the sea" referred to; or, the Arabian Gulf may be that "arm of the sea," and "the east and the west of the country looking into it" may be its commercial outlets, viz., Aelana and Petra leading to Syria in the east, and Berenice, Leukos and Myos Hormos leading to Alexandria in the west.

[2] The "Coral Sea" of the Nestorian Inscription (M 1).

the sea, answers to the Persian Gulf. *Hai-hsi-kuo* is, therefore, the country of the Red Sea (cf. C 3, E 1, P 7, et passim) ; and vessels sailing from T'iao-chih to Ta-ts'in have to cross the "western part of the sea" (=Hai-hsi, P 6). On the other hand, *hai-tung-chu-kuo* means "the countries on the eastern arm of the sea," "the countries on the Persian Gulf" (P 44, 69; Q 27). *Hai-pei*, or "the country north of the sea," I am led to assume on the ground of passages E 40 (*hai-pei-chu-kuo*, "the countries north of the sea," to which one crosses by the bridge north-west of Antioch, P 64, Q 75, *i.e.*, the bridge across the Euphrates at Zeugma), P 13 and P 50, is either Mesopotamia or the north of Syria.

The length of the sea-route from T'iao-chih to Ta-ts'in, *i.e.*, from a port on or near the mouth of the Euphrates (Babylon, Velogesia, Hira, Orchoë, Charax Spasinu?) to Aelana, the sea-port of Petra or Rekem, is described as measuring over 10,000 li (I 3, 22, Q 5, 64). In the text of the *Wei-shu* (I 22) this distance is given as "over 40,000 li," and the *Pei-shih*, a revised edition of the *Wei-shu*, corrects this figure into 10,000. The larger amount (40,000) would very nearly correspond to the length of the passage in stadia; out as the tradition of the text seems to be strongly in favour of 10,000 li, we have to interpret this expression as having a general sense like the latin *sexcenti*, *i.e.*, as meaning an indefinite large number. The sailors on the Parthian frontier,

I presume, were inspired by the spirit of the ancient Phœnician merchants in that they would not help anyone to collect information which might possibly create competition in trade and become ruinous to their own business;[1] for, as they were probably the employés of Syrian shipowners engaged in the carriage of Chinese goods from Parthia to Syria for the Roman market and *vice versâ*,[2] it would have been quite against their interest to let a political agent of the Chinese nation proceed to the west, as he might gossip about the real price of silk in China and learn the real price of glass nicknacks and jewelry in Syria, from which their employers made such an enormous profit [tenfold E 28, *hundredfold* F 16,[3]—we learn from these passages that a highly profitable *sea* trade existed between Ta-ts'in and An-hsi (Parthia) and T'ien-chu (India)]. It is probably for this reason that they told Kan Ying, who as a native of north-western China, and being

---

[1] A similar explanation of Kan Ying's failure in reaching Ta-ts'in is given by the author of the *Hai-kuo-t'u-chih*, Ch. 18, p. 19.

[2] *See* E 28. From this passage it certainly appears that the people of Ta-ts'in (Syria) traded by sea with India and China, and that the profit derived from this trade was theirs; as the *Chin-shu* words it (F 16), the Parthians and Indians seem to have come to them; according to the Liang-shu (H 1) the Indians carry on the trade with Parthia and Ta-ts'in. Whatever nationality the carrying vessels may have belonged to, it seems clear that it was in their interest to keep a Chinese explorer in the dark regarding the particulars of their trade.

[3] "Nec pigebit totum cursum ab Aegypto exponere nunc primum certa notitia patescente. digna res, nullo anno minus HS |DL| imperii nostri exhauriente India et merces remittente quae apud nos *centiplicato veneant*." Plin., VI, 23 (26), 101

accustomed to travelling on land-roads hitherto, was just the greenhorn to be taken in by the cunning skippers, that "there was something about the sea which caused one to long for home; that those who went out could not help being seized by melancholy feelings; if the Chinese envoy did not care for his parents, his wife and children, he might go." The Chin annals, with a shade of humour, state that under the circumstances "Ying could not take his passage" (F 19). On that occasion they probably supplied him with what could be news to none but a Central-Asiatic hero, the information that "the water of the great sea which was crossed on the road to Ta-ts'in, was salt and bitter, and unfit for drinking purposes" (F 18); and also, "that, with favourable winds, the passage lasted two months;[1] that, with slow winds, it could last two years; and that those who risked their lives in such an adventure, had to be supplied with three years' provisions" (D 20). I cannot suppress an after-thought that this last piece of information was given him in order to justify a big price as passage-money, which may have had as powerful an effect on Kan Ying's mind as the horrors of the sea described to him in such drastic language.

The shortest duration of the sea journey from the mouth of the Euphrates, or Hira, to Aelana, according to the *Wei-lio*, was two months. If

---

[1] "Two months," according to the *Wei-lio* (P 6); "three months," according to the passage quoted from the *Hou-han-shu* (D 20).

we assume the sailing track from Hira to Aelana to have measured 3,600 nautical miles, the speed of navigation would have been during the third century A.D., the period represented in the *Wei-lio*, 60 nautical miles *per diem* as an average; the passage of three months, as described in the *Hou-han-shu* during Kan Ying's time (A.D. 97), would give us an average of 40 miles; and the two years, which the passage may have possibly lasted according to Kan Ying's informants, a much smaller figure. It would be a mistake to compare these averages with what we know about the speed of ancient navigation in the Mediterranean. Friedlaender, in a former edition of his celebrated work (*Sittengeschichte Rom's*, Vol. II, ed. 1864, p. 15) computed the daily average for a favourable passage in the Mediterranean at 1,000 stadia, *i.e.*, about 80 nautical miles, and Peschel (*Gesch. d. Erdk.*, ed. Ruge, 1877, p. 20), in collecting accounts of quick sea passages made by ancient sailers, shows that the quickest passage on record was made at the rate of 8 miles in an hour. In a later edition of his Vol. II, (third edition, 1874, p. 26 seqq.) Friedlaender struck averages from a considerably increased number of examples quoted from ancient authors, and arrived at a still higher average speed, viz., 100 to 180 miles within 24 hours. It will be seen that even the quickest passages made according to Kan Ying's informers are left behind considerably by these figures. Yet, I quite believe in the truthfulness of the Chinese record; for, in the first instance, navigation in these unknown waters could not fairly compete with the traffic say between Rome and Alexandria; the Persian Gulf, especially, must have been a dangerous sea to sailers, and the river or canal passage through Chaldaea probably took up more than ordinary time; finally, we learn from the peripli of the Erythraean Sea, that numerous ports of call were entered by these ships, and it seems natural that the delay caused thereby should have been included in the total length of the trip by Kan Ying's informants, who, moreover, may be suspected to have rather exaggerated, than under-stated, the hardships of the joruney. The fleet of a hundred and twenty-five vessels which sailed from Myos Hormos to the coast of Malabar or Ceylon, annually, about the time of the summer solstice, traversed the ocean, with the periodical assistance of the monsoons, in about forty days.[1] The forty days' journey reckoned on this trip represent, according to Pliny,[2] the distance between Ocelis in the Bab-el-Mandeb and Muziris on the coast of Malabar, *i.e.*, a track measuring about 2,000 miles. The average speed, then, must have been 50 miles a day in the Indian Ocean, and that is all we may desire to confirm the correctness of Kan Ying's report.[3]

---

[1] Gibbon, Vol. I, ch. 2; Priaulx, l. c., p. 294; cf. Plin., VI, 23 (26), 101 seqq.

[2] Indos autem petentibus utilissimum est ab Oceli egredi. inde vento hippalo navigant diebus XL ad primum emporium Indiae Muzirim. . . . Plin., VI, 23 (26), 104.

[3] It appears that the *Wu-shih-wai-kuo-chuan* 吳時外國傳 (=Account of Foreign Countries at the time of Wu, A.D., 222 to 277), quoted in the *Yüan-chien-lei-han* (ch. 386, p. 43), alludes

We may conclude from the hints contained in the earlier Chinese histories, that this route (Central Asia, Hekatompylos, Acbatana, Ktesiphon, Hira, mouth of the Euphrates, Persian Gulf, Indian Ocean, Red Sea, Aelana and Petra with its bifurcation to Gaza along the Phœnician coast and to Bostra, Damascus, etc.) was the principal channel of trade between China and Syria as the representative of the Far West from the beginning of commercial relations till up to the year A.D. 166. We are told in records as old as the *Hou-han-shu* and the *Wei-lio* (E 1 and P 5) that Ta-ts'in and Li-kan are one and the same country, and it is clear that Li-kan is the older name of the two. It apparently first occurs in the *Shih-chi* (ch. 123). When Chang Ch'ien had negotiated his treaties with the countries of the west, the king of An-hsi (Parthia) sent an embassy to the Chinese court and presented large birds'-eggs, probably ostrich eggs, and jugglers from

---

to a trip similar to that from Muziris to Ocelis. It speaks of "ships provided with seven sails by which they sailed from Ka-na-tiao-chou (加 郍 調 州), and with favourable winds could enter Ta-ts'in within *over a month*.' I presume that the city (country, province?) here mentioned was on, or near, the Indian West Coast. During the Wu period a traveller called K'ang T'ai (康 泰) was sent to Fu-nan (Siam and adjoining countries?), who afterwards reported on his journey (cf. Ma Tuan-lin, ch. 331, p. 19). The *Hai-kuo-t'u-chih* (ch. 17, p. 7) quotes from his account of Fu-nan: "South-west from Ka-na-tiao-chou, entering the Great Gulf, you arrive at a distance of 700 or 800 li at the mouth of the great river Chih-hu-li; crossing the river, you pass to the west, and at the extreme end of the journey, come to Ta ts'in."

Li-kan (A 1-5 and B 1-5).[1] Various conjectures have been made on the sound of this word. "Regnum" and "hellenikon" (Edkins, *J. N.-C. Branch, R. A. S.* Vol. XVIII, p. 3; cf. ib. p. 19), "legiones" (Taintor in *Notes and Queries on China and Japan,* Vol. II, p. 62), "Lycia" (Pauthier, see Bretschneider in *Notes and Queries,* Vol. IV, p. 59); βασιλικήν ("the royal city"; *Notes and Queries,* Vol. IV, p. 8), and other etymologies have been thought of. With regard to these, as to all identifications of names, I wish to say that most of the writers on the subject seem to have been a little rash in declaring identity on the ground of mere similarity in sound. The name of a place ought to be the last thing we should think of. If, after we have recognised a locality by its characteristic features, a reasonable etymology suggests itself for its name in Chinese, the additional evidence it affords is certainly a welcome help; but we should be careful not to jump at linguistic conclusions before

---

[1] This name is represented by different characters in the various records mentioning it. It appears as 黎軒 *li-hsien* in the *Shih-chi*, *Wei-shu* and *Pei-shih;* as 犂軒 *li-kan* in the *Ch'ien-han-shu* and *Wei-lio;* as 犂鞬 *li-kien* (*li-kin*) in the *Hou-han-shu* and *Chin-shu*. Ma Tuan-lin, who(Q 1) adopts the *Ch'ien-han-shu* style of writing the name, describes the sound by 居言 (*kü* and *yen,=ken*), and in another passage (the account of Wu-i-shan-li, ch. 337, p. 25) by 巨連 (*kü* and *lien,=kien,* old sound : *kin*). The first syllable of *Rekem* could have only been represented by *li* in Chinese; the substitution, in the Chinese sound, of a final *n* for *m*, must be explained by the fact that the Chinese, who first wrote the name down, did not hear it on the spot, but probably through the medium of an informant speaking a dialect of the Aramaean language differing from that spoken at Petra.

having examined the facts underlying them. We have seen that with some probability the oldest trade route to Ta-ts'in touched the territory of this country at Aelana, the port of the great oriental emporium Petra or Rekem. *Rekem*, we may assume, was the city which being connected by direct navigation with the shipping-port in T'iao-chih (Vologesia, Hira, Orchoë?) must have become first known to Chinese travellers (such as Chang Ch'ien, or Pan Ch'ao and Kan Ying) through Parthian informers as the market for Chinese silk. A Chinese supercargo asking the question at Hira: "where do you ship our silk for?" would have received the reply: "to Rekem." Rekem was the landing dépôt for the oriental goods destined for the Phœnician manufacturing towns, just as Berenice and Myos Hormos, or Koptos, may be regarded as receiving-stations for the Alexandrian market; it was the next station after T'iao-chih, and, from an oriental point of view, was the entrance of Ta-ts'in or Syria. At this stage I may be justified in offering the conjecture of Rekem being identical with Li-kan of the *Shih-chi* and the *Ch'ien-han-shu*, which is plausible enough from a linguistic point of view as all those acquainted with the Chinese transliteration of foreign names will admit, and which is, moreover, based on suppositions suggested by facts.

During the period when the name Li-kan was in use for the westernmost country to which Chinese commercial relations extended, *i.e.*, the time following Chang Ch'ien's expedition or about 120 B.C., the Nabathaean kingdom of which Petra or Rekem was the capital commanded a powerful position in western Asia. Mommsen (*Röm. Gesch.*, 7th Ed., Vol. III, p. 138), referring to the time of Pompeius, even speaks of the Nabathaeans as "the real lords in the empire of the Seleucidae, together with the Jews and the Bedouins." Chinese records of the ante-Christian period repeatedly mention the two countries T'iao-chih and Li-kan together, so that, for a long time, they were believed to be neighbouring countries. We have seen that T'iao-chih probably occupied the territory of ancient Babylon, the country about the Chaldaean Lake, which, as the terminus of sea navigation, was considered part of the western sea. Now, there is nothing more natural than that intimate relations, political and commercial, existed between the Chaldaeans and the Nabathaeans, or in other words, between T'iao-chih and Li-kan. For, although these two nations were separated from each other on the one hand by the Syrian deseit, on the other hand by the Indian Ocean with its two gulfs, close relationship existed between them. Mommsen (*l.c.*, Vol. III, p. 141), says with regard to the Nabathaeans: "This remarkable nation has been frequently confounded with their eastern neighbours, the vagrant Arabs; but they are nearer related to the Aramaean branch than to the Ismaëlites proper. This Aramaean—or as occidental nations call it, Syrian -tribe must, at a very early period, have sent out a colony from its oldest residence about

Babylon to the northern coast of the Arabic Gulf, probably for trading purposes: these are the Nabathaeans on the peninsula of Sinai between the Gulf of Suez and Aïla, and in the neighbourhood of Petra (Wadi-Musa). It was in their ports that goods coming from the Mediterranean were exchanged for Indian produce; the great southern caravan-road running from Gaza to the mouth of the Euphrates and the Persian Gulf, led through Petra, the Nabathaean capital, where the palaces and tombs cut in rocks, having retained their magnificence up to the present day, are better witnesses of Nabathaean civilisation than the almost forgotten historical tradition."

The sea route from the Persian Gulf to Rekem, it appears from what we may gather, was the principal channel for the silk trade up to the time of the Parthian war conducted under Marcus Aurelius Antoninus by Avidius Cassius during the years A.D. 162 to 165; whereas the bulk of oriental articles which had nothing to do with further treatment (dyeing, embroidering, re-weaving) in Phœnicia, probably went to Alexandria, for distribution over the Roman Empire. It is probably not an accidental coincidence that just at the conclusion of this war which terminated with the capture of Seleucia and Ktesiphon by the Romans in A.D. 165, a mission went forward from Ta-ts'in by sea to the Far East which arrived at the court of

China in October A.D. 166.[1] Up to this time the Parthians had monopolised the trade between China and Ta-ts'in as we learn from the *Hou-han-shu* (E 32), the *Wei-lio* (P 24), and other records. It may be surmised therefrom that, at a time when battles were fought on the banks of the Euphrates and Tigris, when two of the cities which lay on the road from Central Asia to the shipping-port on or near the coast of the Persian Gulf, the cities of Ktesiphon and Seleucia, were captured or destroyed with their magazines, a commercial crisis may have created much anxiety amongst the Syrian merchants at Antioch, Tyre, Sidon or Petra; their connection with the Chinese market through their Parthian friends—for friends they had been in trade, if not in politics—had been cut off by the armies of their own, the Roman, government; the bales of silk piece-goods they were accustomed to expect did not arrive, nor did their own dyed and mustered piece-goods, their glass nicknacks, their real and imitation precious stones, reach their

---

[1] See *Hou-han-shu*, Ch. 7, p. 4. Ma Tuan-lin (Q 36) places this mission at the beginning of the Yüan-chia period of Huan-ti, *i.e.*, A.D. 151, and the *Chu-fan-chih* (R 21), at the beginning of the Yen-hsi period, *i.e.*, A.D. 158; but this is clearly an oversight, as the year A.D. 166 is supported by two passages in the *Hou-han-shu* (the passage above quoted and E 33), and the authority of the *Liang-shu* (H 5). I may add that the year A.D. 166 is mentioned in the *Han-shu* edition of A.D. 1243, printed about half a century previous to the time when Ma Tuan-lin wrote (*see* facsimile copy of the Ta-ts'in account of the *Hou-han-shu*.)

destination in China.¹ What was, under the circumstances, more natural than that a mercantile mission should be sent through the Indian Ocean and the China Sea to open up direct communication with the Chinese themselves? It is true, the Chinese records speak of the king of Ta-ts'in, An-tun, as the sender of the embassy, and as, at the time, Marcus Aurelius Antoninus was emperor at Rome, it is quite in order to identify his name with the An-tun of the embassy. However, if we examine the two-fold point of view, that of the emperor at Rome and that of the silk merchants in Syria, *vis-à-vis* the Chinese nation, if we apply the *cui bono* question to the sending of a mission to a distant continent which could be in none but commercial connection with the western world: have we really reason to assume that, at a time when the frontier provinces had to be kept

---

¹ The difficulty created through the Parthian war must have been aggravated by the fact that a plague, the most terrible one on record during antiquity, had broken out in Babylonia, which the Roman army, returning from the seat of war, carried all over the empire ("ab ipsis Persarum finibus adusque Rhenum et Gallias cuncta contagiis polluebat et mortibus." Ammian. XXIII, 6, 24). Medical authorities (Krause, *Ueber das Alter der Menschenpocken*," and A. Hirsch, *Handb. der geogr. Pathologie*, quoted by Friedlaender, *Sittengesch.*, Vol. I, ed. 1873, p. 36) declare the epidemic to have been small-pox. The Han annals (*Hou-han-shu*, ch. 7, p. 3) contain the record of a pestilence (chi-yi 疾瘦) and of a famine, the latter having caused 40 to 50 per cent. of the population to die from starvation in Yü-chou (豫州), the present Ho-nan province. Unfortunately, the Chinese term used for this, as for other epidemics, recorded in ancient times, is somewhat vague and contains no clue whether small-pox, or cholera, or the real plague, is meant.

at peace with great effort, the Roman government should have thought of seeking the friendship of the Emperor of China for political reasons? Is not the commercial interest, the "ten" and "hundred-fold profit" which the Syrian merchants had lost since the termination of the Parthian war, a much more powerful inducement to look out for new connections? I am for this and other reasons inclined to believe that the mission of A.D. 166 was not an embassy, but a private expedition.[1] Merchants who were accustomed to trade to India and Ceylon, took passage further on to Annam. They had probably originally neither credentials nor presents nor tribute for the Chinese emperor; any piece of papyrus covered with Greek or Latin writing would do for the former, and the tribute—as we conclude from the nature of the goods presented—was bought up in Annam, where they perhaps made up their minds to play the part of imperial messengers, in order to obtain the trading privileges sought for. Their tribute, we are told (E 33), consisted of ivory, rhinoceros' horns and tortoise-shell,—Annamese articles, as even the author of the *Hou-han-shu* must have suspected, who says "their tribute contained no jewels whatever, which fact throws doubt on the tradition."[2] As true mer-

---

[1] Cf. Klaproth, *Tabl. hist. de l'Asie*, p. 69, also Letronne, in *Mém. des inscr. et belles lettres*, Nouv. Serie, T. X, p. 227, quoted in Friedlaender, *Sittengesch. Rom's*, Vol. II (ed. 1874), p. 63.

[2] or "which makes us suspect that the messengers were at fault." Cf. Q 36 and R 21.

chants, it appears, the pseudo-ambassadors had disposed of their Ta-ts'in jewels[1] wherever the best prices were offered, and bought the presents for the emperor of China from part of the proceeds on the spot, in Annam. It is very likely that part of what we read in the *Hou-han-shu*, especially the remarks concerning commercial traffic with China, was taken from the record written in the daily chronicles when the Ta-ts'in ambassadors were examined by means of interpreters. I am inclined to believe that they brought Roman coins to China, which being explained by them, induced the chronicler to make his remark about the Ta-ts'in gold and silver coins, the relation between which is that of ten to one (E 27). They probably alluded to the subject of their mission by saying: "we have had trade with An-hsi (Parthia) and T'ien-chu (India), from which we have had tenfold profit; we are honest and havé no double prices, etc." Perhaps they even mentioned that "in Ta-ts'in foreign ambassadors are driven by post from the frontier to the capital and were presented with golden money on arrival," in order to show what the Chinese might have done to honour them. They probably further stated that "their kings always desired to send missions to China (*i.e.*, to carry on direct trade), but that the Parthians, who would not lose the profit they made out of the silk trade, would

---

[1] Ma Tuan-lin's version (Q 36) and the *Chu-fan-chih* (R 21) clearly hint at the possibility of their having suppressed the jewels and curiosities which the Chinese expected from a country like Ta-ts'in.

not allow them to pass through their country, until now they had come by sea direct to trade with China" (E 28 to 33). All this reads much more like the arguing of commercial pioneers, travelling on behalf of a wealthy guild in Antioch or Alexandria, than the letter of credence issued by a monarch like Marcus Aurelius Antoninus, who—from what we may conclude from the various passages occurring in classical authors with regard to the Seres—cared about as little for his colleague in Chang-an-fu as the latter cared for him. After the difficulties experienced in his wars with the Parthians, the Roman Cæsar could not dream of ever penetrating to such a distance with his legions, nor would it have served Roman interests to seek an alliance with China against Parthia, as the Chinese under Huan-ti were scarcely able to keep their western frontier in order, not to speak of the Hsiung-nu nation, their great and powerful enemy.

The Han Annals do not say whether the direct sea-route was after that used as the main channel for trade; but we may read between the lines that it was so; for "from that time," they say, "dates the direct intercourse with this country" (E 33). Goods, I presume, then went by junk from Annam to Ceylon, the ancient Taprobane, or the coast of Malabar, whence they were transhipped to the Red Sea.[1]

---

[1] For an abstract from the principal western sources on the ancient trade with China *see* Reinaud, *Relations Politiques, etc., de l'Empire Romain avec l'Asie Orientale*, p. 184 seqq., and the several accounts in Yule's *Cathay and the Way Thither*.

During the two Wei dynasties, *i.e.*, about between the 3rd and 6th centuries A.D., another route was largely used, especially for the importation of goods from Ta-ts'in. It is stated in the *Wei-shu* that "there is also connection by water with the principalities of Yi-chou and Yung-ch'ang" (I 19; cf. Q 62), and in the *Wei-lio* (P 50), that "after the road from Ta-ts'in had been performed from the north of the sea by land, another road was tried which followed the sea to the south and connected with the north of the outer barbarians at the seven principalities of Chiao-chih (=Cochin China);" and that "there was also a water-road leading through to Yi-chou and Yung-ch'ang,"—both these districts being in the present Yünnan. "It is for this reason," the *Wei-lio* adds, "that the curiosities [of Ta-ts'in] come from Yung-ch'ang." The route here described takes us to a sea-port on the coast of Pegu whence one of the two rivers, the Salwen or the Irawaddy, offered a channel for traffic with the confines of Yünnan. Perhaps the southeastern route along the bed of the latter river, the Ta-ho, which has during the last twenty years become known as the scene of distinguished travelling, saw lively traffic in those days, as it must have connected a considerable portion of the interior of China with the ports on the Gulf of Bengal. According to the *Hou-han-shu* (C 2 to 4), natives of Ta-ts'in, musicians and jugglers, found their way to the court of a king of Shan, whose possessions must have been near the borders of the Yung-ch ang principality (the Vochang of Marco Polo). This king, who had previously (A.D. 98; *see* C 1) been endowed by the Chinese emperor with a golden seal and a purple ribbon, the emblems of a tributary prince, presented his liege-lord with a number of Syrian artists who somehow or other had got into his power. On New Year's Day A.D. 121 they gave a performance in the presence of the youthful emperor An-ti.[1]

The journey across Parthia and the sea has probably never been completely performed by a Chinese traveller; but the Chinese must have been aware that their goods were forwarded in this direction, for so, it seems, we have to explain the words of the *Sung-shu*, which says (G 1): "although the envoys of the two Han dynasties have experienced the special difficulties of this road, yet traffic in merchandise has been effected, and goods have been sent out to the foreign tribes, the force of the winds driving them far way across the waves of the sea."

During the Wei period, *i.e.*, during the third century A.D., we may conclude from remarks occurring in the *Wei-lio*, the trade to ports on the Egyptian coast was known to Chinese authors. The Ta-ts'in of this period must be assumed to comprise Egypt, for so I understand the following passage in the *Wei-lio* (P 7): "This

---

[1] The passage (C 4), literally translated, means; "At the new year's meeting (*yüan-hui*) of the following year, An-ti made music (*tso-yo:* gave a musical entertainment?) at court."

country is on the west of the sea, whence it is commonly called Hai-hsi. There is a river coming out from the west of this country, and there is another great sea" The "west of the sea" I have pointed out is the Red Sea; the river referred to in this passage I believe is the Nile, and the other great sea is the Mediterranean. The *Wei-lio* continues (P 9): "In the west of that sea there is the city of Ch'ih-san." The old sound of these two syllables may be assumed to have been Disan,[1] which I venture to explain as a Chinese corruption for the name of the great city of Alexandria on the mouth of one of the Nile branches. The *Wei-lio* further says (P 10): "From below the country one goes straight north to the city of Wu-tan." The phrase "from below the country" may mean "before one arrives in the country," and the Chinese author may write from the standpoint of a traveller entering the Red Sea. He would have to sail in a northerly direction in order to reach the port of Myos Hormos, which may have been called Wu-tan[2] locally. South-west of it the commercial route

---

[1] Ch'ih (達) stands for Sanscrit di in Koundikâ. Julien, *Méthode pour déchiffrer*, etc., IV, No. 1876.

[2] Old sound: Odan, Otan, Utan, Odam, etc. (?) See Julien, *l. c.*, Nos 1313-1315 and 1700-1701. From a linguistical point of view, there could be no closer relationship between the sound of this name and ancient Adana, the modern Aden the existence of which name during antiquity has been testified by Philostorgios (died A.D. 430), *Hist. Ecc.* III, 5 p 478 quoted by Müller ad Anon. Peripl. Maris Erythr., § 26, in *Geogr. Graec. Min.*, Vol. I, p. 276; but unless we assume the text to have been corrupted, it will be impossible to unite the sense as it appears to me at present with the situation of the city of Aden. Regarding the probable site of Myos Hormos *see*

joined the river Nile near the city of Koptos, and the remark made by the Chinese author, that it took a day to cross the river in the south-west, (P 11) may be a hyperbolic allusion to its size. The next paragraph in the text (P 12), which in this portion (P 8 to 14) seems to describe the route to Syria (Antioch, Tyre or one of the other Phœnician cities) by way of Egypt (Myos Hormos, Koptos, Alexandria), says that the country contains three great divisions, and thereby may allude to the division of Egypt, the country of the city of Ch'ih-san, into three sections (Delta, Heptanomis, Thebaïs). The *Wei-lio* further says (P 14): "At the city of Wu-ch'ih-san you travel by river on board ship one day, then make a round at sea, and after six days' passage on the great sea arrive in this country." As I now understand this passage, it describes the journey from Alexandria to Antioch, the capital of Ta-ts'in. The old sound of the characters representing the name Wu-ch'ih-san may be described as Odisan, the *Wu* or *O* being the only additional part in the name otherwise identical with Ch'ih-san above mentioned. I consider this a very descriptive rendering of the sound "Alexandria." The distance from this city to Antioch, which place could be reached by sea, as the Orontes is stated to have been navigable in ancient times as far as Antioch, is about 400 nautical miles. This track sailed through at the rate of 70 miles a day,

---

Müller, ad Agatharchid. De Mari Erythraeo, *l.c.*, Vol. I, p. 167 seqq.

would have occupied about 6 days.[1] The one day's river passage preceding the six days on sea may be explained by the preference being given as an outlet from the river to the Ostium Heracleoticum at the town or suburb Canobus which, being connected by a navigable canal with the small inner harbour Kibotus, was about 15 miles distant from that point, thus causing a day to elapse between the lifting of anchors and the putting to sea.[2] I am inclined to believe that goods coming from China or India by the Nile route, and destined for Antioch or any other Syrian port, did not enter any of the sea harbours of Alexandria at all, but were transhipped previous to passing the Customs station (τελώνιον) which, according to Strabo, guarded the inward and outward river traffic, so that a traveller might well enjoy himself either in the city or in its eastern suburbs, without having to embark on the Mediterranean side of the city for the continuance of his journey.[3]

The reader who has followed me so far in tracing the various routes by which a traveller may have reached Syria from China, may now fairly ask :

---

[1] To quote a practical example : the passage from Tyre to Antioch, which represents just about half the distance from Alexandria to Antioch, occupied *three* days. *Hist. Apollon. Regis Tyri*, ed. Riese, VII, p. 8 : Thaliarchus (starting from Tyre) "tertia navigationis die attigit Antiochiam."

[2] Cf. Strabo XVII, p. 800.

[3] According to Pliny the terminus of navigation for the oriental traffic viâ Koptos was not at the city of Alexandria itself, but at a (river ?) port called Juliopolis, 2,000 paces distant from Alexandria. Plin., VI, 23 (26), 102.

what has become of the overland routes from Babylonia to the west? We know from western authors that connection existed by caravan routes between the mouth of the Euphrates and Petra; there must have, further, been a road through the desert from some station in the neighbourhood of Babylon to Emesa or Damask *viâ* Palmyra; and, finally, the highway to western Asia, the old Via regia, and the route from Seleucia to Antioch through Mesopotamia *viâ* the bridge at Zeugma. It would, indeed, be strange if the existence of these routes, the beaten tracks of oriental traffic, had escaped the notice of the informants to whose accounts the compiler of the *Hou-han-shu* was indebted for the details of his Ta-ts'in chapter. I believe that the end of the account referred to (E 38 to 40) may be fairly interpreted as describing an overland route on Ta-ts'in territory, and since it contains certain allusions which may be traced to the Mesopotamian road from Seleucia to Antioch, it may be surmised that this road was not unknown to the Chinese of the later Han period. I am somewhat doubtful as to the interpretation of the passage E 37, which I have translated as follows: " It is further said that, coming from the land-road of An-hsi [Parthia], you make a round at sea and, taking a northern turn, come out from the western part of the sea, whence you proceed to Ta-ts'in." This passage, one of the most ambiguous in the *Hou-han-shu* account, has been interpreted by Bretschneider (*Chinese Recorder*, Vol. III, p. 30) as meaning: "From An-hsi, Ta-ts'in is reached by land, by travelling round the northern shore of the sea." " Here," he continues to say, "we have referred to, either the going round the Mediterranean through Asia Minor, or round the Black Sea through the Caucasus." Mr. E. H. Parker, (*ibid.*, Vol. XVI, p. 14) though not sharing the last-named author's view of the identity of Ta-ts'in with Italy, joins him in rendering the term *jao-hai* (繞海), which I have translated by "making a round at sea," by "to surround" as a transitive term. His interpretation of the passage is, "that, if you prefer the land-road, you must coast the Caspian Sea north of the Elburz mountains, and go northwards in the direction of Antioch in north Syria, through South-Armenia, leaving as you go the Mesopotamian region altogether." The reason why I cannot agree to this view is that, whatever *jao* (繞) may mean in other phrases, such as *jao-shan*, "to surround a hill," or *jao-ch'êng*, "to surround a city," said of a river, the two characters *jao-hai* do not mean, "to surround the sea on land," but "to turn round oneself on the sea;" or, as a native scholar consulted on the subject expressed it, one cannot *jao-hai* except on board ship. I may support this view by the passage P 14, where the same term occurs in a context entirely excluding the idea of a *terra firma* journey. *Jao*, like the cognate terms *chou* (周) and *hui* (迴), may be used both in the transitive and the intransitive sense. In the last sense it means, "to pursue a curved route, to meander about." The literal rendering of the passage, as I originally translated it, would be: *ts'ung* (從) coming from *An-hsi lu-tao* (安息陸道) the land-road of An-hsi, *jao-hai* (繞海) you make a round at sea and *pei-hsing* (北行) going north, *ch'u-hai-hsi* (出海西) come out from the west of the sea."

However, the Chinese language can be very ambiguous, and I shall show directly that another sense is yet possible apart from Mr. Parker's, who is perhaps right in suggesting that, the sea-route from the Persian Gulf to Aelana being sufficiently well authenticated by other passages [see D 20, 22; F 18, 19; I 3, 22; P 6; Q 5, 64], there is no necessity for seeking to strengthen it by forcing on to a strong chain weak links fairly belonging to quite another chain. This other chain of links may be found in the following passages (E 38 to 40); but, instead of adopting Mr. Parker's version, I would attempt to interpret the doubtful passage as follows: "coming from the land-road of An-hsi [Parthia] you *jao* (繞) pursue a curved route, meander through, or to, *hai-pei* (海北) [the district so called=Mesopotamia, or the north of Syria proper, *cf.* E 40; P 13, 50] and *hsing-ch'u* (行出) going, come out at *hai-hsi* (海西) Hai-hsi, *i.e.*, Ta-ts'in."[1]

---

[1] This passage has been contracted in the *Wei-lio* (P 29) into: *ts'ung An-hsi jao hai-pei tao ch'i kuo*, "from An-hsi [Parthia] you bend through Hai-pei [and so] arrive in this country." The ambiguousness is not removed, though, as we are equally free to translate (as I have done on p. 70): "coming from An-hsi [Parthia] you make a round at sea and, in the north, come to this country."

This overland-route through the district called "Hai-pei" is alluded to in the *Wei-lio* (P 13 and P 50); and the following passages may in every respect be understood to apply to travelling in Mesopotamia. This part of Asia was indeed densely populated, and yet most likely to be infested with lions; for, Strabo (XVI, p. 747) calls the Mesopotamian landscape not only εὔβοτος, "rich in pasture-ground," but also λεοντοβότος, "full of lions"; and, in the passage E 40, mention is made of a most characteristic feature of this road, the flying bridge, by which one crosses to "the countries north of the sea," i.e., *Hai-pei-chu-kuo*. This bridge, as I conclude from the fact of its being situated within 2,000 li or stadia north-east of the capital of Ta-ts'in (P 64; Q 75), can be no other than the bridge across the Euphrates at the city of Zeugma which was in the north-east of Antioch and, according to Strabo (XVI, p. 749), 1,400 stadia distant from the Gulf of Issus.

Overland routes can be clearly traced in the *Wei-lio*. From the city of An-ku (Orchoë?), it is stated (P 13), you can proceed to Ta-ts'in in three different directions of the compass. The northern route is apparently the road through Mesopotamia; the western one, a caravan-road through the Syrian desert, possibly the road *via* Palmyra; whereas, "you go due south" by sea, i.e., through the Persian Gulf, just as one travels south by sea from Yü-lo (Hira; D 22). Another allusion to the northern or Mesopotamian road must be contained in the passages P 50 and 51, inasmuch as the words "after the road from Ta-ts'in has been performed from the north of the sea by land, the sea-route to Annam, etc., was tried," may mean that the central Asiatic overland route was known previous to the sea-route *via* Ceylon. On the other hand, the following paragraph says that, "formerly only the water-road was spoken of," *i.e.*, the circumnavigation of the Arabian Peninsula, and that "they did not know there was an overland route," *i.e.*, the Mesopotamian or Palmyran route became known later than Kan Ying's intended sea-route. This is the only explanation I can give of these otherwise conflicting passages. Thus interpreted they furnish a sort of history of routes as known to the Chinese; these were—

1st.—Kan Ying's intended route, overland to T'iao-chih and thence by sea to Ta-ts'in;

2nd.—after Kan Ying (A.D. 97), but previous to the introduction of the direct sea-route *via* Ceylon (A.D. 166): the overland route on *terra firma* entirely;

3rd.—since A.D. 166 (*i.e.*, since the An-tun embassy), the direct sea-route.

The sketch of the geography of dependent states which follows (P 53 to 76) clearly shows that some of the land-roads from Babylonia to Syria had become known in China during the third century. Nearly all the dependent states mentioned as belonging to Ta-ts'in may be assumed to have been stations on the road to Antioch.

The *Hou-han-shu* (E 4; cf. Q 9) says: "of dependent states there are several times ten," which statement is repeated in the *Hsin-t'ang-shu* (L 12). In the *Wei-lio*, the same remark is clothed in the words: "they have several times ten small kings" (P 33). The same record enumerates some of these states, all of which, if I am not deceived by my topographical intuition, must be looked for near the eastern confines of Syria amongst the out-stations of the Roman empire facing the frontier of Parthia. Their names are (P 41): Tsê-san, Lü-fên, Ch'ieh-lan, Hsien-tu, Ssŭ-fu and Yü-lo. The last named I have ventured to identify with the city of Hira in the Chaldaean Lake, and as one of the shipping-ports in T'iao-chih. The *Wei-lio* adds: "of other small kingdoms there are very many; it is impossible to enumerate them one by one."

The above-named "dependent kingdoms,"— probably so called because they were cities with adjoining territories under their original chiefs (*hsiao-wang*, P 33, 41) paying tribute to the Romans, are separately described (P 58 seqq.), but it is difficult to define their exact position. I would, for this very reason not guarantee the correctness of my translation, which may have to be modified after we shall have once got hold of the key to this problem. Pending further special researches I wish to put forward, not very confidently, though, my present view regarding the position of some of them.

Tsê-san (old sound Da-san?[1]) may have been another Alexandria, Ἀλεξάνδρεια ἡ πρὸς Τίγριδι, which was at one time the name of Charax Spasinu, the principal emporium of trade at the mouth of the Euphrates. Its position was "in the middle of the sea" (P 59; Q 74), which may mean that it was surrounded by arms of the Euphrates. Tsê-san was, further, "nearest to the city of An-ku in An-hsi (Parthia)" (P 60; cf. Q 74). An-ku, we may conclude from another passage (P 6), was a shipping-port, like Yü-lo or T'iao-chih, on or near the coast of the Persian Gulf; and if, as I conjecture, it was identical with the city called Orchoë or Erek, Tsê-san may well have been a district on the entrance to the river (Mesene?). Tsê-san, like all these ports, was a place from which you could take passage by sea to the Red Sea, for "south-west [*i.e.*, south, and then west] you go to the capital of Ta-ts'in, we do not know the number of li" (P 61; Q 74)[2]. Whatever its special site may have been, it is

---

[1] The character 擇 *tsê*, which is now identical in sound and tone with the 澤 *tsê* of the name Tsê-san, is used to represent the syllable da in Sanscrit Pandaka. Julien, *Méthode pour déchiffrer*, etc., IV, No. 2147.

[2] The passage L 13 should be interpreted as an attempt to repeat the facts stated in the *Wei-lio;* but, in order to avoid copying literally, the writer has there chosen to invert the directions of the compass by saying "north-east" for "south-west," etc. In thus trying to improve the reading of an ancient text, mediaeval authors, who like the modern Chinese had no idea of the real configuration of western countries, will

stated that "north you go by water half a year, with quick winds a month, to Lü-fên" (P 60; Q 74). This would take us, after a lengthy river passage, to some region near the upper course of the Euphrates; let us say the kingdom of Osrhoëne, with the then Roman cities of Edessa, Nicephorium, etc.[1] The city of Lü-fên was 2,000 li distant from the capital of Ta-ts'in. The distance from Nicephorium to Antioch *via* Apamea and Zeugma may be fairly represented as measuring 2,000 stadia.[2]

---

be often found to practice what we Germans call "verballhornen." If we are lucky enough to trace such passages back to the original from which they are derived, we can easily remedy the blunder by ignoring it. The country of Shan in the south-west of China is a useful example for illustrating what I mean. The *Hou-han-shu* (C 3) says that in the south-west of Shan one proceeds to Ta-ts'in, alluding, of course, to the direction in which vessels steer when starting for Ceylon, and disregarding entirely the remainder of the journey. Mediaeval authors and modern encyclopaedists would pick from this passage the fact that "Shan is in the north-east of Ta-ts'in," which it is dangerous for Europeans to repeat. We should in all such cases of divergency be guided by the reading of the older text, except when we have reason to assume that the later author has had a still earlier text before him, which is not often the case.

[1] Kiepert, *Lehrb. d. Alt. Geogr.*, p. 155 seq.; cf. Gibbon, ch. VIII.

[2] The distance from the Gulf of Issus to Zeugma was, according to Strabo (XVI, p. 749), 1,400 stadia; that from Antioch to Zeugma may be set down as less, as the Amanus range of hills probably forced travellers to pass Antioch, in order to reach the Gulf. Thus 1,100 stadia may be considered a fair estimate in the sense of Strabo for the road from Antioch to Zeugma. From the city on the opposite shore of the Euphrates, Apamea, I compute 31 schoeni (=930 stadia) to Nicephorium according to the itinerary of Isidorus Characenus (Müller, Vol. I, p. 244 seqq.; cf. Prolegomena, p. LXXXVI). The total of the two distances sufficiently approaches the 2,000 li or stadia of Chinese records to support this identification.

"West from the city of Lü-fen is the flying bridge for crossing the sea in Ta-ts'in, 230 li in length" (P. 63; Q 75). The Chinese frequently speak of "crossing the sea," where you actually cross "a river." To cross the Pearl River at Canton is up to the present day called *kuo-hai*, and not *kuo-ho;* and a comparison of the passages P 73 and P 75 shows that the same water is in almost the same paragraph spoken of as a river and as a sea as well; we may, therefore, be allowed to interpret this passage as meaning: "west of the city of Lü-fên you cross the *river* (the Euphrates) in a flying bridge." The length of the bridge is not to be taken, of course, as so many li, nor even as so many stadia; but we have to assume that the number of paces (passus) has been erroneously translated into the corresponding number of li. The flying bridge, I conclude from the situation described (west of Lü-fên, on the road to the capital of Ta-ts'in), was identical with the bridge built by Seleucus, the founder of the two cities facing each other on either side of the Euphrates, Apamea and Zeugma.[1] Out of

---

[1] Zeugma ... transitu Euphratis nobile. ex adverso Apameam Seleucus, idem utriusque conditor, ponte junxerat. Plin., V, 24 (21), 86. Pliny speaks also of an iron chain, by means of which Alexander the Great had established a bridge between the two shores at Zeugma ("ferunt ... exstare ferream catenam apud Euphratem amnem in urbe quae Zeugma appellatur, qua Alexander Magnus ibi junxerit pontem, etc.," XXXIV, 15 (43), 150). If this second passage refers to the same Zeugma as the first, it appears that the river was actually crossed by means of a flying bridge (*fei-ch'iao*) as indicated in the Chinese record. Regarding the three places of passage across the Euphrates in that neighbourhood, and the bridge at Zeugma, see Bunbury, *l.c.*,

the several well-known cities of the district Osrhoëne I would have given the preference to Edessa for identification with "the city of Lü-fên," but for the passage P 64, which says that "the road, if you cross the sea [river], goes to the south-west; if you make a round at sea [on the river], you go due west." This suggests the existence of a double route from Lü-fên to Antioch, one by land and the other by river. The city of Samosota would answer this description well enough; however, it was probably not one of the stations on the road to Antioch, for which reason I would prefer the city of Nicephorium, which lay on the road, and whence you could reach the capital by going due west by river, or by land *via* the bridge at Zeugma with its south-western road to Antioch.

Ch'ieh-lan, I venture to suggest from the description of the roads in that part of Asia made in the *Wei-lio*, was some region in the east of Syria, per-

Vol. II, p. 107. The bridge referred to in the *Hou-han-shu* and in later records is apparently the Zeugma near the site of the present town of Birehjik. Professor Sachau (*Reise in Syrien und Mesopotamien*, p. 178), speaking of the débris of an ancient city found a few miles north of the ferry at Birehjik, says: "Bemerkenswerth ist auch, dass von jener Seite ein dammartiger Steinbau in den Euphrat hineinragt, der wie der Rest einer alten Brücke aussieht." This may have been the eastern wharf or landing-pier of a flying bridge. I regret not to have found anywhere a statement as to the breadth of the river at that spot, as this may possibly confirm the length of the bridge, stated in Chinese records to have been 230 or 240 li (=here *passus; see* P 64 and Q 75). I recollect having read extracts from a letter written by Count von Moltke during his Asiatic travelling period, commenting on the rocky nature of the soil near Birehjik as an argument suggesting that the present shores of the famous river passage must be the same as those seen by ancient travellers.

haps Palmyra (Tadmor). Ssŭ-t'ao mentioned in the passage referred to (P 66) may possibly be Sittake on the right bank of the Tigris, whence a road may have led due south to the site of Babylon on the Euphrates[1]; or, as the *Wei-lio* says, "coming from the country of Ssŭ-t'ao you go due south and cross the river, then go due west to Ch'ieh-lan 3,000 li; when the road comes out in the south of the river, you go west." The road across the desert actually left the banks of the Euphrates at a considerable distance from the probable place of passage opposite and southwest of Sittake near the little town of Is. Its length may be fairly set down as 3,000 stadia, as the distance from Palmyra to Seleucia is given by Pliny (V, 25, (21), 88) as 337,000 paces, *i.e.*, about 4,500 stadia. The distance of 600 li or stadia laid on in a westerly direction, takes us right into Syria. "Coming from Ch'ieh-lan you go again straight to the country of Ssŭ-fu on the western river 600 li" (P 67). The mention of a "western river" would point to Emesa, on the right bank of the Orontes; but, as all ed'tions do not contain

---

[1] I am well aware how uncertain our knowledge regarding this portion of the country is at present. Sittake, which is mentioned by Xenophon, may, or may not, have existed during the third century A.D., the period described in the *Wei-lio*. Certainly the district Sittakene existed at Strabo's time. See Bunbury, *l.c.*, Vol. I, pp. 349 and 370. Possibly the structure known as the Median Wall, some remains of which were discovered by Lieut. Bewsher (Bunbury, *l.c.*), forced travellers to go south instead of west and to cross the Euphrates nearer the site of Babylon than would have been necessary under ordinary circumstances.

the word *ho* 河, and, as the better read ng appears to be *hsing* 行, I would not lay stress on this point. Emesa is the city at which the Palmyran road through the desert joins the "southern road" leading from Petra north to Antioch. The Chinese account further says that "where the southern road joins Ssu-fu (*i.e.*, the road to Ssu-fu), there is the country of Hsien-tu in the south-west." This last-named locality might be identical with Damask, the site of which was slightly south-west of Emesa. The *Wei-lio* continues (P 68): "Going due south from Ch'ieh-lan and Ssŭ-fu, there is the "Stony Land" (Chi-shih,="accumulated stones)." This, it appears, is merely a descriptive name of the rocky portion of Arabia Petraea, the country about Petra. This conjecture is supported by the remark that "in the south of the Stony Land you come to the great sea which produces corals and real pearls;" by this sea none but the Red Sea could be meant, if our other identifications are correct.[1]

The following paragraph in the *Wei-lio* (P 69) describes in broad features the general direction of the principal mountain ranges in western Asia. "In the north of Ch'ieh-lan (Palmyra?), Ssŭ-fu (Emesa?), Ssŭ-pin (Ktesiphon?), and A-man (Acbatana?) there are [ranges of] hills extending from east to west; in the east of Ta-ts'in [*i.e.*, of Hai-hsi, the country on the west of the sea, the country on

---

[1] Cf. "the Coral Sea," M 1; and "the Coral Islands south-west in the Chang-hai," Q 29. Both corals and pearls were to be found in the Red Sea, as will be shown hereafter.

the Red Sea] as well as of Hai-tung [the country on the Persian Gulf, *i.e.*, the countries on the Euphrates and Tigris] there are [ranges of] hills extending from north to south." The range running east to west in the north of Emesa, Palmyra, Ktesiphon and Acbatana must be the Taurus; the range running north to south in the east (?) of Ta-ts'in may be the Libanon with its northern and southern spurs; the range in the east of Hai-tung is the Zagrus Mons with its spurs, and the various ranges running parallel with the river in the east of the Tigris.

The account of dependent states as given by the *Wei-lio*, and the explanation I have attempted to make of it, may, so far, be considered satisfactory. But the paragraphs that follow [P 72 to 76] become a great puzzle indeed, inasmuch as in them the route previously described is connected with localities clearly belonging to quite another quarter. It is there said that "from Hsien-tu (Damask?) you go 600 li north-east to Ssŭ-fu (Emesa?), and that from Ssu-fu (Emesa?) you go 340 li north-east to Yü-lo, taking sea (or river) passage." This last-named place I have tried to identify with Hira. How could Hira come to be in the north-east of Emesa, or, indeed, in the north-east of any place in that neighbourhood, if Ssŭ-fu were perchance identical with some other region in the north-west of the Palmyran desert? To make sense of this account we are bound to assume that our Chinese text, or the original text on which it is based, has suffered some kind of mutilation, resulting in this confusion being made of an otherwise intelligible digest.

All that follows is quite intelligible again, and supports my conjecture as to the identity of Yü-lo and Hira. It is said (P 74) that "Yü-lo is subject to Ta-ts'in," and (P 75) that "north-east of it you cross a river to Ssŭ-lo, and north-east of this you again cross a river." Ssŭ-lo (P 76) is said to be "subject to An-hsi (Parthia), and to be on the boundary of Ta-ts'in." The eastern boundary of Roman territories has varied, of course, with Roman success in Parthian and Persian warfare; but the city of Seleucia may, better than any other, be considered a boundary city between the two empires. To reach Ssŭ-lo from Yü-lo (Hira) you had to cross the Euphrates and travel north-east; and beyond Ssŭ-lo you crossed a river again, the Tigris, which separated it from Ktesiphon, the winter residence of the Parthian kings. The city had, it is true, been repeatedly laid waste, and, after its destruction by Avidius Cassius in A.D. 165, had not recovered its ancient grandeur as the chief centre of Parthian commerce; but a new city, sometime known under the name of Koche,[1] had grown out of its ruins, which, with Ktesiphon on the left bank of the river was united into the city of Madain, the capital of Persian rulers since Artaxerxes. As the Arsacide dynasty had, since its overthrow by the Sassanides in A.D.

---

[1] *Chôche*. Kiepert, *l.c.*, p. 148.

226, ceased to rule on the banks of the Tigris, it looks like an anachronism to find Parthian (An-hsi) cities spoken of in the *Wei-lio*, which is supposed to cover the period A.D. 220 to 264. We have to assume, therefore, that the informants who furnished this account silently transferred the name of the old rulers (An-hsi, Arsacides) to the new government. It appears from Ma Tuan-lin's account of Persia (*Po-ssŭ* 波斯 ch. 339, p. 6) that the new Persian empire was first brought into contact with China during the After Wei dynasty (A.D. 386-543); the city of Madain is in this account clearly mentioned as the western capital under the name Su-li (宿利城).[1] It lies on the banks of the Ta-ho-shui (達曷水, in Cantonese *Tat-hot* = Tigris, arm. *Deklath; Diglito*, Plin., VI 27 (31), 127; Greek root: ΤΙΓΡΙΔ?), and the river passes through the middle of the city, flowing south. The country south and down river is there said to be identical with ancient T'iao-chih (有河經其城中南流即係支之故地也), which may be considered an additional proof in support of the Chaldaean identification of that country.

---

[1] Called Su-lin (蘇蘭) in the *Sui-shu*. Bretschneider (*Notes and Queries*, Vol. IV, p. 54) identifies this place with "ancient Susa, in proximity to modern Shuster," on the ground that this was the capital of the Sassanides in the time of the Sui dynasty (A.D. 581-618). I am not aware that this was the case; moreover, the proximity of the site of ancient Susa to modern Shuster has, since the excavations carried on in 1852 by Mr. Loftus at Sus, been abandoned by the scientific world. *See* Loftus, "On the determination of the River Eulaeus," in *J. R. G. S.*, Vol. XXVII, p. 120 seqq.

One of the dependencies, according to Chinese records, was the city of Ch'ih-san, which is called a royal city (*wang-ch'êng*) by Ma Tuan-lin (Q 11). I have already attempted to identify this place with the city of Alexandria in Egypt (*see* p. 181). Its first mention is apparently found in the *Wei-lio* (P 9 and 14), which seems to show that its importance as an emporium of trade became known in China during the first Wei dynasty (A.D. 220 to 264), though we have no proof whatever that this was not the case several centuries sooner. Ma Tuan-lin may have had an earlier authority before him when he said (Q 10 seq.): "In the west [of Ta-ts'in] there is the Great Sea. On the west of the sea there is the royal city of Ch'ih-san." I have been determined to make this identification chiefly on the ground of the description made of its situation in the *Wei-lio*, and I am strengthened in my assumption by a passage in the *Hsin-t'ang-shu* (I 6 and 7), purposing to describe the eastern and western boundaries of Fu-lin: "In the west, the country borders on the sea with the city of Ch'ih-san; in the south-east it borders on Po-ssŭ (Persia)." Neumann (*Asiat. Studien*, p. 172) intimates that "in the *T'ang-shu*, Constantinople is distinctly mentioned under the name Tschy or Sy san, *i.e*, Byzantium." Bretschneider (*Arabs*, etc., p. 24) calls the first character of this name a misprint (運 *ch'ih* instead of 避 *pi*) and tries thus to reconstruct a name Pi-san (=Byzantium). I make use of this opportunity to say that the assumption of misprints in Chinese texts should not be resorted to except in cases where very urgent circumstantial evidence enforces such a proceeding. The circumstances in this case would not permit us to identify Ch'ih-san with Byzantium, even if Fu-lin could be proved to have been the Eastern Empire; moreover, the occurrence of the name in the *Wei-lio* is a strong argument against such a supposition, as this record refers to the third century, when, after its destruction in the contest between Niger and Severus (A.D. 196), "the destined capital of the east subsisted only as an open village" (Gibbon).

Amongst the dependencies of Ta-ts'in, or Fu-lin, we find mention made of the countries of the Amazons and the Pygmies. These accounts, we must assume, were not based on reality; they are but pieces of western folk-lore, imported into China with the accounts of other countries, which the informer, whether Chinese or Roman, had never visited himself. The Amazons and the Pygmies must have impressed the Chinese imagination, so susceptible of the wonderful, and this may have caused these traditions to be preserved in their records, whereas accounts of other matters, existing in reality, but being less wonderful, were consigned to oblivion.

According to the *Hsin-t'ang-shu* (ch. 221, lieh-chuan 146 B, p. 6), an island in the south-west [*sic*] of Fu-lin is inhabited by a tribe called Hsi-nü ("western women"), who are all females. "The country contains many precious articles and is a dependency of Fu-lin. The rulers (chün-chang) of Fu-lin send males to them every year to couple with them. It is their custom not to bring up male children they have born." The same authority (ch. 221, lieh-chuan 146ᴬ, p. 6), speaking of the Tung-nü ("eastern women") in Central Asia, says: "On the western sea there are likewise women with a female government, which is the cause of these [in Central Asia] being called eastern women." A parallel passage is contained in the *Ta-t'ang-hsi-yü-chi*,[1] the account of Hsüan Chuang's journeys, chiefly derived from Sanscrit sources, and completed in A.D. 648,[2] *i.e.*, several centuries before the compilation of the *Hsin-t'ang-shu*. One is, in the face of the identity of this account (as well as of part of what the *Hsin-t'ang-shu* says about Persia) with the text of Hsüan Chuang's work, in a temptation to assume that much of the information received in China regarding Fu-lin, perhaps also regarding the ancient Ta-ts'in, has

---

[1] Ch. XI, p. 23. Fu-lin is there written 拂懍 and is said to border on the north-east of Persia, the passage referred to occurring in an account of that country. Julien, *Voyages des Pèlerins Bouddhistes: Mémoires de Hiouen-Thsang*, Livre XI, p. 180, translates as follows : "Dans une île située au sud-ouest du royaume de *Fo-lin*, se trouve le royaume des femmes d'Occident. On n'y voit que des femmes, et pas un seul homme. Ce pays renferme une grande quantité de choses rares et précieuses que l'on vend dans le royaume de *Fo-lin*. C'est pourquoi le roi de *Fo-lin* leur envoie, chaque année, des hommes pour s'unir avec elles ; mais si elles donnent le jour à des garçons, la coutume du pays ne leur permet point de les élever."

[2] Julien, *Vie de Hiouen-Thsang*, Préface, pp. V and LXX.

come thither through Indian sources translated by Buddhist linguists,—a view lately put forward by Dr. Edkins[1]. There is certainly no doubt that, Hsüan Chuang's being the older work and not a compilation[2] like the *T'ang-shu*, the account of the Amazons must have been derived from it.

The account here given of a nation of women agrees in many respects with what we read in Strabo (XI, p. 503, seq.) regarding the Amazons. But the Amazons of Strabo were said to occupy some region on the coast of Lake Maeotis, and not in the "south-west of Fu-lin," nor were they said to be living on an island; their neighbours who sent them males to couple with were not the Syrians but the Gargareans who lived at the foot of the Caucasus. Ma Tuan-lin (Q 52), quotes from the *Tu-huan-hsing-ching-chi:* "In the west [of Ta-ts'in] there is the country of women who, being affected by the influence of water, give birth to children (perhaps: "who are born out of water," like the Venus Anadyomene of Cyprus).[3]

Under the name of Hsiao-jên (Dwarfs) the Pygmies are described by Ma Tuan-lin (Q 70).

[1] "What did the Ancient Chinese know of the Greeks and Romans;" by Joseph Edkins, D.D., in the *Journal of the N.C. Branch of the R.A.S.*, Vol. XVIII, pp. 1 to 19.

[2] Cf. Julien, "Notice Bibliographique sur le Si-yu-ki," in *Mémoires sur les Contrées Occidentales*, etc,, Vol. I, p. XXIII.

[3] I have not seen Paravey's *Dissertation sur les Amazones dont le souvenir est conservé en Chine* (Paris, 1840), but presume this work treats on the same subject.

"These are in the south of Ta-ts'in. They are scarcely three ch'ih (say 4 feet, Engl.) large. When they work in the fields they are afraid of being devoured by cranes. Whenever Ta-ts'in has rendered them any assistance the dwarfs give them all they can afford in the way of precious stones to show their gratitude." This is the old legend of the dwarfs in Africa told over again with all its details. The little folks were living in the south of Ta-ts'in or Syria. This quite agrees with the position assigned to them by Pomponius Mela who (III, 8 81,–Frick), speaking of the inhabitants of the west coast of the Red Sea, says: "fuere interius Pygmaei, minutum genus, et quod pro satis frugibus contra grues dimicando defecit." Gellius (*Noct. Attic.*, IX, 4, 10,–Hertz) describes their size by saying:—"quorum qui longissimi sint, non longiores esse, quam pedes duo et quadrantem." It is not improbable that the Akka nation discovered by Schweinfurth[1] were the real basis of all these accounts, the Chinese version of which has perhaps found its way to the Far East through a similar channel as the legend of the Amazons. It is remarkable that, whereas our Latin authority (Gellius) apparently exaggerates by giving the largest of these dwarfs no greater size than $2\frac{1}{4}$ feet Ma Tuan-lin's account is much more in accordance with reality, if not in the lapse of centuries intermarriage with larger tribes has considerably increased their average height. The

---

[1] *The Heart of Africa*, Vol. II, p. 122 seqq.

Chinese author gives them three ch'ih, which corresponds to 3½ feet English. Schweinfurth furnishes in his work the portraits of two Akka dwarfs whose height was 4 feet 1 inch and 4 feet 4 inches respectively; he adds (p. 140): "I never saw any instance in which the height materially exceeded 4 feet 10 inches."

The *Hsin-t'ang-shu* (L 46 to 49) mentions the countries of certain black tribes in the south-west. To arrive at these countries, called Mo-lin and Lao-po-sa, one had to cross the desert in the south-west of Fu-lin. This is no doubt the desert of Sin on the Peninsula of Sinai. Ma Tuan-lin (Q 53) specifies its situation by saying that it is in the south-west of the country of Yang-sa-lo, which is perhaps a Chinese transcription of the name Jerusalem.[1] On having crossed the desert you arrive in the countries referred to at a distance of 2,000 li. The inhabitants are black and of a violent disposition; the country is malarious, and has no vegetation; cereals are scarce (Q 55); the inhabitants feed their horses on dried fish; men eat *hu-mang*, which name is explained as meaning the Persian date. Ma Tuan-lin (Q 57) adds that the hill tribes which one has to pass in pursuing the overland road of these countries are of the same

---

[1] 羅 *lo* is used in the contracted word *lo-mo* (羅 磨), "pour la terminaison *lam*." Julien, *Méthode pour déchiffrer*, etc., IV, No. 1045. The final character may have been dropped, which may be frequently observed in polysyllabic names.

race. We are probably right in assuming that the countries here described extend along the west coast of the Red Sea as far as the former Troglodytae or Ichthyophagi, the fabulous fish-eaters of ancient renown. I certainly prefer the barren parts of the eastern coast of Egypt as being more likely to have furnished dried fish in quantities as fodder for horses than some territory in the interior of Africa. The Red Sea coast of Egypt was quite prominently known for its barrenness, and the date palm, as in other parts of Egypt, furnished the main part of man's daily food. We find statements almost analagous with that made in the *T'ang-shu*, regarding certain tribes on the coast of Oman, visited and described by both Marco Polo and Ibn Batuta, the former noticing the large consumption of dates and fish as articles of food, the latter, "the surprising custom of feeding cattle of all sorts upon small fish."[1] Oman was, unfortunately, situated in the south-east and not in the south-west of Fu-lin, and too far distant from Fu-lin, so as to exclude the idea of this country being meant. We have to fall back on the Egyptian coast, therefore, say the country about Myos Hormos,[2] which may have become known to travellers disembarking there for continuing the route by way of Koptos and Alexandria. Strabo (XV, p. 720)

---

[1] Yule, *Cathay and the Way Thither*, Vol. II p. 400.

[2] 2,000 stadia along the coast south of Arsinöe, which may be considered as the terminus of the road from Jerusalem across the south-western desert, take us to the neighbourhood of the probable site of that port.

also mentions the date palm amongst the principal trees, and the habit of feeding cattle upon fish: τοῖς δ᾽ ἰχθύσι χρῶνται καὶ αὐτοὶ καὶ θρέμματα. Lieut. Kempthorne ("Notes made on a Survey along the Eastern Shores of the Persian Gulf in 1828," in *J. R. G. S.*, Vol. V, p. 270) says, with regard to the opposite coast: "The inhabitants still live entirely on fish, the cattle having much the same diet as their masters, for the country is wholly destitute and barren, and yields no sort of grass. Vast stores of oysters, crabs, and all kinds of shell-fish, are found on the coast. In many places, both here and in Arabia, the cattle are fed entirely on dried fish and dates mixed together, on account of the great scarcity of grass in these sunburnt and sandy regions." We are pretty safe in transferring all that has been said with regard to the Ichthyophagi of the Arabian coast of the Persian Gulf to those in the neighbourhood of Myos Hormos or Berenice; for, the two classes of tribes described under this common name are in every respect similar as regards the country they inhabit and their mode of life, as has been insinuated by Agatharchides,[1] the principal authority regarding them. I quote from Müller's revised Latin version: "Ac primum de Ichthyophagis Aethiopibus (qui piscibus nutriuntur) dicemus, quibus maritima habitatur regio a Car-

---

[1] Müller, *Geogr. Graec. Min.*, Vol. I, p. 129 seqq. (Agatharch. § 31; for further literary reference *see* Müller's note on p. 129, and Prolegomena, p. LIX seqq.).

mania et Gedrosia ad extremum usque recessum sinus Arabici, qui in mediterranea incredibili prope spatio excurrens, ad ostium a duabus continentibus, hinc Arabia felice, illinc Autæis, qui sunt ad extremum sinus Arabici secessum, quem magnum includit mare, usque ad Indiam et Gedrosiam et Carmaniam et Persas insulasque memoratis gentibus subjectas ubique habitant Ichthyophagi (homines ex piscibus victitantes); qui nudo, tam feminæ quam viri, sunt corpore, et *communem sobolis procreationem habent;* naturali quidem voluptatis et molestiæ cognitione, sed *turpium et honestorum ne minima quidem præditi notitia.*" The last paragraphs may serve as a key to the mysterious passages L 50 and Q 59, which have probably suffered some slight corruption in the text. Mr. Parker proposes to translate (L 50) as follows: "They are not ashamed of incest, and in this respect they are the worst among the barbarians," and I quite agree to this change in my version as it brings us another step nearer to the classical tradition regarding the Ichthyophagi.

The Chinese ancient records, as preserved in the contemporaneous annals and in certain extracts compiled by later authors, contain a series of details regarding the capital of Ta-ts'in, which it would be most interesting to compare with what has been handed down in western authors with regard to the antiquities of the city of Antioch; for, Antioch, as the residence of the

Roman pro-consul ruling over the whole orient (Syria, Egypt and Asia Minor), must be considered the capital of Ta-ts'in. Such details have been collected in a well-known work, the "*Antiquitates Antiochenæ*" by Otfried Müller (Göttingen, 1841); but my attempts to procure a copy of it from Europe have failed, and I am obliged, for the present, to confine myself to placing together the principal statements, regarding the subject, scattered over the Chinese accounts of various ages.

The capital of Ta-ts'in was, during the Wei dynasty, called An-tu 安都 (I 2 and Q 3). Pauthier[1] has justly referred this name to the city of Antioch. Colonel Yule[2] remarks: "With reference to this name, apparently indicating *Antioch*, it is curious to read in Mas'udi that, at the time of the Mussulman conquest there remained of the original name of the city only the letters *Alif*, *Nún* and *Tá*." This would be a sufficient argument to account for the Chinese name containing no *k* at the end; for, whatever principles we may follow with regard to ancient sounds of Chinese characters, there is nothing in the authorities quoted in K'ang-hsi's 都 *tu* which would justify the assumption of the old sound of this word having been *tuk*. But An-tu is, in my opinion, quite a sufficient Chinese equivalent for the sound· Antiochia. The *Atlas Antiquus*, by Spruner and Menke, (Map No. IX) contains a plan of the city, probably

---

[1] Pauthier, *de l'Authenticité*, etc., p. 34.
[2] *Cathay*, etc., Vol. I, p. CCXLI.

based on data contained in Müller's work; and, although I am not in the position to furnish the proof of its accuracy by quoting the necessary classical passages regarding all details, the reputation of its compilers warrants it being a fair representative of the views held by the learned world with regard to the general outlines of the city and its parts. The rough sketch I have drawn from it will suffice to illustrate the Chinese description of the city. I have made no addition of my own, excepting the dotted lines enclosing the "suburbia" in the north-east of the royal city.

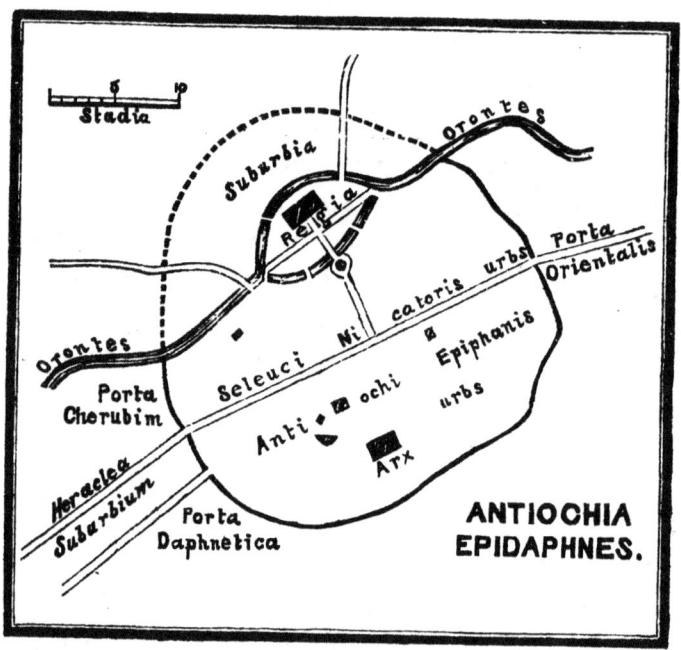

According to the *Wei-shu* (I 9), "the royal capital is divided into five cities, each five li square."

It appears from the following passages that the five subdivisions of the city here mentioned were properly four, with a fifth, the king's city in the middle. For, "the king resides in the middle city" (I 10), and "in the royal [*i.e.* the middle] city there are established eight high officials who divide among themselves the government over *the four cities*" (I 11). The four cities which remain, if we assume the fifth, or middle, city to have been the residence of city magistrates, made up the tetrapolis of Antioch described by Strabo.[1] The division into four cities having each a separate wall (for such is the meaning of the Chinese *ch'êng* here used for "city"), the whole being surrounded by a general wall, is a characteristic feature of the city of Antioch which, if all other arguments failed, would be alone sufficient to distinguish it from any

---

[1] Ἔστι δ' ἡ μὲν Ἀντιόχεια καὶ αὕτη τετράπολις, ἐκ τεττάρων συνεστῶσα μερῶν· τετείχισται δὲ καὶ κοινῷ τείχει καὶ ἰδίῳ καθ' ἕκαστον τὸ κτίσμα. Strab., XVI, p. 750. The king's city, that part which had been built by Callinicus and which contained the Regia, occupied an island in the Orontes. Three principal divisions, surrounded by walls, extended south of the river, and these made up the tetrapolis together with the royal city. The fifth part, *i.e.*, that part which is not counted by the classical authors who speak of a "fourfold city," is the suburbium in the north of the river. It must have occupied a considerable area; for, Pliny (V, 21 (18), 79) says that the city "is divided by the Orontes;" this seems to show that a considerable portion of it must have occupied the northern shore, to which the tetrapolis proper does not extend. The Regia, which may be said to occupy the middle, if we count the northern "suburbia" as one of the four cities, was the seat of government; for, τὸ βασίλειον ἐνταῦθα ἵδρυτο τοῖς ἄρχουσι τῆς χώρας. (Strab., *l.c.*)

other large city of the ancient west, especially the rival cities of Rome and Alexandria.[1]

The circuit of the "capital city" is stated to have been—

1.—"over a hundred li" during the Han, Wei and Chin dynasties, *i.e.*, about during the first three centuries A.D. (E 13; P 34; F 4);

2.—"sixty li" during the northern Wei dynasty, *i.e.*, A.D. 386 to 556 (I 9); and

3.—"eight li" during the T'ang dynasty, *i.e.*, during the seventh and following centuries; for, "the city wall is eight li broad" (L 15), and "the royal city is eighty li square" (Q 47).

The city of Antioch had since its foundation in B.C. 301 by Seleucus Nicator received several extensions, until up to the time of Antiochus Epiphanes (died B.C. 163) it had increased in size so as to contain four separate walled cities apart from its suburbs. But the height of its prosperity reaches far into the Christian era. Several Roman emperors spent part of their lives at this, their eastern, capital, and under the emperors it was the permanent residence of the proconsul ruling over the Roman "Oriens," comprising Asia Minor, Syria and Egypt. From the plan of the city, as furnished by Spruner and Menke, referring to the second century B.C., it will

---

[1] Ancient Syracuse, which also contained five subdivisions, cannot be seriously thought of, as, quite apart from all other points being at variance with the Chinese description, it was, at the beginning of the Christian era, merely a provincial town of no importance.

be seen that "a hundred stadia or li" in circumference is by no means an exaggeration, if we include the suburb in the north-east. It was during the fifth century A.D., *i.e.*, during the time when the northern Wei ruled in China, that the city began to decay; and just at the close of the Wei dynasty (A.D. 532) a terrible earthquake became fatal to its glory; and, although Justinian rebuilt the city at enormous expense, he was not able to revive its old grandeur. This is the period when we find the lowest circuit, 60 li or stadia, in the Chinese record. Under the Arabs the city recovered to a certain extent; and, accordingly, we find it to measure 80 li or stadia again during the T'ang dynasty.

Whatever the extent of truthfulness of the figures preserved in Chinese records may be, there is no doubt that Antioch could at its best times fairly compete in size with any of the large cities of the ancient world. Friedlaender (*l.c.*, Vol. I, 4*th* ed., 1873, p. 6) is inclined to give it, with its suburbs, the circumference of 18,072 paces (=144 stadia), whereas Alexandria is set down at 16,360, and Rome at 14,120 paces. The circumference of the city of Byzantium, which was divided into 14 regions, is reported to have been under Constantine (A.D. 330), when it was rebuilt and considerably enlarged, not more than 7 miles (=56 stadia).

" The walls of the capital are built of stone and are of enormous height (K 14; cf. E 5 and P 17);

in the east of the city there is a large gate, the height of which is over twenty chang (=over 235 feet);[1] it is beset with yellow gold from top to bottom, and shines at a distance of several li (K 17; cf. L 16). Coming from outside to the royal residence there are three large gates beset with all kinds of rare and precious stones (K 18; cf. L 17). On the upper floor of the second gate they have suspended a large golden scale; twelve golden balls are suspended from the scale-stick by which the twelve hours of the day are shown. A human figure has been made all of gold of the size of a man standing upright, on whose side, whenever an hour has come, one of the balls will drop, the dingling sound of which makes known the divisions of the day without the slightest mistake (K 19; cf. L 18)."

We know that the city walls of Antioch were exceptionally high. As to the East Gate, I am not now in the position to identify the fact handed down in the Chinese record.[2] The mechanism described further on must have been a clepsydra;

---

[1] Probably this measure, like the li of itineraries, is not to be taken in the Chinese sense.

[2] "A large part of the walls built by Justinian still remains, and they may be traced round a circuit of four miles. But the city before Justinian's time occupied a much larger area. The walls, which were greatly injured by the earthquake of 1822, are from 30 to 50 feet high, 15 feet thick, and flanked by numerous square towers." "The *eastern gate* is called Bab Boulous, after St. Paul [=the ancient Porta Orientalis?]; part of the ancient pavement still remains." "The remains of an *aqueduct* exist to the south of the city." *English Cyclopædia*, Vol. X, p. 383.

as such at least the Chinese have recognised it, the *Yüan-chien-lei-han*, ch. 369, p. 34, quoting the description of the *T'ang-shu* under the heading K'o-lou (刻 漏), *i.e.*, "Clepsydras."

We are told in the *Wei-lio* (P 16) that the capital of Ta-ts'in was situated on the banks of a *ho-hai*, a river-sea, which term I have ventured to translate by "river estuary;" it probably means a river (*ho*) accessible to sea going vessels. Such, indeed, was the Orontes, the river of Antioch, by which the city could be reached from the sea coast within a day.[1]

The facts stated in connection with the size of Ta-ts'in and Fu-lin would be clear enough but for the doubtfulness of the expressions used in all Chinese records in describing them. The *Hou-han-shu* (E 2) says: "its territory is *fang shu-ch'ien li*," and the question arises, how have we to interpret these words? Former translators agree in rendering them by "several thousand li square;" but this is not the orthodox meaning of the phrase. We read in Mencius (I, II, 2,–p. 29, Legge): 寡人之囿方四十里 *kua-jên chih yu fang ssŭ-shih li*, "my park contains only forty li." We have to translate thus, and not "forty li square," because this would amount to 1,600 square li, which would be a very handsome area for a park, whereas the speaker in Mencius, as may be concluded from the

---

[1] Strab., XVI, p. 751: Ἀνάπλους δ' ἐκ θαλάττης ἐστὶν εἰς τὴν Ἀντιόχειαν αὐθημερόν.

context, wishes to say that his is a very modest park. This passage is, moreover, so explained in the Chinese commentaries as to call for a translation in the above sense.[1] On the other hand, Legge translates in a similar passage (*Lun-yü*, XI, 25, 5,–p. 111) "sixty or seventy li square," and in this case, as the context shows, the orthodox rendering would go against the general sense. This seems to show that such phrases as *fang shu-ch'ien li*, *fang liu-ch'ien li*, etc., should not be considered as having a definite meaning. To give an idea what an ancient author may mean by them, comparison with better known territories is perhaps the safest means. In the *Sui-shu*,[2] written during the beginning of the 7th century, the country of Ch'ih-t'u (赤土國), described as being a part of Fu-nan (扶南), or Siam, is stated to be *fang shu-ch'ien li*, *i.e.*, exactly the size given to Ta-ts'in in the *Hou-han-shu*. Whatever the real size of this country may have been, it is certain that it cannot be compared in extent to the Roman Empire. For, Ch'ih-t'u was but a part of Fu-nan, and Fu-nan, again, was but one out of a number of countries occupying the peninsula between the Bay of Bengal and that of Tungking, even the whole of which would correspond to not too large a portion of the Imperium Romanum. In the *Liang-shu*,[3] the country of

---

[1] *See* Legge's note ad *l. c.*

[2] *Hai-kuo-t'u-chih*, ch. 5, p. 16.

[3] *Ibid.*, ch. 6, p. 1

Tun-hsün (頓遜). being one of the countries on the Malayan Peninsula (*tsai hai-ch'i shang* 在海崎上) and identified with Malacca of the *Ming-shih*, is said to be *fang ch'ien li*. This clearly shows that a country "several thousand li" in extent, as described by the Chinese phrase referred to, can at the best be a province of Rome, but not the empire itself.[1] We must assume that, in the oldest days of their trade with the Far West, the Chinese were not aware of the extent of the country which bought up their silks. During the Han dynasty, their descriptions probably comprise the whole of Syria; a few centuries later, as we may conclude from the accounts applying to the time of the Wei dynasty, other parts were added, probably Egypt, as I conclude from the allusion to what I have tried to trace as the River Nile and the city of Alexandria (P 8 to 14) and from the modified statement of the size of the country which, in the *Wei-shu* (I 6), is said to contain 6,000 li,[2] while the *Chin-shu*, describing a period preceding that of the Wei, says: "in this country several thousand li in all directions of the compass are covered with cities and other inhabited places" (F 3; cf. Q 8). It appears that, during the later Wei period, reaching up to the middle of the sixth century, the territory formerly belonging

[1] The territory described by these doubtful phrases is still further curtailed if we translate *li* by "stadia."

[2] The *Wei-lio* (P 15) makes it "several thousand li in all directions of the compass."

to the prefecture called "Oriens," and being under the jurisdiction of the proconsul residing at Antioch, was comprised in these descriptions. The territory of Fu-lin is stated to amount to 10,000 li (K 3; L 8). This fact is in broad contradiction with the theory of Ta-ts'in being the Roman Empire, and Fu-lin being its continuation under the Byzantine emperors. For, if Ta-ts'in, as described during the period when Rome enjoyed its largest extent, contained 6,000 li, Fu-lin ought to have been given a much smaller territory, if it had really covered the Eastern or Byzantine Empire which, during the T'ang dynasty, had been curtailed by more than half the extent of the old empire. But Ta-ts'in was merely a province of Rome, and Fu-lin was the same province (Syria) under Arab rule. The 10,000 li mentioned in the *T'ang-shu* probably cover territory belonging to Khalif rulers soon after the conquest, in the middle of the 7th century. The *Tu-huan-hsing-ching-chi*, quoted by Ma Tuan-lin (Q 47), says that Fu-lin "in all directions measures several thousand li," which brings it back to the size of old Ta-ts'in, and this account must be understood to refer to Fu-lin previous to the Arab conquest, as it is stated further on (Q 49) that "they have constantly to provide against the Ta-shih (Arabs)," and as the boundaries are there clearly defined as those of Syria (Q 50).

However, vague these statements may be, they tend to show that Chinese authors were not aware of the real size of the political territory of which the country they describe physically was merely a subdivision. On the other hand, there is no doubt that the power of Rome in its full extent must have prevailed on the informants of the Chinese to tell them that "this country is the largest west of the Ts'ung-ling" (P 55).

According to the *Hou-han-shu* (E 3), Ta-ts'in contained over four hundred cities (cf. P 15 and Q 9). The *Chin-shu* simply mentions that it is "covered with cities and other inhabited places" (F 3), and the *Wei-shu* says, "that human dwellings are scattered over it like stars" (I 8). Both the *T'ang-shu* (K 4 and L 9) copy the older records, and we must assume that the statements there made in this respect are all derived from the older source. Four hundred cities (*urbes, municipia*) would have been a trifling number for the Roman empire, as ancient Italy is alone said to have contained 1,197 cities;[1] and "for whatsoever æra of antiquity the expression might be intended," Gibbon adds, "there is not any reason to believe the country less populous in the age of the Antonines, than in that of Romulus." Gibbon further says: "Under the reign of the Cæsars, the proper Asia alone [*i.e.*, the countries under the proconsul of Antioch, or the territory of Ta-ts'in] contained five hundred populous cities, enriched with all the gifts of nature, and adorned with all the refinements

[1] Gibbon, Vol. I, ch. II.

of art."¹ The five hundred cities of Asia proper may possibly have been the very same as those described in the *Hou-han-shu* by the words *ssŭ-pai yü ch'êng*, meaning "over four hundred cities." The populousness of Syria must have been enormous during the middle ages, as, under the military government of the Mamelukes, the country was supposed to contain sixty thousand villages.²

The records of the Han dynasty contain various remarks which show clearly that the informant of the Chinese, whether a Chinese or a foreigner, had himself travelled in the country. I am inclined to assume that the road from which he received his impression regarding the facilities for travelling in Ta-ts'in was the overland route through Mesopotamia from Ktesiphon to Zeugma. The description given of it in the *Hou-han-shu* (E 39), repeated in various later records (cf. P 32, Q 16, etc.), says that, "although one is not alarmed by robbers, the road becomes unsafe by reason of fierce tigers and lions, who will attack passengers, and unless travelling be done in caravans of a hundred men or more, or under the protection of military equipment, one is liable to be devoured by those beasts." Beasts of prey are repeatedly alluded to; tigers and lions,

---

[1] Cf. Joseph., *Wars of the Jews* II, 16, 4 (transl. Whiston): "What is the case of five hundred cities of Asia? Do they not submit to a single governor, and to the consular bundle of rods?"

[2] Gibbon, *ibid*.

to start with, in the passage just quoted. There was, further, the Ts'ung, the ferocious quadruped mentioned in the *Hsin-t'ang-shu*. It has the size of a dog,[1] is fierce and repulsive, and of great strength (L 39), and, according to Ma Tuan-lin's version, may be domesticated (Q 22). Bretschneider (*Arabs*, etc., p. 24), referring to this animal, says: "Probably the hyæna, which is not found in Eastern Asia, and is, therefore, unknown to the Chinese:" perhaps rightly so, though it may be suggested that the jackal answers the Chinese description as well, and must have been quite as common in Syria. The Black Bear (玄熊) is another beast of prey mentioned as occurring in Ta-ts'in in the *Wei-lio* (P 49) and by Ma Tuan-lin (Q 21). None of these animals would have attacked a traveller on any of the roads of Italy during the time of the emperors; if existing at all in Italy, as some species of bears probably did, the latter had withdrawn long ago into the hills, where they continued to be the sport of imperial "venatores:" lions and tigers, however, which in Syria (Mesopotamia) forced travellers to go in caravans, were so much in demand in Rome, whither they were

---

[1] 有 獸 名 賓 大 如 狗, etc. Bretschneider (*Arabs and Arabian Colonies*, p. 24) is not fortunate in translating: "In Fo-lin occurs a wild beast, *Pin-ta*, which is very strong and wild, and resembles a dog." The character *Ts'ung*, which, it is true, occurs only once, *i.e.*, as the name of this animal, in Chinese literature somewhat resembles the character 賓 *pin;* but the following *ta*, great, as the tertium comparationis is here dependent on 如 *ju*, and does not form part of the name.

imported from the African and Oriental provinces for use in the imperial plays, as to render Italian roads quite clear of them. These were not infested by beasts, but by robbers and outlaws,[1] the very absence of which scourge distinguished the caravan road described in the *Hou-han-shu*.

We learn through the *Hou-han-shu* and other ancient records that the country of Ta-ts'in enjoyed the comfort of roads for travelling, and postal arrangements "like the Chinese" (P 28), and that postal routes existed between certain parts of the frontier and the capital; for, "when the embassies of neighbouring countries came to their frontier, they were driven by post to the capital" (E 31, etc.)[2] The means of conveyance probably consisted in carriages of various descriptions, one kind of which was provided with a wide canopy (E 11).

The postal roads, it appears, were lined with postal stations, and with mile-stones of an ornamental character, as they were covered with plaster (E 6). All these institutions would answer well

---

[1] *See* Friedlaender, *Sittengesch. Roms*, Vol. II (ed. 1874), p. 44 seqq. Pliny, VIII, 16 (17), 45) states distinctly that lions were found in Europe merely in certain parts of Northern Greece. "In Europa autem inter Acheloum tantum Mestumque amnes leones esse, sed longe viribus praestantiores iis quos Africa aut Syria gignant." Pliny's "Syria" here no doubt refers to the Mesopotamian district, which, according to Strabo, was full of lions. *See* p. 187.

[2] The fact here stated is quite in accordance with the spirit of Roman postal administration. The use of the posts was allowed to those who claimed it by an imperial mandate, and only exceptionally indulged to the business or convenience of private citizens (Gibbon).

enough to the postal system of the Romans, and may be applied to Italy as well as to any of the Roman provinces.[1] But the *Hou-han-shu* contains some other details in connection with postal matters which, it seems to me, constitute a broad hint as to the oriental position of the country described. It is said there (E. 38; cf. P 31, etc.) that "every ten li of a road are marked by a t'ing (pavilion, pavilion-shaped mile-stone?), and every thirty li by a chih (resting-place)—or hou, [so called by Ma Tuan-lin (Q 15) and in the *Chu-fan-chih* (R 14)]." It appears to me that this remark describes in the fewest possible words the milliary system of the country. It shows that the unit for measuring roads (chih or hou) was divided into three smaller distances (t'ing), and into 30 of a still smaller kind (li). I cannot discover any similarity between this and the Roman system.[2] The roads of Italy starting at the *milliarium aureum* erected by Augustus, were lined with *lapides* (milliary columns) at distances of 8 *stadia*, corresponding to 1,000 paces, and there was no division into three or thirty. The only ancient mile which may be compared to that described

---

[1] The well-known "royal road" from Sardes to Susa described by Herodotus (V, 52) was lined with "royal stations," σταθμοὶ βασιλήϊο, and excellent inns, καταλύσιες, all along, and the whole road was through an inhabited and safe country.

[2] Visdelou (in d'Herbelot, *Bibl. Or.*, IV, p. 420) says: "les maisons bâties d'un mille ou d'une lieue à l'autre, et ces postes de 3 en 3 maisons, que sont-elles autre chose si-non ces pierres ou colonnes dressées de mille en mille pas, et couriers établis d'un certain nombre de colonnes à l'autre?"

in the *Hou-han-shu* is the Asiatic mile, *i.e.*, the Persian parasang. The parasang has been the principal road-measure throughout western Asia from the time of Herodotus till up to the present day Herodotus himself (II, 6; V, 53; and VI, 42) distinctly states that the parasang is divided into *thirty* stadia. "Hesychius and Suidas give it the same length, and Xenophon must have calculated it at 30 stadia, as he says (*Anab.*, II, 1, § 6) that 16,050 stadia are equal to 535 parasangs. The Arabic geographers (*see* Freytag, *Lex. Arab.*, s. v. Fàrsakh) reckon it equal to three [Arabian] miles."[1] The readiness with which these measures may be compared, and the close relation in which Greek civilization stood with that of western Asia from the time of Alexander's campaigns, almost challenged a system corresponding to the one described in the *Hou-han-shu*, viz:—

1 *chih* or *hou* = 1 parasang.
= 3 *tʻing*, or Arabian miles.
= 30 *li*, or stadia.

---

[1] *English Cyclopædia*, s. v. Parasang. Cf. Doursther, *Dictionnaire Universel des Poids et Mesures Anciens et Modernes*, Bruxelles 1840, s. vv. "Parasange: Egypte et Syrie," and "Mille: Arabic, antiquité:" "le mille des Arabes était le ⅓ de la parasange." The modern Farsang, the Agatsch of the Turks, is divided into 3 Berri.—"Parasang is a Persian word, and is derived from the ancient farsang, which is pronounced in modern Persian, ferseng. It has been changed in Arabic into farsakh. Various etymologies of this word have been proposed. Its latter part is supposed to be the Persian *song*, a stone, and the word might thus be derived from the stones which were placed to mark the distances in the road. Bohlen (quoted by Rödiger) supposes the first part to be the preposition *fera*, and compares the word with the Latin *ad lapidem*." (*Engl. Cycl.*, l.c.)

Several of my identifications have been based on the supposition that the distances given in li by Chinese writers must be understood to be stadia in the sense of western classical authors,[1] and I would recall to the reader the following statements, occurring in Chinese records, which must be admitted by every student of ancient geography to compare most favourably in point of exactness with any similar statement occurring in the most trustworthy classical author:

1. Antiochia Margiana (*Mu-lu*)
   to Hekatompylos (*An-hsi*),
   passing the Hyrcanian hills. 5,000 *li* or stadia.

2. Hekatompylos (*An-hsi*) to
   Acbatana (*A-man*) . . . 3,400 ,, ,,

3. Acbatana (*A-man*) to Ktesiphon (*Ssŭ-pin*), passing
   the Mount Zagros ranges . 3,600 ,, ,,

4. Ktesiphon (*Ssŭ-pin*) to Hira
   (*Yü-lo*) . . . . 960 ,, ,,

---

[1] The distances given in ancient itineraries are not to be taken as the crow flies, in a straight line, but we have to add in every case a certain percentage to make up for the meandering of a road and détours of all kinds. Ancient measures in this respect somewhat resemble the Chinese mode of reckoning distances (see *China Review*, Vol II, p. 276 seq.). The Rev. G. Rawlinson remarks (in a note in his edition of Herodotus,—quoted *Engl Cycl.*, l.c.), that the parasang, like the farsakh, was originally a measure of time, not of distance, and consequently varied according to the country passed over. It is, therefore, natural that "the tendency to *over*-estimate distances in travelling should be much more frequent than the contrary error." *See* Bunbury, *l.c.*, Vol. I, p. 359, seqq.

5. Antioch (capital of Ta-ts'in)
to the city of Lü-fên beyond
the bridge of Zeugma . . 2,000 *li* or stadia.
6. The caravan road from the
place where it leaves the
banks of the Euphrates to
Palmyra (*Ch'ieh-lan*) . . 3,000 ,, ,,
7. Palmyra (*Ch'ieh-lan*) to
Emesa (*Ssŭ-fu*) . . . . 600 ,, ,,
8. The circumference of the
city of Antioch (*An-tu*) . 100 ,, ,,

The tenfold (E 28) and hundredfold (F 16)[1] profit the traders of Ta-ts'in made on their sea-borne commerce with India and China may be easily accounted for by the nature of the merchandise they carried to and fro. We may assume that the bulk of the exports from China to Ta-ts'in was silk; and of this one pound is stated to have been considered equal in value to as much weight in gold.[2] This may be nothing more

---

[1] *See* note 3 on p. 165.

[2] Vita Aureliani, c. 45, in *Scriptt. Hist. Aug.*, quoted by Friedlaender *l.c.*, Vol. III (5th ed., 1881), p. 70. This Roman myth regarding the price of silk has its counterpart in ancient China. The *Shuo-wên* (說文), published in A.D. 100 (*see* Wylie, p. 8), explains the character *chin* (錦), an old name for the finest ornamental silk textures, as being composed with the radical *chin* (金), *i.e.*, gold, "because its price was then equal to that of gold." (*Ko-chih-ching-yüan*, ch. 27, p. 4). Pliny (XXXIV, 14 (41), 145) speaks of *iron* and *skins* as articles imported by the Seres. "Ex omnibus autem generibus," he says with regard to the various kinds of iron found on the Roman market, "palma

than a *façon de parler*, and have no definite sense at all; but, whatever the real price of silk has been, there can be no doubt that the statement referred to involves that heavy sums were spent in this commodity. According to Pliny (VI, 23 (26), 101, *see* note 3 on p. 165), India alone drew out of the Roman Empire every year not less than 55 millions sesterces (=about £600,000); and in another passage (XII, 18 (41), 84) he says that, at the lowest

Serico ferro est. Seres hoc cum vestibus suis pellibusque mittunt." Iron, as well as skins, were produced in abundance in the north of China. The iron industry as well as the iron trade was since ancient times in the hands of the people of Liang (梁), which district comprised part of the present Shen-hsi, Hu-pei, Kan-su, and Ssŭ-ch'uan (see *Shih-chi*, ch. 129, lieh-chuan 69, p. 17, in palace ed. d. d. 1739). The iron industry received the most careful attention at the hands of the Chinese governments from a very early period, as a study of Ma Tuan-lin's chapters 15 and 16, containing a history of the salt and iron monopolies in China, will show. Ma Tuan-lin gives the names of forty principalities (*chün*), mostly in the northern districts, at which at the time of Wu-ti (B.C. 110), inspectors of government iron works (*t'ieh-kuan*) were stationed. In another passage (ch. 20, p. 4) the same author has an opportunity to mention the principal articles of trade and the districts in which they were chiefly produced at the time of Chao-ti (B.C. 86-73). This list may give us an idea what goods could be drawn from the Chinese market, provided there was a demand for them in the west. The districts Lung (隴) and Shu (蜀), *i.e.*, the present provinces of Kan-su, Shen-hsi and Ssŭ-ch'uan, were noted for cinnabar and woollen cloth (?'毛羽); Ching (荊) and Yang (揚) in the present Hu-pei and Chiang-su respectively, for skins (皮) and hides (or leather, 革) besides *ku-hsiang* (骨象,–bone and ivory ware?); Chiang-nan (江南) furnished certain kinds of wood and bamboo arrows; Yen (燕) and Ch'i (齊) in the present Chih-li and Shan-tung: fish, salt, rugs and furs; the districts Yen (兗), Yü (豫) and Ho (河), *i.e.*, Shan-tung, Ho-nan and Kan-su (?), varnish, silk, hemp or grass-cloth. This shows that silk, the foreign demand for which is now supplied from districts in the neighbourhood of Canton and Shanghai, was then chiefly produced in the north-west of China, and that skins and hides (Pliny's *pelles*) were also near at hand in Hu-pei.

calculation, 100 millions sesterces (=about a million £ sterling) were taken away from the empire annually by India, China and Arabia ("minima computatione miliens centena milia sestertium annis omnibus India et Seres et paeninsula illa [Arabia] imperio nostro adimunt"). Both these amounts (£600,000 and £1,000,000) would be trifling, indeed, if they really represented the whole value of the trade with the countries named; and if silk was really paid with its weight in gold, the quantity imported, according to this estimate, must have been very insignificant. Several attempts have been made to remove the difficulty contained in these two passages. Höck (*Röm. Gesch.* I, 2, 288, quoted by Friedlaender, *l. c.* Vol. III, p. 68, note 3) represents the sums mentioned as applying to the importation into the city of Rome, and not into the Roman Empire; but Friedlaender seems to be right in rejecting this as well as Marquardt's proposal who (*Röm. Staatsverwaltung*, II, 266) assumes that a hundred million sesterces for pearls imported from India were not included in the estimate of Indian trade. As I understand Pliny's words, he does not mean to give the total value of the trade with these countries at all; he merely says: "the trade with India, etc., costs us so much annually," *i.e.*, so much money in addition to the goods exported from the Roman Empire; for, thus we have to interpret the words *exhauriente* and *adimunt* in the two passages respectively. In other words, the author wishes to say that the balance of trade is in favour of India, China, and Arabia. I look at Pliny's computation as an indirect proof that a considerable portion of the goods received from China was paid for in kind. And which, we may now ask, were the articles given to the Chinese in exchange? The reply may be gathered from the list of Ta-ts'in products: glass, carpets, rugs, embroideries, and other piece goods, and the precious stones a merchant could take away from Syria and those he could pick up *en route*, in addition to a few drugs and fragrant woods.

Enormous profit must have been made on the importation into China of small vessels, such as cups and bottles, and beads, of coloured glass. We learn from the *Wei-lio* (P 49^{bb}) that ten kinds of glass were produced in Ta-ts'in. The colours were: carnation, white, black, green, yellow, blue or green, purple, azure, red, and red-brown.[1]

Glass is, in the passage referred to, called liu-li (琉璃), whereas in other places it is called po-li (玻璃, 頗黎, etc.) From what I learn in dealing with vendors of curiosities in China, it appears that the difference between the two substances is this: po-li

---

[1] Cf. Pliny, *Nat. Hist.*, XXXVI, 26 (65), 191 seqq. It is stated in the *Yüan-chung-chi* (元中記), quoted in the *Yüan-chien-lei-han*, ch. 364, p. 41, that red glass was the most valuable kind produced in Ta-ts'in, and the articles of tribute offered by the embassy of A.D. 643 contained red glass (K 34; L 41; Q 66). According to Pliny, the dearest quality was the uncoloured, transparent glass. The red kind referred to in the Chinese authors may have been an imitation murrhine. Cf. A. Nesbitt, "Glass" in Maskell's *South Kensington Museum Art Handbooks*, London, 1878, p. 22.

is transparent, liu-li is opaque. The latter substance is also vulgarly called liao (料), whence liao-ch'i (料器) is the name for "glass-ware" in the Customs Tariff. It appears to me that Pfizmaier ("Beiträge zur Geschichte der Edelsteine und des Goldes" in *Sitzungsber. d. phil.-hist. Cl. der Kais. Akad. d. Wissensch.*, Wien, March 1868, Vol. LVIII, p. 199) has not been fortunate in translating liu-li by rock crystal (Bergkrystall), and that Geerts, on pp. 471 and 475 in Vol. II of his work *Les produits de la Nature Japonaise et Chinoise*, is misguided by his Japanese authorities in translating liu-li (riu-ri) by Lapis lazuli, and po-li (ha-ri) by "Gemme Vitreuse Bouddhique." The Chinese were accustomed to consider both kinds of glass as precious stones and to place them on a level with the other gems constituting the "Seven Pao" (七寶) of Buddhistic lore, as long as they were ignorant of the real nature of these articles; but since they learned to produce them in their own country, the meaning of these terms as applied to reality was 'glass," whatever their use may have been in a historical or poetical sense. Metaphorically, liu-li may come to be the name of substances similar to opaque glass in respect of transparency. General Mesny informs me that in some parts of Kuei-chou sheets of semi-transparent horn used for lamp and lantern shades are called liu-li; the same name is also given to the glazing of porcelain and earthen-ware, in which sense the General says it is a synonym of yu-li

(泊璃?). The origin of the name liu-li, it appears to me, has to be looked for in the languages of Central Asia. The *Kuang-ya*, quoted in the *Han-shu hsi-yü-chuan pu-chu* (漢書西域傳補注), i.e., "Supplementary Comments on the Record of Western Countries in the *Ch'ien-han-shu*," by Hsü Sung-hsiao (徐松學), a Secretary of the Grand Secretariat under Tao-kuang (?), says that the original name for liu-li was pi-liu-li (璧流離) or fei-liu-li (吠瑠璃). The former is mentioned in the account of Chi-pin (罽賓國) contained in the Hsi-yü-chuan of the *Ch'ien-han-shu*, and has been wrongly interpreted as meaning two different substances (pi, a kind of jadestone, and liu-li). The syllables pi-liu-li or fei-liu li, the old sound of which may have been *beloli*, are explained as *fan-yin* (梵音), which term is not necessarily confined to Sanskrit sounds. Pending a better suggestion from somebody else, I would refer this term to the word *belor* or *bolor*, meaning glass or crystal in several central Asiatic languages. Possibly even po-li, the name for transparent glass, probably of later origin, but occurring as early as A.D. 643, as the passages K 43 and L 41 may prove, has to be referred to this root. There is certainly no connection between this word and the Portuguese vidro as Williams suggests (*Syllab. Dict.*, p. 704), the Portuguese having come to China at a much more recent period.

According to the *Pei-shih* (北史) it was during the time of T'ai-wu of the northern Wei dynasty

(A.D. 424-452) that traders came to the capital of Wei from the country of Ta-yüeh-chih (大月氏), bordering on the north-west of India[1] who said that, by fusing certain minerals, they could make all colours of liu-li. They then gathered and digged in the hills, and fused the minerals at the capital (near the present Ta-t'ung-fu in Shan-hsi). When ready, the material so obtained was of even greater brilliancy than the liu-li imported from the west. The *Pei-shih* specially states that, after this event, articles made of glass became considerably cheaper in China than they had been before. Grosier (*Description de la Chine*, edition of 1787, Vol. II, p. 464) quotes the "grandes annales" (meaning, I presume, the *Sung-shu*), according to which "le Roi de Ta-tsin envoya à l'Empereur Tai-tsou, des présents très-considérables en verres de toutes les couleurs, et quelques années après, un verrier qui avait l'art de changer au feu des cailloux en cristal, et qui en apprit le secret à des disciples; ce qui acquit beaucoup de gloire à ceux qui étaient venus et qui viennent de l'Occident." T'ai-tsu was the name commonly used in the earlier Sung annals for the Emperor Wên-ti of the Sung (A.D. 424 to 454), the contemporary and rival of T'ai-wu, under whose reign the art of making glass was said to have been introduced from Ta-yüeh-chih, or from India. We have, therefore, to

---

[1] According to the *Wei-shu*, quoted in the *Yüan-chien-lei-han*, ch. 364, p. 31, they came from India (天竺國). Cf. Pliny, *l. c.*, § 192. "Auctores sunt in India ex crystallo fracta fieri et ob id nullum [*sc.* vitrum] comparari Indico."

deal with a two-fold tradition as regards the introduction of glass-making in China, each of the two rival dynasties (Sung and Wei) claiming to itself the honour of having introduced the art. We are thus, it is true, left in doubt as to whether Syrian or Indian artisans helped to establish the first factory; but the very discrepancy existing in the tradition as regards the origin, strengthens my belief in the correctness of the date, of its introduction, as the reign of the two monarchs referred to fell within very nearly the same period, dating from A.D. 424.

It is obvious that merchants as shrewd as the Syrians, the successors in the history of commerce to the ancient Phœnicians, made the most of this article which, produced on the coast near Sidon from minerals near at hand, was brought with little trouble overland to Aelana for shipment to the Persian Gulf, connecting with the ancient overland route through Parthia, or later on to Ceylon for transhipment to Chinese or Annamese junks. From all we may conclude from the passages, regarding glass and glass-ware, handed down in ancient Chinese authors, and collected by the compilers of the various cyclopædias (*lei-shu*), both liu-li and po-li were considered most precious substances previous to their being manufactured in China, *i.e.*, before A.D. 424. The *Chêng-lei-pên-ts'ao* (證類本草, ch. 3) probably repeats words originally written previous to that date, in saying that "glass (po-li) is *hsi-kuo chih pau yeh* (西國之

寶也), the precious stone of western countries."
Ancient Chinese folk-lore considers that ice, when
a thousand years old, turns into glass,[1] and the
botanical work just quoted says that it ought to be
classed with jadestone. The poet Li T'ai-po
(quoted in *Ko-chih-ching-yüan*, ch. 51, p. 7), who
wrote during the 7th century, speaks of the fairy
lady T'ai-chên (*see* Mayers, *Manual*, p. 212), who
poured grape wine into cups of "glass and the
seven precious substances" (gold, emerald, jade,
etc.),[2] which seems to show that the first-named
material was held in no light estimation. A
modern poet would certainly not be allowed to let a
fairy lady touch any but a gold, silver, jade, or crystal cup. During the Ta-ts'in period that peculiar
fancy for *objets de vertu* which, in Chinese life, has
at all times taken the place of other luxuries, was
not yet absorbed by the porcelain industry, which
probably did not begin to assume larger dimensions
previous to the T'ang dynasty. Clumsy copper
censers and other sacrificial implements, imitating
the then archaic style of the Chou dynasty, mono-

---

[1] Or crystal. See *Yüan-chien-lei-han*, ch. 364, pp. 36 and 41, and the *Ko-ku-lun* (格古論), quoted in *Ko-chih-ching-yüan*, ch. 33, p. 11: 千年冰化爲水晶. This Chinese popular belief regarding the origin of crystal may possibly have been imported from the west together with the article itself. Pliny, at least, entertains a similar prejudice, in saying (XXXVII, 2 (9), 23): Contraria huic caus crystallum facit, gelu vehementiore concreto. non aliubi certe reperi- tur quam ubi maxime hibernae nives rigent, glaciemque esse certum est, unde nomen Graeci dedere.

[2] Regarding the "Seven Pao" (七寶), *see* Geerts, *l. c.*, Vol. II, p. 468.

polised the attention of the rich together with the so-called precious materials (寶物, *pao-wu:* gold, silver, jade and other precious stones, ivory, pearls, tortoise-shell, etc.). A large portion of the latter came from Ta-ts'in, and glass is in all the older records mentioned amongst them; whereas, *e. g.*, the *Chêng-lei-pên-ts'ao*, published A.D. 1108, classes it under "minerals of the first class (玉石部上品 *yü-shih-pu, shang-p'in*)," the *Pên-ts'ao-kang-mu*, half a century later, even under "metals" (金 *chin*). This shows the gradual depreciation of a formerly very valuable article. It is most probable that small implements such as beads, cups, bottles, vases, etc., made of coloured glass fetched much better prices in China than in Rome, and that this trade was particularly profitable to the Syrians, who were perhaps less upright in their dealings than their reputation amongst the Chinese (E 21) seemed to indicate.

As to *precious stones* in general, glowing accounts of their marvellous abundance in Syria were apparently circulated in China as well as they were circulated and believed in the west. Numerous passages show that Ta-ts'in was considered *the* country where everything nice and valuable in the way of jewelry and mineral curiosities was to be had.[1] It has to be considered that Syria was specially well situated as a market for the districts

[1] *See* the passages D 23; E 26; F 14; G 3; H 2; I 20; K 31 and 32; etc.

IDENTIFICATIONS.

then known to produce real precious stones. Syria occupied a central position amongst the principal producing districts in Asia Minor, Cyprus, Egypt, Armenia, Media, etc., and possessed from remote antiquity all the facilities for monopolising the trade in emeralds, rubies, opals, sapphires, carbuncles, jaspers, lapis lazuli, sards, agates, topas, etc.; and the city of Alexandria which, under the Romans, had inherited the commercial grandeur of the Phœnicians and Syrians, had become the chief factory for all the industries connected with the cutting and polishing of precious stones. Wm. Jones (*History and Mystery of Precious Stones*, London, 1880, p. 346 seq.) justly remarks of ancient Syria: "Seldom are toys and jewels mentioned by Homer, but with this additional circumstance, that they were either of Sidonian workmanship or imported in a Phœnician ship." The same author (*l. c.*, p. 165) says: "The treasures contained in the ancient Syrian temples were immense, ivory and precious stones included. That of Astarte, at Hierapolis, abounded with gold and jewels, precious stones of all colours, sardonyx, hyacinth, emerald, brought from Egypt, Æthiopia, India, Media, Armenia and Babylonia. On the brow of the goddess shone a marvellous carbuncle. Lucullus took from Armenia magnificent gemmed vases which filled a car drawn by camels, etc." The fact cannot be doubted that, whatever show the Roman Emperors made of pearls and precious stones, their luxury was chiefly made up from the plunder of their Asiatic provinces. Jones (*l. c.*, p. 350) speaks of things seen in Syria rather than in Italy when he says: "At the beginning of the third century the extravagant luxury of the Romans was at its culminating point. An example was set by the monster Elagabalus,[1] who styled himself a priest of the sun. His apparel was costly in the extreme. He never wore a garment twice; his shoes were decorated with pearls and diamonds; his bed was covered with gold and purple, decorated with costly jewels. The path on which he walked was strewed with gold and silver powder,[2] and all the vessels in his palace were of gold.[3] The splendour of the sun-worship at Emesa, under the name of the voluptuous emperor, was almost incredible; the black stone which it was believed had fallen from heaven on the site of the temple set in precious gems, was placed on a chariot drawn by six milk-white horses richly caparisoned." Till late in the middle ages Syria enjoyed the reputation of being an inexhaustible source of precious stones, as, in spite of the thorough plundering of the Romans, there was so much left for the crusaders who, generally, did not return from their adventures amongst the infidels without a good load of portable property. Wm. Jones (*l. c.*, p. 356) says:

---

[1] Of Syrian extraction. He spent part of his life in Emesa, the seat of his family.

[2] Possibly the *lü-chin-ching* offered to the Court of China in A.D. 643 (*see* K 34; L 41; and Q 66) was "gold-powder," like the one mentioned above, which need not necessarily be real gold-dust.

[3] Cf. R 19.

"The amount of precious stones, spoils of the Crusades, was enormous. The immense wealth of King Tancred is stated by an old German historian quoted by Scheidius, to have been almost fabulous. When, after his death, the Emperor Henry entered the palace, he found the chairs and tables made of pure gold, besides one hundred and fifty mules' loads of gold, silver, and precious stones," and (p. 339) "Henry the Lion, who went on a pilgrimage to the Holy Land in 1172, returned with an enormous amount of riches, especially in jewels."

These camels' and mules' loads of precious stones show that Syria was even then credited with being a very rich country indeed. I cannot help feeling somewhat sceptical at these accounts. The ancient world was very credulous, and the suspicion may be justified that much of the gold was gilt copper, and that many of the jewels were coloured glass. The *Hou-han-shu* account of Ta-ts'in winds up by giving utterance to this suspicion in saying (E 41): "The articles made of 'rare precious stones' produced in this country are sham curiosities and mostly not genuine." Pliny (XXXVII, 7 (26), 98), speaking of carbuncles, says: "adulterantur vitro simillime, sed cote deprehenduntur, sicut aliæ gemmæ, etc." This clearly shows that glass imitations, though easily discovered by the connoisseur, were commonly made, and it seems natural that, in a country where the glass industry was quite unknown, as it must have been in China up to about the year A.D. 424, such spurious articles could fetch prices far beyond their real value.

It is for this reason that the alleged profuse employment of crystal for certain architectural purposes finds an easy explanation. The *Hou-han-shu* (E 15; cf. P 39 and Q 4) states that "crystal is used in making pillars in the palace buildings." According to the *Chin-shu* (F 6), crystal is merely used in making the pedestals of pillars, whereas walls are adorned with opaque glass. The *Chiu-t'ang-shu* (K 6) adds to the pillars, "the eaves and window-bars;" and the *Hsin-t'ang-shu* (L 19), "the king-posts of their roofs," as parts of palaces adorned with either rock-crystal or glass. The *Wu-wai-kuo-chuan* (吳外國傳), quoted in the *Ko-chih-ching-yüan* (ch. 20, p. 26) states that, even "the tiles of the royal palace in Ta-ts'in were made of crystal." Bretschneider (*Chinese Recorder*, Vol. III, p. 30) says: "It is clear that the columns of rock-crystal are a Chinese exaggeration." I have several reasons for not joining in this opinion. I do not, in the first instance, consider that the wording of the passage Mr. Bretschneider had before him (*Hou-han-shu* E 15), which had been so sadly misunderstood by de Guignes (*see* Introduction, p. 28), necessarily involves that pillars were made out of solid rock-crystal; for, even the very literal translation *à la* Julien merely says that, "*i* [employing] *shui-ching* [crystal] *wei* [they make] *chu* [pillars]," *i.e.*, that crystal is one of the materials employed in making pillars. I presume that pieces of rock-crystal were, like other precious stones, merely fastened on the outer surface of pillars as they were fastened on the surface of walls and other parts of palatial residences. Rock-crystal must have been more common in Syria than in other countries, as it was one of the local products of the neighbourhood.[1] I have quite recently read an account of the natural resources of the modern province of Aleppo, in which it is stated that rock-crystal is found in the district of Harim. The list of products of the *Wei-lio* (P 49 *e*) contains rock-crystal as a separate article, and the country probably produced sufficient quantities of it to allow of its being used as an ornament in the manner indicated, *i.e.*, so that pillars were not made entirely out of crystal and that their surfaces were but partly covered with it. It is still more likely, however, that both the crystal and the precious stones employed were in reality glass imitations. Glass and crystal are frequently confounded by Chinese authors. The *Po-wu-yao-lan* (博物要覽), quoted in the *Ko-chih-ching-yüan* (ch. 33, p. 11), says: "no hot soup or boiling water should be poured into a vessel made of *shui-ching* (rock-crystal), lest it will burst as if it were smashed to pieces;" and the *Ko-ku-yau-lun* (格古要論)

---

[1] *See* Pliny, XXXVII, 2 (9), 23, who mentions Orthosia (in Syria), Alabanda (in Caria), Cyprus, and an island in the Red Sea, as places where crystal was found.

(*ibid.*) speaks of "imitation *shui-ching* made by burning drugs" (假水晶用藥燒成者). The *shui-ching* in both cases seems to have been nothing better than glass.

The reason which led Mr. Bretschneider to declare the crystal pillars of Ta-ts'in a Chinese exaggeration, was probably this, that, in ancient Rome, he considered them more or less out of place.[1] The practice of using gems and precious stones, whether real or made of glass, was originally a local feature of ancient Syria. I quote from Heeren's *Historical Researches* (Vol. I, Asiatic Nations: Phœnicians. English ed. of 1846, p. 345): "From the small number of glass houses, the use of glass would seem to have been much less general in antiquity than amongst us. While the mildness of the climate in all southern countries, as well as all over the east, rendered any other stoppage of the windows unnecessary, except that of curtains or blinds, goblets of the precious metals or stones were preferred as drinking-vessels. This, however, seems in some measure to have been made up for by the early introduction of a singular kind of luxury in the stately edifices of these countries, that of covering the ceilings and walls of the apartments with glass. The various significations,

---

[1] To see glass mosaic work employed in vaults was a novelty in Rome at Pliny's time (Plin., XXXVI, 25 (64), 189); later on ornaments of glass and precious stones were as common a luxury there as they were in the Orient. Friedlaender, *l.c.*, Vol. III, 5th ed., 1881, p. 85 seqq.

however, in which the Greek ύαλος is made use of, and which properly means any transparent material, as crystal, various kinds of stones, and the like, render it impossible to determine with certainty whether glass itself or some other transparent substance is spoken of."

As regards the different kinds of gems and precious stones specified in Chinese records, it is not in all cases possible to determine what they really were. Some of them are sufficiently well known nowadays to pronounce their identity, while the names of others are not in use now, but have to be identified by means of the information collected in works like the *T'ai-p'ing-yü-lan*, the *Yüan-chien-lei-han*, the *Ko-chih-ch'ing-yüan*, and others. Professor Pfizmaier of Vienna has published, amongst the papers of the Austrian Academy of Sciences, translations regarding the subject, from the first-named Cyclopædia, viz., "*Beiträge zur Geschichte der Edelsteine und des Goldes*" (1868), and "*Beiträge zur Geschichte der Perlen*" (1868). It is to be regretted that the author of these otherwise valuable papers has chosen to translate the names of Chinese works quoted in a manner which renders it difficult even to sinologues to identify them without comparing the German version with the Chinese text. Who would recognise the *Hsi-ching-tsa-chi* (西京雜記) under the title "Vermischte Erzählungen von der Mutterstadt des Westens,' or the *Shih-i-chi* (拾遺記) under that of "Die Geschichte des Auflesens des Hinterlassenen?" I would here refer readers who take interest in the gem question to the two volumes published of the late Mr. A. J. C. Geerts' work, "*Les Produits de la Nature Japonaise et Chinoise,* etc." (Yokohama, 1878 and 1883), the author of which has combined the literary point of view, by translating some of the Chinese and Japanese data regarding each article, with that of the practical mineralogist.

Amongst the stones mentioned here and there in the various records, the *Yeh-kuang-pi*, or "jewel that shines at night," has apparently more than all others taken possession of the imagination of the Chinese, as it is mentioned in all the principal records. I am not, from my own experience, able to decide whether any and what stones do really shine at night; but this, it seems to me, is less important than the question: what ideas did the ancient world entertain with regard to shining stones? For, the Chinese belief in the existence of such curiosities may have just as well originated from the reports regarding the wonders believed to exist in Ta-ts'in as from their having been actually seen by Chinese observers in China or abroad.

The River Sangarius, in Asia Minor, according to Plutarch, produced a gem called Aster, which is luminous in the dark and called by the Phrygians "Ballen," "the king." Streeter (*Precious Stones and Gems*, London, 1877, p. 173) refers this to the gems known under the name of star-stones or Asteria. "When light shines upon these stones," this author says, "stars of six rays are seen,

an appearance which attracts much attention, etc."
"These star-stones, according to their colour, are designated Star Ruby, Star Sapphire, or Star Topaz." If these stones give off rays merely when light shines upon them, as seems to be the case from the passage just quoted, Plutarch's Aster has perhaps merely lent its name, but not its chief quality, that of shining in the dark, to the modern Asteria. Possibly the Chinese name "jewel that shines at night" is an allusion to the ancient name *carbunculus*[1] (*i.e.*, the "little coal"), corresponding to the Greek ἄνθραξ (=coal), the name given to the garnet, one of the favourite stones of ancient luxury, owing to its brillancy which, as in the Greek and Latin names, may have been exaggerated into luminousness. The shining stone *par excellence*, however, seems to be the Chlorophane (in German Pyrosmaragd), an emerald possessing the power of reflecting after dark the rays received from the sun during the day time. If the text of Herodotus, II, 44, has been handed down correctly, a temple in Tyre, in Phœnicia, dedicated to Hercules, contained "two pillars, one of fine gold, the other of emerald stone (σμάραγδος), both shining exceedingly at night;" and Pliny (XXXVII, 5 (17), 66) tells us the wonderful tale of the sepulchre of King Hermias, in the island of Cyprus, on which is a lion formed of marble, but with eyes of emeralds, which shone so brightly on the surround-

---

[1] *Yeh-ming-chu* (夜明珠) is the usual name for "carbuncle," according to Bridgman, *Chrestomathy*, p. 503. Cf. Giles, *Record of the Buddhistic Kingdoms*, p. 92, note 8.

ing sea that the tunny fish were frightened away; the fishermen, having long observed this phenomenon, resolved to remove this disadvantage, and so have replaced the emeralds by other stones which have not this property of sparkling brightness. Ordinary emeralds could certainly be obtained in Syria from the rocks near the city of Koptos (*see* Pliny, *l. c.*); but there seems to be no passage proving whether and where "luminous" emeralds were found. So much seems certain that, if not in reality, at least according to the local folk-lore (in Phrygia according to Plutarch, in Tyre according to Herodotus, and in Cyprus according to Pliny) luminous gems were quite at home in the Levant.

I shall leave it to the hands of scholars possessing a better knowledge than I possess of precious stones and pearls, to deal with this question, and I have no doubt that a connoisseur of these articles who is thoroughly acquainted with their history in the Syrian or Alexandrian market, may, after some research in the Chinese cyclopædias in connection with enquiries made in native curiosity shops, throw considerable light on the question.

In attempting to prove the existence in ancient Syria of certain articles mentioned in the Chinese records as "coming from" (出) Ta-ts'in, we need not necessarily assume that these were produced on the spot. It is well known that Phœnician merchants, previous to the rise of Alexandria, monopolised the trade in *gold* and *silver*. *Amber*, though imported from the coast of the Baltic, if not from Sicily,[1] could perhaps be found in greater quantities in the magazines of Syrian merchants, whose ancestors had imported this article for centuries, than even in the producing districts themselves. Probably the greater part of the gems brought to China "from Ta-ts'in" were not the immediate produce of the country, but were procured from the gem cutting and polishing factories of Alexandria, whither they had been brought from all parts of the western world.

---

[1] *See* O. Schneider, "Zur Bernsteinfrage" in "*Naturwissenschaftl. Beiträge zur Geogr. u. Kulturgesch.*, Dresden, 1883, p. 177 seqq. Fraas, "*Drei Monate im Libanon*" (Stuttgart, 1876), p. 94, comments on the frequency of amber in the neighbourhood of Sidon. This author considers that we are going too far in assuming the Phœnicians to have sailed to the Baltic for cargoes of amber. " Die kunsterfahrenen sidonischen Männer, welche die Halsketten von Bernstein den Frauen der Helden vor Troja brachten, werden wohl nicht erst durch die "Quellen des Okeanus" hindurch zu den mitternächtlichen Kimmeriern gefahren sein, um dort Steine zu holen, die sie vor den Thoren von Sidon haben konnten." Though there is apparently much force in this argument, the many proofs we possess of the existence of Roman enterprise in the amber trade across the European continent to the coast of the Baltic at a later period cannot be easily denied. *See* Friedlaender, *l. c.*, Vol. II, p. 63. Foreign amber may be assumed to have first come to China through Central Asia as Klaproth's derivation of the Chinese term *hu-p'o* (in Cantonese: *fu-p'ak*, in the Amoy dialect: *hu-p'ek*) from Uiguric *chuʋich* (*see* "Sprache u. Schrift der Uiguren," in Appendix to *Verzeichniss*, etc., p. 22) seems to indicate. Klaproth's list of Bokharic words (*Asia Polygl.*, p. 252) contains the word *Keherbai* for amber, which looks as if it could be related to either the Chinese or the Uiguric root. According to Pliny (XXXVII, 2 (11) 37) a spindle-whirl (verticillus) made of amber, was called *harpox* in Syria, "quia folia paleasque et vestium fimbrias rapiat." Could there be any connection between this Greek root *harpag* and the Asiatic names *keherbai*, *chubich* and *hu-p'ek*?

Corals were apparently fished for in the Red Sea during the time of the T'ang dynasty; so we may judge from the account L 37 in the *Hsin-t'ang-shu*. The sea called "Coral Sea" in the Nestorian stone inscription (M 1) and "the sea which produces corals and real pearls" according to the *Wei-lio* (P 68) are apparently identical with the Red Sea. An account resembling the one contained in the *Hsin-t'ang-shu* is quoted from the *Hou-wei-shu* (後魏書) in the *Yüan chien-lei-han* ch. 238, p. 20. The coral fisheries are there stated to be *hsi-nan-chang-hai chung* (西南漲海中, *i.e.*, "in the south-western gulf (?) sea") at a distance of about 700 or 800 li (cf. Ma Tuan-lin's version, Q 29). 800 Chinese li on the open sea may correspond to about 260 miles,[1] which distance, if calculated from the port of Aelana, would carry us to the neighbourhood of Koseir or the ancient Leukos. The best corals of antiquity, it is true, came from the Mediterranean; but the Red Sea did not stand back, though its produce may have been of a different colour. Pliny (XXXII, 2 (11), 21), speaking of the coral, says: "gignitur et in Rubro quidem mari, sed nigrius, item in Persico – vocatur lace – laudatissimum in Gallico sinu circa Stoechadas insulas et in Siculo circa Aeolias ac Drepana;" and, to quote

---

[1] The distance would be somewhat short if reckoned in stadia. However, the original statement may have been given in so many days' sailing, and afterwards been converted into real Chinese li, about three of which make a nautical mile.

quite a modern authority, Klunzinger,[1] speaking of the neighbourhood of Koseir, says: "Der ganze nördliche Theil des Rothen Meeres ist mit einem der Küste parallelen *Korallriff* gerändert, das sich bald als Saumriff, bald als (durch eine Lagune vom Land getrenntes) Wallriff darstellt."

As to *Pearls*, the occurrence of which in the Red Sea is insinuated in the *Wei-lio* (P 68), it is well known that Pearls and Mother-of-pearl are now important articles of trade at Suakim, Massowa, Djeddah and Hodeida; and Koseir, the port just mentioned in connection with corals, is stated to be a market for pearls also.[2] But, what I have said of gems may be said of this article and of all other goods of intrinsic value: it is not necessary to assume that the "curiosities and rare precious stones" said to have come from Ta-ts'in were actually produced in the country; it is sufficient to know that Ta-ts'in merchants commanded the market.

The articles of trade next in importance to gems, pearls, etc., were the *textile fabrics* produced in the eastern provinces of the Roman Empire. The list of piece-goods furnished by the *Wei-lio* alone contains eighteen varieties. Some of these are

---

[1] *Zeitschr. d. Ges. f. Erdkunde*, Vol. XIV, Berlin, 1879: C. B. Klunzinger, "Die Umgegend von Qoseir am Rothen Meere," p. 411.

[2] *See* C. Kallenberg, "Der Handel mit Perlen und Perlmutterschalen im Rothen Meere" in *Oesterr. Monatsschr. f. d. Orient*, March 1884, p. 86.

stated to occur in five colours (P 49 *jj*, *kk*, *yy* and *bbb*), whereas one variety is stated to occur in nine colours (P 49 *ll*). I read in an older edition of Pierer's *Universal Lexikon* (Altenburg, 1861) *s. v.* "Purpur," that "of simple purple the ancient world knew nine colours, and of mixed purple, five."[1] I have not hesitated, therefore, to translate the expression *wu-sê* (五色), which, under ordinary circumstances, means "of *all* colours, of *all* descriptions," literally, as in opposition to *chiu-sê* (九色), "nine colours."

The various names of piece-goods mentioned in the *Wei-lio* list are partly descriptive, partly phonetic. Such names at least which do not seem to convey any definite meaning in Chinese, *e.g.*, Fa-lu" cloth, "O-lo-tê," "Pa-tsê" and "To-tai" cloth, may be assumed to be Chinese corruptions of foreign sounds. I cannot discover from my classical recollections, any similarity between any of these sounds and any Greek or Latin words denoting classes of piece-goods; but further research may possibly lead to the discovery that some of these names are derived from some other ancient language of western Asia, say Persian or Syriac, if not from Greek or Latin. The Chinese language is full of foreign words denoting technical objects introduced from abroad, and the names

---

[1] "Welches die eigentliche Purpurfarbe der Alten gewesen sei, lässt sich schwer sagen, da die Alten selbst neun Arten einfachen u. fünf gemischten Purpurs kannten." I regret not being able, at the present time, to quote any more immediate authority than this German Cyclopædia, which is generally well-informed on classical topics.

for the principal piece-goods now on the market are foreign. Thus, *to-lo-ni* (哆囉呢), now signifying "broadcloth," is probably derived from *tow-lo*, a textile material of India (*see* Mayers, in *Notes and Queries*, Vol. II, 1868, p. 95); *ha-la-ni* (哈喇呢), the name for Russian Cloth, from Mongolian "khara" [black]. The word *ni* (呢) itself, in its present meaning of "broadcloth," must be of foreign origin, to judge from the composition of the character.

Of the descriptive names the expression *huo-huan-pu* (火浣布), the "cloth that can be cleaned by fire" (P 49 *ss*; cf. E 23, F 14, G 3 and M 2), cannot possibly be mistaken. It must be the asbestos cloth (asbestinum *sc.* linum) of antiquity which, according to Pliny (XIX, 1 (4), 19 seq.) is produced in the rainless deserts of India.[1] According to old Chinese traditions, a special account of which, collected from numerous ancient works, will be found in the *Ko-chih-ching-yüan* (ch. 27, p. 23 seqq.), the article known as *huo-huan-pu* was considered to be the hair, only two to four inches in length, of an animal which lived in fire and died in water, was of the size of a rat, and weighed a hundred catties, the

---

[1] "Nascitur in desertis adustisque Indiæ locis, ubi non cadunt imbres, inter diras serpentes." Marco Polo (ch. XXXIX) fell in with a district producing asbestos in Central Asia. An early Latin text of his travels describes the substance as follows: "Et in ista montana est una alia vena unde fit salamandra. Salamandra autem non est bestia sicut dicitur quæ vivat in igne, sed dicam vobis quomodo fit salamandra, etc."

animal being either red or white in colour. It came, according to one authority, from an island in the sea which shone at a distance of over 300 li, and the shining was produced by that animal, the hair of which was as fine as silk and could be woven into a kind of cloth. Of this cloth garments were made that did not perish, though exposed to the fire, but would come out of the flames as white as snow. According to others, the cloth was made from the bark of a tree that grew out of the fire. Such and similar fabulous ideas regarding its origin prevailed in China throughout the ancient period. At Marco Polo's time, its real origin must have been known, as in the *Yüan-shih* (元 史), the Annals of the Yüan dynasty, it is called *shih-jung* (石 絨), *i.e.*, "stone wool" (see *Ko-chih-ching-yüan*, *l.c.*, p. 24). If the philosopher Lieh-tzŭ (Faber's Licius), whose writings are said to date from the 4th century A.D., can be trusted, asbestos cloth was known in China as early as a thousand years before Christ. Lieh-tzŭ, quoted in the *Yüan-chien-lei-han*, ch. 366, p. 4, says that King Mu of the Chou dynasty (B.C. 1001–946) received as tribute from the Western Tartars (*Hsi-jung*, 西戎) a sword made of *k'un-wu* (錕 鋙) steel, which would cut jadestone like mud, and asbestos cloth (*huo-huan-pu*). The joke practised at the court of the Emperor Charles the Fifth, who treated his guests after dinner with the sight of an asbestos table-cover being washed in a chimney fire, was performed in China long before his time. The *Wei-chih*, quoted in the *Ko-chih-ching-yüan*, *l.c.*, tells us a story how the scoundrel Liang Chi, who murdered the youthful Emperor Chih-ti, and as the favourite of Huan-ti became virtually the ruler of China for nearly twenty years (died A.D. 159, Mayers), had an unlined garment made of asbestos. Having assembled a circle of guests, he soiled it by spilling a cup of wine, and then, as if in anger, took it off his body, exclaiming, "burn it." When the garment was placed into the fire, it began to simmer like ashes, and when the dirty matter on the cloth was burnt off and the fire was extinguished, it had turned into a brilliant white. Besides the article of dress in the possession of Liang Chi, which according to some was a napkin,[1] the Chinese had handkerchiefs which "were not different from common linen ones, except that they were of a bluish and blackish (青黑) colour;" they had also "lamp-wicks that would never finish."

All these articles were not manufactured in China, but came from the foreign countries beyond the sea (*hai-wai-chu-kuo*, 海外諸國) either by sea or by land. According to the *Wei-chih* (l.c.),

---

[1] *Tui-chin* (帨巾). See the quotation from the *Fang-chou-tsa-yen* (方洲雜言) in *Ko-chih-ching-yüan*, *l.c.*, p. 24. A napkin is certainly more likely to have been made of this expensive stuff than an article of dress. Moreover, napkins (mappæ) made of asbestos as instruments for convivial pleasantry, seem to have been in vogue in those times. Pliny, *l.c.*, says: "Ardentes in focis convivium ex eo vidimus mappas, sordibus exustis, splendescentes igni magis, quam possent aquis."

asbestos cloth was received at the Chinese court as tribute from the western countries (*hsi-yü*) in A.D. 238. Several countries are mentioned in the Cyclopædia, from which the above facts are derived, as producing asbestos, but as I am not able to identify their names, I confine myself to stating that its being mentioned in connection with Ta-ts'in products, makes it probable that Syrian (Antiochian, Tyrian, Alexandrian) merchants were in the habit of exporting it to China, together with their other piece-goods.

The list of piece-goods which, from the fact of their being mentioned with so much detail, we must assume to have represented part of the ancient Chinese import trade in these articles, contains a broad hint with regard to the identification of Ta-ts'in. For, just as the mere perusal of a list of the woollen or cotton goods met with on the China market at the present day will naturally suggest to anyone familiar with the geography of modern commerce the idea of their being principally the manufacture of Manchester looms, the perusal of the list of piece-goods in the *Wei-lio* (P 49*jj* to *bbb*) points to the factories where cloth of all kinds was woven, embroidered, or dyed. These were about all on territory belonging to the district called "Orient;" I mean the manufacturing cities of Tyre, Sidon, Berytos and others of ancient Phœnician renown, certain districts in Asia Minor, and, not amongst the last, the commercial capital of the empire, Alexandria. Syria and Egypt probably supplied the greater part of the articles forming the trade in textile fabrics; their principal rivals in this respect were "the countries on the east of the sea" (*hai-tung-chu-kuo*), which I understand to be the countries on, or near, the Persian Gulf. Babylonian rugs and carpets have at all times commanded a high position on the oriental market;[1] but, as the *Wei-lio* (P 44; cf. Q 27) assures us, the colours of those manufactured in Ta-ts'in, *i.e.*, those of Syrian and Alexandrian looms, are preferable in colour. This is probably prominently the case with Tyrian manufactures, owing to the purple-dyeing industry having been practised throughout antiquity on the Phœnician coast; but also with the various embroidered textures, amongst which the gold-thread embroideries are specially mentioned in Chinese records (*see* Index to Translations, etc. p. 125, *s. v.* Cloth). The art of weaving gold-thread into cloth was of very ancient origin. I quote from the Very Rev. Rock's "Textile Fabrics" (*South Kensington Museum Art Handbooks*, No. 1, p. 23): "The process of twining long narrow strips of gold, or gilt silver, round a line of silk or flax, and thus producing gold-thread, is much earlier than has been supposed; and when Attalus'

---

[1] "Colores diversos picturæ intexere Babylon maxume celebravit et nomen imposuit." Plin., VIII, 48 (74), 196. "Babulonica peristromata," Plaut. Stich., 378 (Fleckeisen). "Babylonica," *i.e.*, "Babylonian goods," was the name for certain kinds of bed-covers and carpets of superior texture.

name [1] was bestowed upon a new method of interweaving gold with wool or linen, thence called "Attalic," it was probably because he suggested to the weaver the introduction of the long-known golden thread as a woof into the textile from his loom. It would seem, from a passage in Claudian, that ladies at an early Christian period used to spin their own gold-thread." According to the same author, the superior quality of Cyprian gold-thread was known to the mediæval world. *Attalicæ vestes* are mentioned in Propertius, but, as Rock (*l. c.*, p. 14) points out, "the earliest written notice which we have about the employment of gold in the loom, or of the way in which it was wrought for such a purpose, is in the Pentateuch. Among the sacred vestments made for Aaron was an ephod of gold, violet and purple, and scarlet twice dyed, and fine twisted linen, with embroidered work; and the workmen cut also thin plates of gold and drew them small into strips, that they might be twisted with the woof of the aforesaid colours."[2]

The combination of several materials (silk, wool, linen, byssus) in the same texture [P 44] was well known in ancient manufacture, and the Syrian school of art is especially known for the great

---

[1] *Cf.* Plin., *l. c.*

[2] In the passage E 22, the term which I have rendered by "gold-embroidered rugs," means, literally translated: "cut gold (剪金) embroidery (縷繡) woven into (織成) gold-embroidered rugs (金縷扇)," which seems to describe as nearly as possible the above-mentioned twisting of strips of gold into the woof of a texture. Regarding the use of gold embroideries, *see* Friedlaender, *l. c.*, Vol. III, p. 61.

variety of musters produced by means of coloured threads. The *I-wu-chih* (異物志, see Bretschneider, "Botanicon Sinicum," in *J. of the N.-C. Branch, R. Asiat. Soc.*, Vol. XVI, p. 154,- No. 236), quoted by K'ang-hsi, *s. v.* 氀 (*sou*), says: "In the country of Ta-ts'in they weave rugs [*ch'ü-sou;* cf. P 44, 49*jj*, and Q 27] from wild cocoons, and by means of wool of different colours, taken from all kinds of beasts, they weave into them birds, beasts, human figures, and [dead] objects; grass, trees, clouds and numerous astonishing tricks [?]." The *Ko-chih-ching-yüan* (ch. 54, p. 14) completes the quotation by adding: "on these rugs they represent cockatoos flying gaily at a distance; the musters show the following ten colours: carnation, white, black, green, red, crimson, gold, azure, jade colour and yellow."[1] These rugs (*ch'ü-sou*), like the articles called *t'a-têng* and *chi-chang* (vestes, vela, peristromata?) are distinctly stated (P 44) to be made of sheep's wool (the stuff derived from the water-sheep described in the T'ang records) together with a substance derived from the bark of trees (fibre; flax, linen?) and the silk of wild silk-worms.

How did the ancient Syrian manufacturers obtain the silk of wild silk-worms? Were they really acquainted with sericulture in all its phases?

---

[1] The translation of these colours is, of course, somewhat vague and can, at the best, give an approximate idea. Cf. the colours of opaque glass and of precious stones described under P 49*bb* and *ii* respectively.

From a superficial examination of the Chinese records one might be tempted to assume that they were, in spite of the tradition, by which the first silk-worms were brought in bamboo tubes from China to Constantinople by Byzantine monks under Justinian.[1] The mulberry tree is said to have been planted in Ta-ts'in both in the *Hou-han-shu* (E 8) and the *Wei-shu* (I 17), and both passages are so worded as to suggest the practice of silk cultivation. The existence of the *morus nigra*, L., which is said to have been indigenous to the districts of Media and Pontus, and its occurrence in the Roman Orient as well as in Italy, may be proved by numerous passages.[2] The species referred to is perhaps identical with the tree described under the name *ch'iung-sang* (窮桑), *i.e.*, "the unproductive mulberry," in the *Shih-i-chi* (拾遺記), a work of the 4th century, quoted in the *Ko-chih-ching-yüan*, ch. 64, p. 20. It grows on the coast of the Western Sea; its leaves were red, and the fruit was of purple colour.[3] Further, the earliest list of Ta-ts'in products, that of the *Hou-han-shu* (E 22), speaks of certain fabrics clearly made of silk, as the very composition of the characters used in the Chinese

---

[1] Yule, *Cathay*, etc., Vol. I, p. CLIX seqq. I regret not being able to consult the often quoted work on this subject: Pardessus, "Mémoire sur le Commerce de Soie chez les Anciens," in *Mém. de l'Acad. des Inscr.*, XV, 1842.

[2] Hehn, *Kulturpflanzen und Hausthiere*, 3rd ed., 1877, p. 336 seqq.

[3] "Sanguineis frontem moris et tempora fingit." Virg., *Eclog* VI, 22.

text may suggest. The one about which the least doubt can be entertained is the "*ling* (綾) of various colours." I have translated this term by "silk-cloth;" but it should be understood that it means a *fine* texture.[1] The same article is mentioned again by Ma Tuan-lin (Q 28), but in a somewhat different connection. It is there said that the people of Ta-ts'in make profit by obtaining the Chinese *chien-su* (縑素). The first of these two characters is explained by K'ang-hsi as meaning a *close-textured* stuff, the second as plain white silk, for which reason I have translated: "the thick, *i.e.*, close-textured, plain silk-stuffs of China." These stuffs, Tuan-lin says, are split, or unravelled, in order to make foreign *ling* (damask, gauze), *kan* (purple-dyed) and *wên* (mustered) fabrics. The passage quoted is apparently drawn from the same source as, but has been more completely preserved than, the corresponding passage in the *Wei-lio* (P 45), which agrees with Ma Tuan-lin's version, but omits the mention of *chien-su* (close-textured silk). The *Wei-lio* simply speaks of Chinese silk unravelled (*chieh* 解) and made into *hu-ling*, foreign *ling* (damask, gauze).

I have enlarged upon the details of these two passages, because they possess considerable importance in confirming a fact which has lately been disputed by an authority in whose judgment in such questions I place otherwise the highest confidence.

---

[1] *Pu-po chih hsi-chê yüeh ling* (布帛之細者曰綾). *Shuo-wên*, s. v. 綾.

Colonel Yule (*Cathay*, Vol. I, Preliminary Essay, CLIV) says, that two passages of Pliny have "led to a statement made in many respectable books, but which he apprehends to be totally unfounded, that *the Greeks and Romans picked to pieces the rich China silks*, and wove light gauzes out of the material." The passages referred to read as follows: "Primi sunt hominum qui noscantur Seres lanicio silvarum nobilis, perfusam aqua depectentes frondium canitiem, unde geminus feminis nostris labos *redordiendi fila rursusque texendi* (VI, 17 (20), 54);" and: "ex grandiore vermiculo gemina protendens sui generis cornuum urica fit, dein quod vocatur bombylis, ex ea necydallus, ex hoc in sex mensibus bombyx. Telas araneorum modo texunt ad vestem luxumque feminarum, quæ bombycina appellatur. prima eas *redordiri*[1] *rursusque texere* invenit in Coo mulier Pamphile, Plateæ filia, non fraudanda gloria excogitatæ rationis ut denudet feminas vestis (XI, 22 (26), 76)." Yule holds that Pliny's words "seem to be merely affected expressions, indicating nothing more than the carding and reeling the *sericum* and the *bombycinum* respectively out of the entanglement of their natural web (as Pliny imagines it) and then re-entangling them again (as it were) in the loom." Yule further quotes a parallel passage from Aristotle (*De An. Hist.*, V, 19), from which it may seem that this author, while speaking of the same *bombycina*, was not aware of the practice

---

[1] *Redordiri:* one of the Paris codices has *retorqueri*. But, even if we could adopt this reading, it would not alter the sense very much.

of picking foreign stuffs to pieces,—"a figment," Yule adds, "which seems entirely based on Pliny's rhetoric." It must be admitted that as long as we had no clear idea as to what kind of texture was meant by Pliny's "telæ araneorum modo textæ," we were free to assume that the stuff "split and re-woven" was either the cocoon itself, or raw silk pressed into skeins. Yet, it seems to me that the passage in the *Wei-lio* and Ma Tuan-lin's extension of it, fully confirm the matter of fact as represented by Pliny. It looks very much, as if the texture called *hu-ling* in the two passages referred to was identical with the thin gauzes[1] of which Seneca (*De Beneficiis*, VII, 9, quoted by Yule, *l. c.*) says: "Video sericas vestes, si vestes vocandæ sunt, in quibus nihil est quo defendi aut corpus, aut denique pudor possit; quibus sumptis mulier parum liquido nudam se non esse jurabit, etc."[2] These *Coicæ*

---

[1] The very word *gauze*, the French *gaze*, is by some authorities derived from the name of the city of Gaza, once one of the principal markets of Indian trade on the coast of Phœnicia, on the ground that these textures were first manufactured there. I regret being unable to verify this statement, which I have seen made in various popular works (*Encycl. Brit.*, s.v. Gauze; Meyer's *Conv. Lex.*, s.v. Gaze; Heyse, *Fremdwörterb.*, etc.). Wedgwood, *Dict. of Engl. Etym.*, Vol. II, p. 139, who refers the word to Teutonic roots, is either not aware of this etymology, or silently disapproves of it. I should be glad to see the manufacture of this texture traced to Syrian soil. Could the Sanscrit *kashâya*, "the gown of a Buddhist priest," which appears in Chinese as *chia-sha* (kasa, 袈裟, Julien, *Méthode*, etc., Nos. 581 and 34) be connected with this root? The corresponding Chinese name stands now for "Cambrics" and "Muslins" in the Customs Tariff.

[2] Cf. Horat. *Sat.* I 2, 101: "Coïs tibi pæne videre est Ut nudam," and the jest ascribed to Varro, who called the dresses made of thi

vestes seem to have been amongst the articles of trade sent to China; they were, of course, of a pattern quite unknown there, and may thus have been credited with being the original produce of Ta-ts'in instead of Chinese produce re-manufactured abroad. We, therefore, find the texture called *ling*, together with certain other silk manufactures mentioned as original produce in the *Hou-han-shu* (E 22), without any explanation as to its origin, which we must assume was unknown to the Chinese up to the second century. After this time, the Chinese must have got acquainted with the fact somehow or other; for, the passage in the *Wei-lio* (P 45) shows that they were aware of the process of their manufacture during the time of the Three Kingdoms. The mistake made previously in the *Hou-han-shu* with regard to the existence of silk culture in Ta-ts'in was, however, not corrected, and, quite in accordance with the spirit of Chinese literature, was copied into the *Wei-lio* as well as into the later records.

I shall not attempt to say the last word with regard to the mystery of the *shui-yang* or water-sheep (K 26; L 40; Q 23). The fact of these animals being connected by their navels with the ground suggests that we ought not to think of ordinary sheep, not even of that breed

---

stuff *togæ vitreæ*. Friedlaender is probably right in assuming that the scandalous fashion of wearing this Coïc gauze was confined to the frail sisterhood. *Sittengesch. Rom's*, Vol. I (1873), p. 476.

of Arabian sheep, mentioned by Herodotus (III, 113), which "has long tails, not less than three cubits, and were they suffered to drag them behind them, they would become sore by rubbing against the ground. The shepherds, therefore, make small carriages, and fasten them under the tails, to each animal one."[3] Nor would Pliny's description of a Syrian breed satisfy me, of which he says (VIII, 48 (75), 198): "Syriæ cubitales ovium caudæ, plurimumque in ea parte lanicii. Castrari agnos nisi quinquemenstres præmaturum existimatur."[4]

Colonel Yule (*Cathay*, Vol. I, pp. LVII and 144), refers these accounts to the stories of the Lamb-plant of the Wolga countries related by Friar Odoric, who speaks of "certain very large melons growing in a certain great kingdom called Cadeli, on the mountains called the Caspean Mountains. When these be ripe, they burst, and a little beast is found inside like a small lamb, so that they have both melons and meat" Odoric adds: "and though some, peradventure, may find that hard to believe, yet it may be quite true; just as it is true that there be in Ireland trees which produce birds." Yule quotes the senior Scaliger's *Exercitationes*, where a similar plant is described. But, although according to

---

[3] Cf. Heeren, *Hist. Res.*, Vol. I, p. 363.

[4] The two passages quoted from Herodotus and Pliny show that to identify the *shui-yang* there was no need to fall back on the Cappadocian sheep of Strabo, if sheep they must be, as is done by Pauthier, *De l'Authenticité*, etc., p. 39.

the *Hsin-t'ang-shu* the "water-sheep" occur in a northen district, the locality referred to by Odoric as well as by Scaliger takes us too far away from the Ta-ts'in territory to consider it as a produce of the country. Moreover, the tradition regarding this vegetable curiosity appears to belong to a period much later than the time when the first allusion to the *shui-yang* was made in Chinese records. Odoric's journeys were made early during the 14th century, and Scaliger's *Exercitationes* are dated A.D. 1537; whereas "the down of the water-sheep," a material which must have been derived from the animal described in the T'ang histories, is mentioned in as early a record as the *Hou-han-shu* (E 24; cf. P 44). It may be safely surmised therefrom that the water-sheep tradition belongs to antiquity, and not to the middle ages.

Bretschneider (*Arabs*, etc., p. 24) says, with regard to the passage L 36, which reads "they weave the hair of the water-sheep into cloth which is called *Hai-hsi-pu*," and which is clearly a transcript of the older passage E 24: "This is perhaps, the *Byssus*, a cloth-stuff woven up to the present time by the inhabitants of the Mediterranean coast, especially in Southern Italy, from the thread like excrescences of several sea-shells, especially *Pinna squamosa*." I am inclined to believe that Dr. Bretschneider has hit upon the right thing; but, to prove the fact, a special inquiry will have to be made into the habits of the Pinna, in order to ascertain whether there was any sense in screening them off to prevent the beasts (large fishes, etc.) from eating them up; whether the animal will perish, if the byssus be forcibly cut off the rock to which it attaches itself; whether it can be induced by certain noises to detach the byssus voluntarily, and whether in doing so it will then yield a sound of alarm, etc. All these facts will have to be enquired into by a naturalist; and philologists will have to answer the question, whether the byssus derived from certain species of Pinna was employed in weaving the texture called *hai-hsi-pu*, which is described in the *Wei-lio* (P 44) and which consisted of this byssus (sheep's wool, water-sheep's wool), the bark of trees (vegetable fibre, linen?), and the silk of wild silk-worms (Chinese silk split for re-weaving).

Amongst the products repeatedly mentioned as peculiar to the country of Ta-ts'in the drug called *su-ho* by the Chinese deserves special attention. I have translated this term by "storax," as an enquiry into the present meaning of this word strongly suggested it. The *su-ho-yu* (蘇合油) of the present day is the article enumerated in the Customs Tariff as "Rose Maloes;" it appears under the same name in the Emperor K'ang-hsi's Customs Tariff of the year A.D. 1687, and is translated by the same term ("Rose Malloes") in the manuscript copy written by a Foreign merchant during the middle of the last century.[1] It has been pointed out by Dr. H. F. Hance (*Notes and Queries*, Vol. III, p. 31) that the term Rose Maloes as applied to this drug must be a misnomer inasmuch as the article imported into China is not the produce of the *Altingia excelsa*, Noronh., "a lofty and most valuable tree in Java, with a close-grained fragrant wood, which is there called *Rasamala*, and yields from incisions in the bark a honey-like sweet-scented resin, hardening by exposure to the air, which, misled probably by the similarity of the name, some have supposed to be identical with the *Rose Maloes* of the Customs Tariff." Dr. Hance justly draws attention to the late Mr. Daniel Hanbury's notes on Storax in connection with the route by which the article referred to is brought to China. Here it now arrives generally from Bombay whither it is imported from Aden, the Persian Gulf and the Red Sea.[2] A specimen of the *su-ho-yu*, which I had procured from a Chinese drug shop at Shanghai, was submitted to a chemist who was perfectly neutral in the question and quite unaware of my own opinion on the matter, and who declared it without hesita-

---

[1] See "The Hoppo-Book of 1753" in the *J. of the N.-C. B. of the R. Asiat. Soc.*, Vol. XVII, p. 221 seqq.

[2] Hanbury ("On Storax" in *Pharm. Journ.*, XVI (1857), reprinted in *Science Papers*, ed. J. Ince, London 1876, p. 143) draws attention to a *Report of the External Commerce of Bombay*, in which the term "Rose Malloes" occurs as that of a drug imported by sea into the Port of Bombay from Aden, the Arabian Gulf and the Persian Gulf. A sample was sent for by Mr. Hanbury and, on examination, proved to be our ordinary *Liquid Storax*.

tion to be *Unguentum Styracis.* It appears therefrom that the modern *su-ho-yu* is Liquid Storax. I do not feel competent to decide whether the Storax of ancient classical writers (Dioscorides and Pliny) was Liquid or Solid Storax. The two kinds of the drug so called are, according to Hanbury (*Science Papers*, p. 129), derived from different plants. The botanical reader will find the question most exhaustively dealt with in Hanbury's papers on Storax in the *Pharm. Journ.* for 1857 and 1863 (reprinted in *Science Papers*, l. c.) It will be seen from the second of these papers that, in the author's opinion, Liquid Storax was probably not known in ancient commerce, in opposition to Professor Krinos of Athens, who assumes that it was known to the ancient Greek physicians. The text of the *Hou-han-shu* does not show what kind of Storax then came to China; but it appears to me that the term *hsiang-kao* (*i.e.*, fragrant or aromatic ointment), in the *Liang-shu* (H 2) suggests the coming from Ta-ts'in of a substance similar to the modern article during the 6th century A.D. Whichever view we adopt, there cannot be the slightest doubt that neither of the two kinds was produced in Italy, as the study of Mr. Hanbury's exact researches will show. The conclusion at which this painstaking scholar arrived after several years' study of the matter, is this:—

1st., as regards Solid Storax:
that the original and classical Storax was produced by *Styrax officinale*, Linn.; that, always scarce and

valuable, it has in modern times wholly disappeared from commerce (*Science Papers*, p. 145); that it was produced in certain localities in Syria, in the south-east of Asia Minor, in Cyprus and Creta (*ibid.*, p. 131 seq.);[1]

2nd., as regards Liquid Storax:
that it is now produced in certain localities in the south-west of Asia Minor.

Su-ho is, according to the *Pên-ts'ao-kang-mu* (ch. 34, p. 54), the name of a country producing the drug; in *fan* (梵), *i.e.*, Sanscrit or Pâli, books it is called *tu-lu-sê-chien* (咄魯瑟劍).[2]

Amongst the aromatic drugs mentioned in the large list of Ta-ts'in products of the *Wei-lio*, we find the incense called *Hsün-lu* (熏陸, P*ggg*). *Hsün-lu-hsiang* is, according to the *Pên-ts'ao-kang-mu*, identical with *Ju-hsiang* (乳香), which is now the Tariff name for Gum Olibanum. The Chinese word *hsün-lu* furnishes

---

[1] Plin., XII, 25 (55), 124: Proxima Judaeæ Syria supra Phœnicen styracem gignit circa Gabala et Marathunta et Casium Seleuciæ montem, etc." Cf. Dioscorid., *de Mat. Med.*, lib. I, cap LXXIX, quoted by Hanbury, *l. c.*, p. 130. According to Pliny the qualities produced in Syria were the best; those of Asia Minor, Cyprus and Creta came after.

[2] According to Nos. 2091, 1083, 1554 and 629 in Julien's *Méthode*, etc., the Chinese equivalent of the Sanscrit sound *turushka* (tourouchka, Julien). It appears from Julien's No. 629 that this word is explained in the *Fan-i-ming-i* (翻譯名義), ch. VIII, p. 7, which I regret not being able to consult at present.

an additional proof towards its identification, as its sound in the Southern dialects, which may have resembled the ancient sound, *hun-luk*, is clearly connected with Turkish *ghyunluk*, the name for Olibanum in that language.[1] The question arises how this word came into the *Wei-lio*, and from what language it was then derived; and, whether it is not a foreign term in the Turkish language. One of the various equivalents mentioned in the *Kang-mu* is the term *Mo-lê-hsiang* (摩勒, old sound: malek?), which name may be derived from a Semitic root (melek, malch, etc.), though I do not wish to do more than draw attention to this possibility. Another name is *tu-lu-hsiang* (杜魯), which may represent the root *thur* of the Latin equivalent *thus*.

There seems to be, with all these linguistic probabilities in connection with the Chinese identification, little doubt that the *Hsün-lu* of the *Wei-lio* is Olibanum or Frankincense. The difficulty is that, far from being produced in Syria, this drug had been imported from remote antiquity by the Phœnicians from Arabia and the neighbourhood of Cape Guardafui for the use of their temples. But Phœnician and Syrian, as well as Indian, traders had no doubt supplies of it amongst their cargoes, and may thus have come to be credited with being the producers. The *Wei-lio* and the *Nan-fang-i-wu-chih*, quoted in *Pên-ts'ao-kang-mu*, ch. 34,

---

[1] The word is quoted as the Turkish name of that drug in Hanbury, *Science Papers*, ed. Ince, p. 142, note 4.

p. 45, are, therefore, probably not literally right in saying that *Hsün-lu-hsiang* comes from Ta-ts'in[1]

I do not intend to speak of all the products mentioned in the lists handed down in Chinese records. But, before closing my remarks on Ta-ts'in drugs, I wish to draw attention to a most characteristic product of the Roman Orient, the "finger-nail flower," called *Chih-chia* (指甲) in Chinese. The *Nan-fang-ts'ao-mu-chuang* says of it:[2] "The Chih-chia [*i.e.*, finger nail] flower grows on a tree, five or six ch'ih in height, with soft and slender branches. Its leaves are like the tender *Yü* (榆). Its snowy whiteness and flavour resemble that of the *Yeh-hsi-ming* (耶悉茗) or *Mo-li-hua* (末利花). It was also brought by *Hu* people (Persians, Arabs?) from Ta-ts'in, who transplanted it to Nan-hai [*i.e.*, Canton]; yet, these flowers are very numerous. They are fine, like half a grain of rice, but rather larger. The people there often pluck them and place them in their

---

[1] The account given of the tree yielding the drug, as given in that ancient botanical work, somewhat explains the origin; it says: "On the sea-coast there grows a large tree, the twigs and leaves of which are straight like those of the *ku-sung* (古松, a kind of pinus?); it grows in the sand. During midsummer, gum will flow out on the sand; it is shaped like the gum (resin) of peach trees. The barbarians (*i-jên*, 夷人) collect it for sale to travelling merchants. If these fail to arrive, they consume it themselves." The allusion to barbarians suggests that the drug was probably not produced in Ta-ts'in itself but that the Ta-ts'in people must have been the "travelling merchants" who brought it on to China.

[2] Cf. E. C. Taintor, "Henna in China," *Notes and Queries*, Vol. II (1868) p. 46.

pockets and sleeves for the sake of their smell. Another name of the flower is *San-mo-hua* (散沫花)." The plant here described has been generally referred to the *Lawsonia inermis*, L., furnishing the Henna of the Levant. A correspondent of *Notes and Queries* (Vol. I, p. 40 seq.) says, with regard to this point:

"In Western Asia and Northern Africa, henna is extensively used as a dye for the finger-nails of women and children, and in some places it is used also by men, and applied to the hands, feet, hair and beard, and also to the manes and tails of horses.[1] Its application as a reddish brown dye for the finger-nails is, however, the most universal; when used for the hair it is changed to black by a subsequent application of indigo. The custom is one of great antiquity; henna is supposed to be the "camphire" mentioned in the Song of Solomon (I, 14, and IV, 13); and the expression in Deuteronomy (XXI, 12) "pare her nails" may be rendered "adorn her nails," and alludes to this practice; evidence of it has also been found in Egyptian mummies. Henna is derived from a tree called

---

[1] Mr. Parker suggested to me the possibility of the expression *pai-ma-chu-lieh* (白馬朱鬣) in the passages I 18, P 49 *h* and *i*, and Q 21, where *mao* (髦), mane, stands for *lieh*, meaning: "white horses with red manes." The above-mentioned habit of dyeing the manes of horses would greatly support this translation as far as matter of fact goes; but, can it be justified that *chu-lieh* as the dependent noun does not precede *pai-ma*? Should not the above words, rendered into Chinese, read: *chu-lieh-pai-ma* rather than *pai-ma-chu-lieh*?

Lawsonia inermis,[1] the leaves of which are beaten into a paste and thus applied.

"*Lawsonia inermis* is a common shrub of cultivation in Kwangtung, and its flowers are extensively used in bouquets and by women to adorn their hair; but numerous enquiries that I have made among a Punti population, have failed to elicit any logical reason for its name, 指甲花 (finger-nail flower), and it is interesting to find that, though not generally known to the Puntis, the custom of dyeing the finger-nails by an application of the pounded leaves of this tree, exactly as has been done for thousands of years, and is done to this day in the West of Asia, is practised by the young girls among the Hakkas of Kwangtung."

The author of the note on p. 46 of Vol. II of *Notes and Queries*, the late Mr. Taintor, draws attention to the curious similarity in name between the flower there mentioned and called in Chinese *Yeh-hsi-ming* (old sound Ya-si-ming?) and the botanical name of the plant it denotes (*Jasminum officinale*, L.?), which is nearly related to the *mo-li-hua* (*Jasminum Sambac*, L.). The *Nan-fang-ts'ao-mu-chuang* devotes an article to this plant also, in which it is distinctly stated that it was brought to Nan-hai (Canton) from western countries (*hsi-kuo*) by *Hu* people (Arabs, Persians?). This foreign name, which is now common to all

---

[1] According to Dr. Hance (*Notes and Queries*, Vol. II, p. 29) the common garden balsam (*Impatiens balsamina*, L.) is also used for dyeing the nails.

European languages, is said to be derived from Arabo-Persian *jâsamîn*, and the occurrence of the word in a Chinese record written about A.D. 300,[1] shows that it must have been in early use. I do not wish to commit myself to any positive statement as to the identification of the term *hu* (胡), very common in Chinese ethnographical records of all ages. This word has probably various senses; but in connection with the extreme west, I am inclined to assume it denoted the inhabitants of the coast of the Persian Gulf, especially those of the Euphrates and Tigris countries, or travelling Arabs. It appears that the *Hu-jên* who brought the Henna plant from Ta-ts'in to China were not Ta-ts'in people, but belonged to another nationality trading between Ta-ts'in and China; they may have had factories at Canton (*Nan-hai*) as, without taking a certain permanent interest in the country, they would not have thought of introducing foreign plants to this distant soil. The two passages quoted from the *Nan-fang-ts'ao-mu-chuang* seem to throw a certain light on the trade with the far east inasmuch as they suggest that Canton (*Nan-hai*) was during that time (about A.D. 300)[2] the terminus of navigation to which

---

[1] *See* Bretschneider, "Bot.-Sin.," *l.c.*, p. 38.

[2] It was very nearly about that time that an embassy, probably like the An-tun mission, a commercial expedition, arrived from Ta-ts'in (F 20; Q 36; R 22), and I am inclined to believe that they opened the way to Canton; for, not too long before, at the beginning of that century, in A.D. 226, the merchant Ts'in-lun still landed in Tung-king, and not in Canton (H 8).

foreigners were in the habit of resorting, and that these foreigners were *Hu* people. Neumann's remarks anent the *Hu* people and the *Hu* writing[1] do certainly not contradict this assumption. However, this question cannot be decided upon all at once, and a special enquiry, based on a large number of ancient passages, will be a great desideratum for this kind of research.

The *Nan-fang-ts'ao-mu-chuang* further contains the following notice: "*Mi-hsiang-chih* (蜜香紙, *i.e.*, honey-fragrance paper) is made of the bark and leaves of the *mi-hsiang* tree; its colour is grayish, and it has spots giving it the appearance of fish-spawn. It is very fragrant, but strong and pliable; it may be soaked in water without spoiling. In the fifth year of T'ai-k'ang of the Chin dynasty (A.D. 284) Ta-ts'in presented 30,000 rolls.[2] The [Chinese] Emperor bestowed 10,000 rolls on the general field-marshal, "Subjugator of the South," the Marquess of Tang-yang Tu Yü (杜預),[3] commanding him to write thereon the works compiled by him, namely, the *Ch'un-ch'iu-shih-lieh* (春秋釋例)[4] and the *Ching-chuan-chi-chieh* (經傳

---

[1] "Zur Geschichte der Schrift bei den tatarischen Völkerschaften" in *Asiat. Studien*, p. 130 seqq.

[2] It is very probable that this paper was brought by the so-called embassy mentioned in the *Chin-shu* (F 20). *See* Note 2 on p. 271.

[3] *See* Mayers, *Manual*, No. 684.

[4] Cf. Bretschneider, "Bot. Sin.," l.c., p. 144: No. 89.

集解), to be submitted to the throne.¹ But Tu Yü died before the paper had reached him; the latter was, therefore, handed to his family by Imperial command to be kept by them."

The above passage from the *Nan-fang-ts'ao-mu-chuang* has given rise to the assumption that a quantity of Roman paper, the produce of the Papyrus plant, took its way to China, as a present from the then reigning Roman emperor. Dr. Edkins, in an article "On the origin of Paper-making in China," in *Notes and Queries*, Vol. I, p. 67 seq., even makes use of it to show that the idea of manufacturing paper was first introduced to China from the west. I do not wish to interfere with all the cherished notions of our writers on ancient civilisation; but as regards this fact, I cannot help saying that I consider it very doubtful. Thirty thousand rolls of paper represent a big cargo, and as the Chinese at that time were already in the possession of a voluminous literature written on paper of silk and other materials which must have suited their own purposes at least as well as the Alexandrian "chartæ," it does not seem probable that a

---

¹ I strongly suspect that Pauthier who (*Mémoires sur l'Antiquité Chinoise*, p. 252) translates an apparently identical passage from the *Chêng-tzŭ-t'ung* (正字通), labours under some kind of misunderstanding in saying: " — — le Ta Thsin vint offrir en présent trente mille pièces de ce même papier. L'empereur des Tçin (Wou-ti, alors régnant) donna, de son côté, à l'envoyé (du Ta Thsin) dix mille larges pièces d'étoffes préparées, et une copie manuscrite du Tchûn-thsiêou (Annales du royaume de Lou, par Confucius), placée dans une enveloppe bois de pêcher rouge."

present of such a bulky nature should have been sent on this lengthy journey, in order to introduce a mission, official or commercial. Pauthier[1] thinks he cannot credit Diocletian with presenting such a valuable gift, and therefore believes the embassy to have come from the Sassanide king. My own personal opinion is that neither the former, nor the latter sent any paper, nor even an embassy to China; but that Syrian or Alexandrian merchants reached Annam via Ceylon in the same way as the so-called embassy of A.D. 166; that, in order to obtain certain trading privileges, possibly the opening to trade of the port of Canton,[2] they had to send presents to the court of China; and, having disposed of their Ta-ts'in goods, they invested part of the proceeds of their sales in the purchase of local (Annam) produce to serve in lieu of original home articles, as a present to the emperor. Such a mode of dealing with the Chinese court would not have been without precedent, since even the very first mission of A.D. 166 presented Annamese goods, *viz.*, ivory, rhinoceros horns and tortoise-shell (E 33, etc). I base this view on the fact that the tree called *Mi-hsiang-shu*, the bark and leaves of which are said, in the *Nan-fang-ts'ao-mu-chuang*, to furnish that kind of fragrant paper "presented by Ta-ts'in," is not men-

---

[1] *Mémoires*, etc., *l.c.* "Le présent de trente mille pièces de 'papier' porté par l'ambassadeur à l'empereur de la Chine n'aurait guère été du goût de Diocletién, en supposant qu'il en ait eu les moyens."

[2] *See* note 2 on p. 271.

tioned in any of the Ta-ts'in records we have examined amongst the products of the country; and that we possess a distinct statement in the very same authority from which the paper account is derived,[1] that this tree grows in Chiao-chih (交趾), *i.e.*, Tung-king.

Amongst the products *realgar* and *orpiment* (P 49*gg*) are almost a speciality of Syria. Pliny (XXXIII, 4 (22), 79) tells us a story how gold was made "ex auripigmento, quod in Syria foditur."

Copper was produced in excellent quality on the island of Cyprus; *gold* and *silver* occurred in the country, but it is probably, as I have insinuated on p. 244, rather owing to the fact of trade in these precious metals having been in the hands of Syrian or Alexandrian merchants that their names became associated with the products of Ta-ts'in. The same

---

[1] *Nan-fang-ts'ao-mu-chuang*, ch. 2, in the account following that of the *Chih-chia* or finger-nail flower. There, eight different *hsiang* or incenses, including the *mi-hsiang*, or honey-fragrance, and the *ch'ên-hsiang* (沉 香), which name stands for Garoo wood (*Aquilaria Agallocha*, Roxb.) in the modern Customs Tariff, are said to be derived from one and the same tree, called *mi-hsiang-shu*. Regarding the *ch'ên-hsiang*, see Hanbury, "Notes on Chinese Materia Medica," in *Transact. of the Linn. Soc.*, 1860-62, reprinted in *Science Papers*, p. 263 seqq. If, as the Chinese authority states, Garoo wood is derived from the same tree which furnishes the paper in question, there can be no doubt that the paper was produced in Annam and not in a western country, where I understand the tree referred to did not grow. The Chinese description of the *Mi-hsiang-shu* answers well enough to the Annamese tree, but not by any means to the Papyrus plant of Egypt or Syria.

reason will hold good for other metals found in the Ta-ts'in list of products, all of which probably came from Alexandria, the central depôt for the Roman trade in metals.

The *Chin-t'ang-shu* (K 36) says that, "in the 2nd year of the period Ch'ien-fêng (= A.D. 667) Fu-lin sent an embassy to China offering *Ti-yeh-ka* (底也伽, old sound: téyaka)."

Mr. Phillips (*China Review*, Vol. VII, p. 414) remarks with regard to this article of tribute: "This, a Chinese scholar informs me, is the same as Shên-k'an, 神龕, that is, a shrine or moveable box in which figures of gods were placed. Another Chinese suggests Kia-lăn, 伽藍, or Tsêng-k'ia-lan, 僧伽藍, Sanscrit *Sangarana*, a temple and a shrine. *Vide* Williams' Dictionary, under character Lan, 藍."

It appears to me that both the Hsien-shêng advising Mr. Phillips were wrong, and I should like to know on what authority they could base their identifications. *Ti-yeh-ka* was a drug, highly valued in western countries, though probably not imported with much success in China. It is apparently first mentioned in the *T'ang-pên-ts'ao*, the pharmacopœia of the T'ang dynasty, published during the middle of the 7th century.[1] The *Pên-*

---

[1] Regarding this work, *see* Bretschneider, Bot. Sin., *l.c.*, p. 44.

ts'ao-kang-mu (ch. 50ᴮ, p. 45) contains a short account of it.¹ It came from the countries of the west, and the people there say that pig's gall is used in making it, that it resembles the *Chiu-huai* (久壞) pill in shape, and that it is red and black in colour.² It was known in Canton during the Sung dynasty. Its taste is bitter and cold; it is not poisonous; its medical qualities are those of a panacea inasmuch as it cures *pai-ping-chung-ngo* (百病中惡), "the evil effects in all diseases," etc.

I do not hesitate to identify this drug with the theriac (Greek τὰ θηριακά =téyaka, *ti-yeh-ka*) of

---

¹ The word is there written with the characters 底野加, *ti-yeh-ka*, identical in sound with the name appearing in the *Chiu-t'ang-shu*.

² The 23rd volume of a manuscript pharmacopœia now in my possession, the *Pên-ts'ao-pin-hui-ching-yao* (本草品彙精要), written in A.D. 1506 by the Imperial Medical College of the Ming, contains besides the text, coinciding in its main points with that of the *Kang-mu*, a water-coloured illustration, apparently describing the moment when a sample of this drug was presented to a Chinese emperor. The figure of the latter, it is true, looks somewhat plain; he sits on a piece of rock instead of a throne, and we could not guess his dignified position but for the figure of a foreigner kneeling before him and holding a dish in his hands, which are covered with a green napkin. The dish contains a number of pills of the size of a billiard ball, red and black in colour. According to the text of the manuscript (and also in my edition of the *Chêng-lei-pên-ts'ao*, printed in A.D. 1523) the western makers mix *chu-tan* (諸膽), i.e., the "gall of *various* animals." It appears that the expression *chu-tan* (猪膽), i.e., "pigs' gall," in the text of the *Kang-mu* is an arbitrary change from the former; for, in the manuscript it is distinctly stated that "various galls" are *ho-ho* (合和), "mixed." The manuscript quotes from the *T'ang-pên-chu* (唐本注) that "foreigners at the time [*i.e.*, during the T'ang dynasty] considered it as highly valuable, and that a trial would prove its efficacy as a medicine. The drug was to be kept in porcelain vessels. Its smell is described as rancid (腥), probably because, by the time it arrived in China, it was spoiled.

ancient and mediæval renown. This celebrated panacea was, according to Pliny (XXIX, 1 (8), 24), "excogitata compositio luxuriæ." It was made of six hundred, *i.e.*, a great many, different ingredients. The same author (XX, 24 (100), 264) has preserved a recipe of the theriac used by Antiochus the Great as an antidote against all poisons excepting that of the viper. It contained no gall, it is true, but it states that the medicine was made into pills of a certain weight ("pastillos victoriati ponderis"). Another recipe will be found in Pliny (XXIX, 4 (21), 70., in which theriac is also made into pills. From later accounts it appears that the composition of the drug varied at different times, and it looks as if the essential point in the matter is, that it was at any time a very complicated, expensive, and fashionable medicine. Pliny (XXIX, 1 (8), 25) seems to consider it an ostentatious humbug, and the Chinese may have been right in not giving it a more prominent place in their materia medica. I have seen later recipes for theriac containing substances which must have imparted to it an intrinsically bitter taste, such as myrrh, snakes' gall and opium. The latter drug probably often entered in large proportions. The Mussulmans of the middle ages who wished to enjoy the effect of either hemp or opium, took this compound in lieu of these drugs themselves; and we may be allowed to conjecture that Opium was first brought to China in this disguise. D'Herbelot (*Bibliothèque Orientale*) says, under the word *Benk*, which is the name used in Western Asia for the hen-bane plant, also applied to the narcotic prepared from hemp-leaves:[1] "Ceux qui usent ordinairement du Benk et de l'Afioun [=Opium], sont nommez par les Arabes, Persans et Turcs Benghi, et Afiúni, et passent parmi eux pour des débauchez: car ces deux drogues qui ôtent la liberté de l'esprit et l'usage de la raison, produisent le même effet que le vin, sont condamnées par les Docteurs Musulmans les plus rigides, quoy qu'il n'en soit fait aucune mention dans l'Alcoran; et parce que la Theriaque quoyque permise, prête souvent son nom à ces deux drogues, le nom de Theriaki ou preneur de Theriaque, s'applique aussi à un débauché." According to Arab historians the best Theriac came from the province of Irák or Baghdad (see d'Herbelot, l.c., Vol. III, p. 453).

The *Hsin-t'ang-shu* (L 38; cf. Q 51 and R 31) contains a curious account of some kind of barter trade said to be carried on "on the western sea." We may be safe in assuming that neither Syrian nor Alexandrian merchants ever concluded a single bargain in this primitive manner in their own country, and the words "on the western sea" seem

---

[1] The Chinese were apparently not unacquainted with this preparation. Western or foreign hemp (胡麻=flax?) was introduced into China by Chang-ch'ien. (*Ko-chih-ching-yüan*, ch. 61, p. 22 B) The effect of eating the juice (汁) of the hemp plant must have been known in China as early as the 4th century A.D., as the *Shih-i-chi* (拾遺記), quoted in the *Ko-chih-ching-yüan* (l.c.), speaks of the juice of hemp, the eating of which causes one to see spirits

to indicate that the custom described existed somewhere on neutral soil as the point of *rendez-vous*. The passage referred to is probably a transcript from some older record, and purports to give a description of the barter trade said to have existed during the first century A.D. between the aboriginal Singhalese and Chinese or Roman (Syrian, Alexandrian) traders. Pliny (VI, 22 (24), 88) mentions an almost identical custom which, according to the reports received from Ceylon ambassadors to the Emperor Claudius as well as from Roman merchants ("nostri negotiatores") prevailed on the island of Ceylon; these reports were to the effect that "fluminis ulteriore ripa merces positas juxta venalia tolli ab his, si placeat permutatio."

We may be allowed to declare the two accounts, that of the *Hsin-t'ang-shu* and that of Pliny, to refer to one and the same subject, the ancient barter trade at Ceylon. The name *kuei-shih*, "spirit-market," or "devil-market" as it may perhaps be as well rendered, can be easily explained by a passage in Fa Hsien's *Fo-kuo-chi* which beyond all doubt refers to Ceylon, and which reads, in Mr. Giles' translation:[1] "This country had originally no inhabitants; only devils and spirits [鬼 神] and dragons lived in it, with whom the merchants of neighbouring countries came to trade. When the exchange of commodities took place the devils and spirits did not appear in person,

---
[1] *Record of the Buddistic Kingdoms*, ch. XXXVIII, p. 93.

but set out their valuables with the prices attached. Then the merchants, according to the prices, bought the things and carried them off."[1]

Sir James E. Tennent refers to both the Roman and the Chinese tradition regarding this barter trade,[2] and, further, traces its existence during antiquity as well as in later times to the shyness of the aboriginal race inhabiting the island. The principal locality where trade was carried on was, according to Tennent, the port of Galle. "Galle," he says,[3] "in the earlier ages, appears to have occupied a position in relation to trade of equal if not of greater importance than that which attaches to it at the present day. It was the central emporium of a commerce which in turn enriched every country of Western Asia, elevated the merchants of Tyre to the rank of princes, fostered the renown of the Ptolemies, rendered the wealth and the precious products of Arabia a gorgeous mystery, freighted the Tigris with "barbaric pearl and gold," and identified the merchants of Bagdad and the mariners of Bassora with associations of adventure and romance. Yet, strange to say, the native Singhalese appear to have taken no part whatever in this exciting and

---

[1] Cf. Ma Tuan-lin's chapter on "The Country of Lions" (*shih-tzŭ-kuo* 師子國 = Ceylon), ch. 338, p. 26; transl. Julien, in *Journ. Asiat.*, 1836, Vol. XXIX, p. 36 (quoted in Tennent's *Ceylon*, Vol. I, p. 587, note 3).

[2] *Ceylon*, Vol. I. pp. 534 and 587, where Fa Hsien's account is quoted from Rémusat's translation.

[3] *l.c.*, Vol. I, p. 568.

enriching commerce; their name is never mentioned in connection with the immigrant races attracted by it to their shores, and the only allusions of travellers to the indigenous inhabitants of the island are in connection with a custom so remarkable and so peculiar as at once to identify the tribes to whom it is ascribed with the remnant of the aboriginal race of Veddahs, whose descendants still haunt the forests in the east of Ceylon."

"Such is the aversion of this untamed race to any intercourse with civilised life, that when in want of the rude implements essential to their savage economy, they repair by night to the nearest village on the confines of their hunting-fields, and indicating by well-understood signs and models the number and form of the articles required, whether arrow-heads, hatchets, or cloths, they deposit an equivalent portion of dried deer's flesh or honey near the door of the dealer, and retire unseen to the jungles, returning by stealth within a reasonable time, to carry away the manufactured articles, which they find placed at the same spot, in exchange."

"This singular custom has been described without variation by numerous writers on Ceylon, both in recent and remote times."[1] "Concurrent testimony, to the same effect, is found in the recital of the Chinese Buddhist, Fa Hsien, who in the third century describes, in his travels, the same strange peculiarity of the inhabitants in those days,

---

[1] For quotations, *see* Tennent, p. 569 with Notes 1-4 on that page.

whom he also designates "demons," who deposited, unseen, the precious articles which they come down to barter with the foreign merchants resorting to their shores."[1]

"The chain of evidence is rendered complete by a passage in Pliny, which, although somewhat obscure (facts relating to the Seres being confounded with statements regarding Ceylon), nevertheless serves to show that the custom in question was then well known to the Singhalese ambassadors sent to the Emperor Claudius, and was also familiar to the Greek traders resorting to the island, etc., etc."

The analysis of the various accounts we possess of the country of Fu-lin, *i.e.*, the Ta-ts'in of the middle ages, shows that we have to distinguish between two classes of statements made in them, viz. :—

    1st, statements which have appeared already in the previous accounts of Ta-ts'in, and which we must, therefore, assume to have been transferred thence by the compilers of the new accounts;

    2nd, statements which have been newly introduced from contemporaneous sources.

If we deduct from these mediæval records all

---

[1] A footnote on p. 570 of the work quoted contains a full record of Chinese passages repeating, or alluding to, the same account. I may add to these the passages referred to in our Ta-ts'in and Fu-lin accounts T. 38, Q 51 and R 31.

old Ta-ts'in information, that which remains bears a certain characteristic stamp which I feel inclined to describe as "ecclesiastical." It is the merit of Mr. George Phillips to have first drawn attention to this, in my opinion the only reasonable, explanation we may attempt of the Fu-lin mystery.[1]

The so-called "King of Fu-lin" must be an ecclesiastical ruler. For, the king who has a tunnel built from his palace to his church, who rarely goes out, but every seventh day performs divine service with the assistance of over fifty attendants (R 16-17), and who sends priests to China as tribute-bearers (K 39),[2] cannot be a worldly monarch. High church dignitaries, such as any of the pa-

---

[1] I refer to Mr. Phillips' unpretending note: "Supposed Mention in Chinese History of the Nestorian Missions to China in the 7th and 8th Centuries," on p. 412 in Vol. VII of the *China Review*, in which the author says with regard to the embassy of A.D. 719: "To me it seems that this Ta-tê-sêng gives us the key as to whom the other Envoys were, and I am inclined to think that the Envoys recorded in the T'ang books as coming from Fu-lin were missionaries of the Nestorian Church." The connection between one of the Fu-lin missions and the arrival of Nestorian missionaries in China as recorded on the Nestorian Inscription had been already conjectured by Yule (*Cathay*, etc., Vol. I, pp. LXIV-LXV).

[2] The *Ta-tê-sêng*, sent in A.D. 720. It is by no means insignificant that these priests were sent, or at least allowed to go with tribute, at a time when a Khalif who was known for his liberality as regards disbelievers, had just taken charge of the government from the hands of rulers more or less inimical to Christianity. Omar the Second followed his cousin Soleiman in A.D. 717; he died in A.D. 720 near Emesa, about 70 miles south of Antioch, on Syrian soil, where he probably spent some time during his reign. *Sêng*, though generally meaning a Buddhist priest, may be a priest of any religion if applied to western countries, just as the Khoran is called 佛經, *Fo-ching*, *i.e.*, Buddha's Canon, elsewhere (see *Yüan-chien-lei-han*, ch. 238, p. 25,

triarchs in the east, commanded a powerful position amongst the people belonging to their community. Their religious zeal would excuse any exaggeration of their worldly influence *vis-à-vis* the distant nations amongst whom they wished to propagate the Christian faith. The Nestorian patriarchs distinguished themselves at an early period by the zeal with which they carried on missionary work in Central and Eastern Asia, and China must have appeared to them a field worthy of their best efforts. The Chinese emperor Yang-ti of the Sui dynasty (A.D. 605–617), who extended his conquests far beyond the limits of the empire of his fathers, tried in vain to open intercourse with Fu-lin (K 33). In doing so, this enterprising monarch may have been guided by the wish to see some of the Nestorian scholars at his court; for his capital, Lo-yang-fu, had, at his instance, become a place of assembly for all the first *savants* of the eastern world, including Taoists and Buddhists. It was not until the second ruler of the T'ang dynasty, T'ai-tsung (A.D. 627 to 650), had ascended the throne that the first Nestorian missionary, by name of O-lo-pên, arrived in China. O-lo-pên, who as we

---

in the article concerning *Medina*). *Ta-tê-sêng*, however, is the priest of a Christian sect, as I conclude from the text of the inscription of *Si-an-fu*, where it is used as an honorary epithet in connection with the personal names of certain Nestorians, *e.g.*, *ta-tê O-lo-pên*, "the Most-virtuous Alopun" (Wylie), something like the English "Reverend" or "Venerable." We may be justified, therefore, to translate *Ta-tê-sêng* by "Nestorian priest." In Buddhistic works the term is used for *bhadanta*, a title like Reverend, given to Buddhist priests (Williams, *Syll. Dict.*, p. 871; cf. Giles, *Buddh. Kingdoms*, p. 100: "a distinguished shaman").

know from the Nestorian stone inscription, arrived in Ch'ang-an, the present Hsi-an-fu, in the year 636 A.D.,[1] was well received at the Chinese court; the religious books he had brought with him were translated under Imperial auspices and, with all the facilities granted to that "luminous religion of Ta-ts'in" (*Ta-ts'in-ching-chiao* 大秦景教) after its first introduction in China, O-lo-pên had become the precursor of a series of missions extending over several centuries. It was through these Nestorian pioneers, I presume, that the accounts of Fu-lin, which country, geographically, coincided with the ancient Ta-ts'in, were brought to China. The name Ta-ts'in had, as a matter of prudence, been revived by these missionaries who were perfectly correct in stating that the Ta-ts'in so well known amongst the Chinese from the accounts of their classical histories was the country they came from; they were further correct in stating that the founder of their religion was born in Ta-ts'in;[2] Fu-lin was merely another name for Ta-ts'in introduced by the Nestorians, and these may have said to the Chinese: "We come from the place where the Messias is born; the name of this place is Fu-lin, and it lies in the country known to you as Ta-ts'in." The name Fu-lin appears to have been first used at about the time when O-lo-pên arrived. I cannot, at least, discover any earlier mention of it than that in an account of Persia, appended to the

---

[1] Cf. Pauthier, *l'Inscription de Si-ngan-fou*, pp. 12 and 13.

[2] *Ibid.* pp. 8 and 9.

Sui-shu, the history of the Sui dynasty, compiled during the reign of T'ai-tsung, in which Persia is stated to be bounded in the north-east by Fu-lin. Yüan-chuang's work, the *Ta-t'ang-hsi-yü-chi*, which was completed in A.D. 646, contains a similar mention, but the name is there[1] written 拂懍國 Fu-lin-kuo. I may add that this *lin* 懍 is identical in sound with *lin* 林. The old sound of the two characters *fu* and *lin* 拂林 was most probably not *po-lin*, as those who wish to refer it to the Greek πόλιν would like to make it; nor *fu-lan*, which would suit the defenders of the "Frank" etymology.[2] It seems to me that here, if anywhere,

---

[1] Ch. XI, p. 23. The *Yen-pao-tan-yü* (偃曝談餘), quoted in the *Ko-chih-ching-yüan*, ch. 33, p. 31, has preserved under the name of *Fo-lin* (佛㝹) an account which I have no doubt refers to our Fu-lin. It says that "when the ambassadors from Fo-lin came to court [the embassy referred to arrived during the period Ching-yu, 景祐, =A.D. 1034 to 1038, as I conclude from K'ang-hsi's quotation of the same passage, s.v. 㝹, Rad. 日, p. 20], they stated that this state at the time had ceased to exist Its territory was very extensive; that it was under seventy-two leaders (*chiu-chang* 酋長); there was in the country a "quicksilver-sea" with a circuit of about 40 or 50 li," etc., etc. I shall refrain from quoting the account of the manner of obtaining the quicksilver, occupying about half a page in the *Ko-chih-ching-yüan*, as it apparently throws no light on the subject. The *Ko-chih-ching-yüan*, ch. 35, p. 19, has a quotation from the same work (*Yen-pao-tan-yü*) in connection with Fu-lin coins, apparently a transcript of the passage N 16; and there the name appears as *Fu-lin* (拂林).

[2] Various more or less unhappy suggestions have been made with regard to the origin of the name Fu-lin. Pauthier (*De l'Authenticité*, etc., p. 42, Note 3) follows the example of Mr. Jaquet, who had long before him (*Nouv. Journ. Asiat.*, Vol. IX, 1832, p. 456 seq., quoted by ron Richthofen, *China*, Vol. I, p. 535) advanced the derivation from the Greek accusative πόλιν as part of the expression εἰς τὴν πόλιν alleged to have been originally used as a name for the capital Constan

Dr. Edkins may be trusted as a guide with regard to the old sound. The phonetic value given by tinople, and supposed to survive in the Turkish *Istanbúl*. True barbarians they must have been, the mediæval Constantinopolitans, who could reply to the question: "where do you live," by εἰς τὴν πόλιν. However, this etymology seems to be universally recognised since Sir V m. Ouseley, in his *Travels* (Vol. III, p. 573) has shown some parallel cases, and it may pass as far as Istanbúl is concerned, although Sádik Isfaháni (transl. J. C. for Orient. Transl. Fund, London, 1832, p. 7) maintains that this word in the Turkish language signifies, " you will find (there) whatever you wish." To connect, however, the sound *polin* with our *Fu-lin*, is not much better than Visdelou's *Hellen* (d'Herbelot, *Bibl. Orient.*, Vol. IV, p. 423; cf. Neumann, *Asiat. Studien*, p. 172). Bretschneider (*Arabs*, etc., p. 23) shows that he was well aware of the old sound of the first syllable having been *bot ;* and yet he agreed (*l.c.*) to Jaquet's conjecture. In a later work (*Mediæval Travellers*, etc., p. 86, Note 131) the same author is at some pains to defend the connection between "Fu-lin" (said to have been pronounced *fu-lan*) and the word "Frank" which, according to von Richthofen (*China*, Vol. I, p. 535) was believed in by de Guignes, and which has been recently revived by Dr. O. F. von Moellendorff (*China Review*, Vol. VI, p. 349). It seems not out of place to refute in detail an error so persistently recurring. As I have stated above, the Chinese name Fu-lin occurs in works written during the first half of the 7th century (*Sui-shu* and Hsüan Chuang's Journeys, *cf.* Introduction, p. 17), *i.e.*, at a time when in my opinion the word *frank* cannot possibly have been known in the east. I doubt whether anyone can find an authority speaking of Europeans as Franks much earlier than the 10th century A.D. Gibbon (Chap. LIII, Wm. Smith, Vol. VII, p. 33) speaks of the end of that century when he remarks: "A name of some German tribes between the Rhine and the Weser had spread its victorious influence over the greatest part of Gaul, Germany, and Italy; and the common appelation of FRANKS was applied by the Greeks and Arabians to the Christians of the Latin Church, the nations of the West, who stretched beyond *their* knowledge to the shores of the Atlantic Ocean." To support his view of the use of this term in a period anterior to the Crusades, Gibbon quotes from Liutprand in *Legat. ad Imp. Nicephorum* [p. 483 seq.]: "ex Francis, quo nomine tam Latinos quam Teutones comprehendit, ludum habuit." "This extension of the name," Gibbon says, "may be his authority[1] to the character *fu* 彿 is *but*, and as this character, according to native dictionaries, belongs to the same phonetic group as *fo* 佛, Buddha, which represents the first syllable *bud* in this Indian name, and is pronounced *fat* in Cantonese, and *butsu* in Japanese, there is apparently sufficient evidence for assuming its old sound to have been *but*, and not *po* or *fu*. The second character, *lin* (棶) belongs to a phonetic group the final of which, in the southern dialects, is *m;* it is pronounced *lám* in Cantonese and *lîm* in the Amoy dialect. The old sound of the name Fu-lin may, therefore, be safely assumed to have been *But-lim* or *But-lám*.[2]

Having thus shown the probable old sound of the name, I come back to what I suppose to be its origin. Just as the Nestorians actually said in their celebrated stone inscription: "we come from the land where the Lord is born; and the Lord is

---

confirmed from Constantine (*de Administrando Imperio*, I. ii, c. 27, 28) and Eutychius (*Annal.*, tom I, p. 55, 56), who both lived before the Crusades. The testimonies of Abulpharagius (*Dynast.* p. 69) and Abulfeda (*Præfat. ad Geograph.*) are more recent." Liutprand, who, in the work quoted by Gibbon, describes the impressions he received from the court of Constantinople during his mission thither in A.D. 968, was born about A.D. 922. Constantine was born in A.D. 905, and Eutychius, the Alexandrian patriarch (*alias* Said Ibn Batrik), was born in A.D. 876.

[1] Ch'ien Ta-hsin (錢大昕), in his work *Shih-chia-chai-yang-hsin-lu* (十駕齋養新錄). *See* Edkins, *Mandarin Grammar* (second edition, Shanghai, 1874), p. 92.

[2] Cf. *Notes and Queries*, Vol. IV, p. 8.

born in Ta-ts'in,"[1] they may have also said: "We come from the land where the Lord is born; and the Lord is born in Bethlehem," the sound of which name could not be better represented than by the two syllables which constitute the name Fu-lin, then pronounced *But-lim*. To see the name of the town of Bethlehem as the birthplace of the Messiah, extended to the country to which it belongs, is by no means singular if we consider that this was done by religious enthusiasts who must have thought it a great privilege to come from the Holy Land. Moreover, the fact would be in perfect analogy with the Buddhistic usage according to which the name Magadha (摩伽陀), originally the birthplace of Buddha, was applied to the whole of India during the T'ang dynasty.[2]

Visdelou (d'Herbelot, *Bibl. Or.*, Vol. IV, p. 423) may not have been so very wrong in comparing the name *Hua-lin* (花林) in the Nestorian Inscription (M 1), which I have translated by "the flowery groves," to the name Fu-lin. If it could be proved that the old sound of these two characters was *wa-lim* or *ba-lim*, if not *wát-lim* or *bát-lim*, it might look as if the term *hsien-ching hua-lin* (仙境花林) could be translated by "the angelic region of Bethlehem,"

---

[1] Pauthier, *l'Inscription*, etc., p. 13, § 11 and p. 7, § 6: 室女誕聖於大秦, "a virgin gave birth to the holy one at Ta-ts'in."

[2] The *Hsin-t'ang-shu* (Lieh-chuan 列傳 ch. 146, p. 23) introduces this name as an equivalent of T'ien-chu-kuo 天竺國, *i.e.*, India.

which indeed occupied the west of Ta-ts'in (Syria, Shám; *cf.* L 5 and note, Q 41, R 24) just as the "coral sea" made the southern, and the Chung-pao-shan (the Taurus range) the northern, and "the Long Winds" and "the Weak Water" the eastern, boundary. I do not know what the "Long Winds" could possibly mean in the east of Syria; but the "Weak Water" may apply to the Euphrates owing to an association with the mythological *Jo-shui* of the Chinese which, like the Euphrates, could be navigated upon in skin-boats. I may here be allowed a departure from the subject in hand, in order to correct a very common misunderstanding which has led to the identification of the "Weak Water" with the Dead Sea. "Weak Water" is not so called on account of buoyancy; for, buoyant water is rather strong than weak. Herodotus (lib. III, 23) describes a fountain in Æthiopia, the water of which is so weak ($ὕδωρ\ ἀσθενές$ = 弱水) that nothing is able to float upon it, neither wood nor such things as are lighter than wood, but everything sinks to the bottom," and the Paradoxographus Vaticanus Rohdii (see *Rerum Naturalium Scriptores Græci Minores*, ed. O. Keller, c. XXXVI, on p. 110 of Vol. I) speaks of a spring called Sille, in India, $ἐφ'\ ἧς\ τὰ\ ἐλαφρότατα\ καταποντίζεται$ (*Cf.* Strab., c. 703). This is indeed the sense in which the Chinese understand their *Jo-shui*. The first mention of the "Weak Water" is apparently made in the *Yü-kung* (I, 10, 72, Legge, p. 123 and Note on p. 124):

"The Weak Water was conducted westwards. The king was led to mingle its waters with those of the Wei (river)." Ts'ai-ch'ên, commenting on this passage, quotes the poet Liu Tsung-yüan (A.D. 773–819) who says: "In the hills (islands or lands) on the western sea there is a water (river) spreading out and having no strength (coherence); it does not carry even a trifling object, and whatever is put on its surface will drop down to the bottom and remain there,—whence it is called 'Weak Water.'" As described in the *Yü-kung*, the Jo-shui must have been a river, and not a lake; it was near the western boundary of China, which at that time meant as much as the western terminus of the world. Ts'ai-ch'ên goes on to quote from other authorities a number of passages relating to the Weak Water (*cf.* the exhaustive notes in the *T'ung-chien-kang-mu*, ch. 25, under 6th year of Wên-ti of the anterior Sung, p. 9), and in due course mentions the Jo-shui of T'iao-chih; "and as this country is yet over a hundred days distant from a place 12,200 li west of Ch'ang-an (Hsi-an-fu)," he argues, "it cannot be identical with the Weak Water of the *Yü-kung*." The Weak Water, as well as the other terms usually mentioned together with it, the Hsi-wang-mu, the Red Water (*Ch'ih-shui*) and the Flying Sands (*Liu-sha*), appear in very old Chinese legends, and although it would be a fruitless task to ascertain their actual whereabouts (*cf.* Mayers, *Manual*, Nos. 236, 330 and 572), so much is certain, that these imaginary abodes of a fairy queen were, according to the ideas of the original legend-writers, neither in T'iao-chih nor in Ta-ts'in. But it looks as if ancient reports received in China from those countries contained certain features recalling associations connected with the still earlier Hsi-wang-mu legends. I have drawn attention to the navigation of the Euphrates as one of the points of contact. Legge (*Shoo king*, p. 124) adds to his note on the Weak Water: "Some accounts say that it can be crossed in coracles of skin, etc." I am indebted to Mr. Kingsmill for the suggestion that the Hsi-wang-mu legends moved farther west in the imagination of the Chinese in the same degree in which geographical discovery opened up new countries in that direction of the compass; they occupied indeed the *terra incognita* beyond the western boundary of the world known by the Chinese at the several periods of antiquity. This will account for all these utopianisms being stated again to exist in the west of Ta-ts'in (E 34, I 21, etc.).

We read in both the *T'ang-shu* (K 34 and L 41), and in Ma Tuan-lin (Q 66) that a mission was sent to China from Fu-lin in A.D. 643 by the king of Fu-lin, Po-to-li. Who was Po-to-li? This name has indeed, ever since the *T'ang-shu* account became known in Europe, been a great puzzle to western sinologues. Pauthier (*l'Inscription*, etc., p. 48) sees in it the name of Pope Theodorus. Bretschneider is at a loss how to explain it, as

Constantinople, at that time, was the residence of the emperor Heraclius Constans. I venture to submit the following solution to the judgment of those who maintain that etymologies are essential in the identification of historical and geographical accounts, and in doing so, I merely follow the example of Mr. Phillips who, indeed, made the very same suggestion years ago (*China Review*, Vol. VII, p. 414).

The old pronunciation of this name was probably *Bat-da-lik* (the modern Cantonese sound is: *Po-to-lik*); and this, in default of any prominent personage being mentioned under a similar name in that period of the history of Syria, I consider as the Chinese form of Arabic *Bathric*. D'Herbelot (*Bibl. Orient.*, Vol. I, p. 380) says: "*Bathrik* et *Bathrirak*, dont le pluriel est *Batharekah*, signifie en Arab, Persien et Turc, le Patriarche des Chrêtiens de chaque Secte et de chaque Eglise." It is further stated by d'Herbelot that, at the council of Constantinople held under Theodosius the Great in A.D. 381, the rank of the patriarchs, the spiritual rulers over large countries, was fixed, and that the patriarch of Antioch was to rank fourth amongst five (*viz.*, those of Rome, Constantinople, Alexandria, Antioch, and Jerusalem).

There is, however, one doubtful point in this assumption: the "patriarch of Antioch" was a Catholic, and the Nestorian patriarch may not have resided at the capital (Antioch), but at Edessa or some other city in the neighbourhood. This doubt is somewhat alleviated by the fact that our account of Po-to-li's mission refers to the period following the Arab conquest; that the Catholic patriarchate of Antioch and the sees of Jerusalem and Alexandria remained practically unoccupied after the Arab occupation for the reason that their possessors, living in the Greek empire, were merely titulars.[1] I am not able to say whether the heads of the Nestorian church were allowed by the Arabs to reside at Antioch, and if they were, whether they made use of the privilege; but, even if this has not been the case, they certainly resided in Syria, and had no reason to contradict the traditions they found in China with regard to the capital of Syria or Ta-ts'in. The Nestorians held such an influential position at the courts of the Khalifs and their satraps that the part attributed to them as mediators between the west and the far east would have met with no difficulty from a political point of view.

The siege of the capital of Fu-lin, as mentioned in the *Chiu-t'ang-shu* (K 35) and in the *Hsin-t'ang-shu* (L 42 and 43) is described in a text narrating certain historical facts in a chronological series. In the first-named work, the facts stated appear in the following order:

1. The emperor Yang-ti wishes to communicate with Fu-lin, A.D. 605-617, (K 33).

---

[1] Gieseler, *Eccles. Hist.*, transl. S. Davidson, Edinb., 1848, Vol. II p. 172.

2. An embassy is sent to China in A.D. 643 (K 34).
3. *The capital of Fu-lin is besieged by the Arabs, and finally submits to Arab rule* (K 35).
4. An embassy is sent to China in A.D. 667 (K 36).
5. An embassy is sent in A.D. 701 (K 37).
6. An embassy is sent in A.D. 719 (K 38).

Although no date is mentioned in connection with the siege of the Fu-lin capital, the strictly chronological order in which these facts are enumerated in the T'ang annals, clearly shows that the event referred to must have taken place previous to A.D. 667. Its being mentioned immediately after the embassy of A.D. 643 strongly suggests that the news regarding the political change having taken place in the country was brought to China by that embassy, and that the siege actually took place previous to A.D. 643. The first siege of Constantinople by the Arabs began in A.D. 668 and lasted till A.D. 675, and although this city escaped conquest likewise by the payment of tribute, the account in the *T'ang-shu* cannot refer to it owing to this difference in time; moreover, Constantinople has never become subject to the Arabs as the capital of Fu-lin has according to the Chinese record. On the other hand, Antioch was besieged by the Arabs in A.D. 638; the "Queen of the East" had to ransom the preservation of life and religious freedom by the payment of tribute, and became a provincial city of the Khalif empire.[1]

The *Chiu-t'ang-shu* (ch. 198, lieh-chuan 148), in the account of Ta-shih, p. 20) says that the Arabs or Ta-shih "got into the possession of grain and flour (*i.e.*, grain-producing countries) on having defeated Pο-ssŭ (Persia) and Fu-lin in the beginning of the period Lung-so (=A.D. 661)."[2] This passage shows clearly that the conquest of Fu-lin was concluded in the year referred to; it is the year in which Muavia had, after a long struggle for supreme power, become sole master of the Khalif empire, *i.e.*, of Persia and Syria with Egypt. The passage may involve that the capital of Fu-lin had been in the hands of the Arabs some time previously; but it excludes in my opinion the assumption of its siege and conquest after the year 661.

In the *Sung-shu* and the *Chu-fan-chih* we find Fu-lin described as a province or satrapy of the Seldjuk empire. It is very probable that the

---

[1] The Arab General sent against Antioch is in both versions of the T'ang annals (K 35, L 42) called Mo-i, which name is clearly the equivalent of that of Muavia, who was born about A.D. 600, and became governor of Syria in A.D. 644. History mentions the generals Abu Ubeida and Chalid as charged with the conquest of Antioch, and I am at a loss how to explain the Chinese statement. I am at present not in the position to say whether Muavia could have possibly taken part in the conquest.

[2] 龍朔初擊破波斯叉破拂菻始有米麪之屬.

Nestorian see had then been removed, perhaps to Edessa; for, south-east of it, you go to Mieh-li-sha, and north and west a considerable journey is to be performed, in order to reach the sea (N 1). The name Mieh-li-sha (old sound: Mi-lik-sha) cannot possibly be misunderstood. It is the name of the Sultan Milikshah who then (*i.e.*, at the time when the Sung embassy arrived in China, or A.D. 1081) was the most powerful ruler in the west of Asia and whose capital was at Baghdad. The characters *mieh-li* (滅力) represent in this name the Arab word *milik* or *melek*, and this will furnish us the key for reading the other mysterious name in the passage N 3, Mieh-li-i-ling-kai-sa. This, I conjecture, is the name of one of the diadochs who had taken possession of Syria as vassals of the Sultan. De Guignes (*Hist. des Huns*, III, p. 162) gives the following account with regard to the titles Sultan and Malek (or Melek): When Mahmud (the Ghaznavide) came back to Ghazna with the title Ghazi or 'Conqueror' (in A.D. 1002), he had to make war against Khalaf, the governor of a neighbouring province, who finally submitted, addressing Mahmud by the title of Sultan, "et ce titre jusqu' alors inconnu devint en usage parmi les princes Mahometans; il plut à Mahmoud qui le porta le premier. Auparavant les princes prenaient celui de *Malek* ou de *Roi*. Dans la suite celui-ci s'avilit et ne fut plus donné qu' à des princes tributaires et soumis aux sultans." Such is the mutual relation of the two rulers mentioned in the accounts of the Sung dynasty. The king of the Ta-shih, who is styled su-tan (sultan) and who sends tribute (R 18), was probably a Seldjuk ruler, as the title Sultan was not in use before the year A.D. 1002. The tribute paid by him to the country of Fu-lin would in this place not have to be looked upon as a sign of submission, but as the necessary support which a feudal lord lends his representative on a minor throne; this view is supported by the remark that the Ta-shih (here Seldjuk) army has to restore order when trouble arises in the kingdom of the ruler of Fu-lin, who is given the title Melek, denoting at this time a "prince tributaire." The King of Fu-lin, whom the mission arriving at the court of China in A.D. 1081 called their lord, and who was styled Mieh-li-i-ling-kai-sa,[1] must have been a Melek, *i.e.*, one of the Seldjuk satraps, perhaps Tutusch, the Sultan's brother, or Soliman, who were both made subkings (Melek) by the Sultan in A.D. 1078. This somewhat lengthy name mentioned in the *Sung-shih* (N 3) has been referred by de Guignes (*l.c.*, I, 67), and with him by Pauthier, Bretschneider and others, to "Michael VII Parapinaces," emperor at Constantinople, and the Chinese expression has been explained as the equivalent of the words "Michaël Cæsar." I cannot understand how so many erudite scholars could repeat such a suggestion. For, the monarch referred to had, in the first instance,

---

[1] Bretschneider reads *sha* 沙 for *i* 伊, for which I can find no authority. (*See* note 1 on p. 62).

abdicated (he had not died as de Guignes says, *l.c.*) in A.D. 1078; and 1078 is not 1081; and then we may fairly ask: what relation can there be between the sounds Michael and Mi-li-i-ling, except their both beginning with the syllable *mi*? I have no doubt that the syllables Kai-sa, at the end of the Chinese term have induced many to declare that it can only apply to the Cæsar of the Roman Empire, for the similarity of these two syllables with Greek Καῖσαρ is indeed very suggestive. But the defenders of this theory forget that, since the Arab conquest of Syria and other Roman provinces, the Roman emperor was not the only ruler claiming this title. D'Herbelot, *Bibl. Orient.*, *s. v.* Caissar, says: "Les Historiens Orientaux donnent souvent par anticipation le titre de Caissar aux princes qui ont possédé les pays, que les Empereurs Romains et Grecs ont depuis conquis dans l'Asie." As the recognised king in a formerly Roman province, the representative of Milikshah would have been right from a Seldjuk point of view, in assuming this title, which may possibly stand for the words "Melek-i-Rûm Kaisar," *i.e.*, "under-king of Rûm and Cæsar." King of Rûm was, indeed, the title of Soliman, whose residence was at Iconium in Asia Minor.

The articles offered by this embassy are characteristic of the country as well as of the time in which they were brought. They consisted in saddled horses, swords, and real pearls,—articles peculiar to the industry of Syria, where the city of Damascus was renowned for its saddlery as well as especially for its sword-blades. Damask blades became celebrated in Europe through the traffic existing with those parts during the Crusades, but this industry dates as far back as the reign of Domitian, *i.e.*, the end of the first century A.D. We need not wonder, therefore, to find swords amongst the *fang-wu* or local produce of Fu-lin. The city of Damask had since the Arab conquest taken the place of Antioch, whose grandeur had sunk into insignificance after its fall. Omar, the second Khalif, resided there and in Mekka; and Muavia and his successors made it their capital from A.D. 660–753. This somewhat explains the importance of Syria amongst the Khalif possessions. Though merely one of the many subjected Arab states, this province was destined to keep up the connection between the West and the Far East just as it had represented the Roman Empire centuries before. We may say, in a few words, *Ta-ts'in* was Syria as a Roman province; *Fu-lin* was Syria as an Arab province during the *T'ang* dynasty, and as a Seldjuk province during the *Sung* dynasty.

We read in the *Hsin-t'ang-shu* (L 34; cf. Q 61) that the physicians of Fu-lin could open the brain and extract worms, in order to cure blindness (*lit.* film of the eyes). This art of opening the brain is most probably the art of trepanning not known in its application to eye-diseases by the Chinese of those days, although the opening of skulls for other purposes appears to have been practised at very early times in China as well as in several other parts of the world. Mr. Giles draws my attention to a passage in the *San-kuo-chih* novel, according to which Hua T'o (華 陀), a well-known physician of the second century, the Æsculapius of China (Mayers, *Manual*, No. 209) cured the great Ts'ao Ts'ao of a cerebral disease by opening his skull. Mayers (*l. c.*) calls it acupuncture, and I am not prepared to say whether it was an operation in the sense of what is now called trepanning. A trepanned skull was found in an Inca cemetery, from which fact it may be concluded that the art was at least not unknown in this secluded civilisation (*see* E. G. Squier, *Peru: Incidents of Travel and Exploration in the Land of the Incas*, New York, 1877, pp. 457 and 577). Broca, the well-known Paris anthropologist, has even drawn attention to the traces of trepanning executed by means of stones on human skulls found in graves of the ante-metallic period (*Archives Générales de Médecine*, 1877, Vol. II, p. 376). The art was, in ancient times, quite at home in Asia, and probably more so here thàn in Italy, as I conclude from a remark made by Galen (*Method. Medend.* VI, 6 *sub fin.*) who, while describing various methods that may be adopted in opening the skull, speaks of a particular treatment after the operation practised by an old physician called Eudemus, and remarks that he (Galen) might have had some experience therein, had he been all his time in Asia, and not spent most of it in Rome. Smyrna, where Galen pursued his Asiatic studies, must have seen many bold operations long before the *Fu-lin* period, and Syrian physicians practising the art at that time would be no curiosity, if the Chinese account did not add that, "by extracting worms they could cure blindness." The worms we may assume have been added by the imagination of the Chinese author; the cure of blindness by trepanning, however, if not effected often, has at least been described. Hippocrates (Περὶ νούσων, Littré VII, 26) speaks of cases in which a kind of brain disease complicated with pain about the eyes, in which the patient ἀμβλυώσσει, and ἡ κύρη σχίζεται, καὶ δοκέει ἐκ τοῦ ἑνὸς δύο ὁρᾶν, and which, if all other treatment fails, is cured by trepanning; and in his book on vision (Περὶ ὄψιος, ch. 8) he recommends a similar process in the case of amaurosis. I quote from Littré's French text (Vol. IX, p. 159): "Lorsque la vue se perd sans maladie apparente des yeux, il faut pratiquer une incision à la région pariétale, disséquer les parties molles, *trépaner l'os*, et évacuer le liquide épanché; c'est là le traitement, et c'est ainsi que ces malades guérissent." I am not able to decide whether such patients could possibly recover; but so much seems certain, that, whether actually practised or not, the art of curing some kind of blindness by trepanning was believed to have existed by those who supplied the information regarding Fu-lin to the court annalists of the T'ang. This comes in very well with our view that all the first embassies sent from Fu-lin during the T'ang dynasty were carried out by Nestorian missionaries. The Nestorians enjoyed a great reputation in Western Asia on account of their medical skill, and what brings them even into closer contact with the somewhat singular theory that blindness may be cured by trepanning, is that they translated Greek medical works into the Arab language and may be fairly supposed to have been acquainted with the remarks Hippocrates made on the subject. D'Herbelot (Vol. I, p. 352), speaking of the three Christian physicians Baktischua, says: "Ils étaient Syriens de nation, et ont traduit plusieurs livres Grecs et Syriens en Arabe, etc." The Baktischua flourished in the 8th, 9th and 10th centuries A.D.

Just as the Chinese annals contain records of alleged embassies from western monarchs which, on close examination, we had to declare to have been private missions, allusions to Chinese embassies to Rome may be found in Roman authors, which, if approached in the same critical spirit, may be shown never to have been sent by the monarch from whom they alleged to come.

Eusebius (*Vit. Const.* I, IV, c. 50, quoted in Gibbon, Chap. XVIII) speaks of an Indian embassy to the court of Constantine the Great (died

A.D. 337), which may possibly be referred to China. He "remarks three circumstances relative "to these Indians: 1. They came from the "shores of the eastern ocean; a description "which might be applied to the coast of China "or Coromandel. 2. They presented shining "gems, and unknown animals. 3. They pro-"tested their kings had erected statues to represent "the supreme majesty of Constantine." This embassy must have arrived during the reign of Ch'êng-ti of the eastern Chin dynasty (A.D. 326-335) who ascended the throne when a child. It appears that Chinese annals are as silent on this point as Roman records are on the various missions to China mentioned in Chinese historical works. I have at least looked in vain for anything like an allusion to it in the *T'ung-chien-kang-mu* covering that period. It is hardly necessary to take the same trouble with regard to the Seres stated in Florus' *Epitome* (IV, 12) to have been amongst the envoys of all countries who came to the court of Augustus (*see* Yule, *Cathay*, Vol. I, p. XLII), as the Chinese Annals clearly insinuate that Kan Ying (A.D. 98) was the first Chinese who ever penetrated as far west as T'iao-chih. The Chinese are, and have at all times been, so well at home in their own literature, that we may depend on this statement as a proof at least of no similar mission being mentioned in any recognised record as having gone further west previous to Kan Ying; and this again implies that no Chinese has proceeded to the

Far West in an official capacity; for such a fact would have been duly noted in the State Annals. If any Chinese subject did at all penetrate to the west, previous to Kan Ying, he must have been a private traveller, and one who either never returned to China, or did so without calling public or official attention to his journey. If the Seres mentioned by Florus were actually Chinese they must have come by way of India, and with the Indian envoys; they did certainly not come from the court of Han. The only official mission which might have gone forward from China to Ta-ts'in direct is that of Ts'in-lun, a Syrian merchant, who had come to some port in Cochin China and was sent on to the emperor of Wu, one of the three states contending for the supremacy during the third century A.D., Sun-ch'üan, *alias* Ta-ti (A.D. 222-252). This monarch asked him for an account of his country; and the details of his reply were perhaps contained in the *Wu-shih-wai-kuo-chuan* (吳時外國傳), regarding which I regret to have obtained no information beyond the fact of its being quoted in certain cyclopedias.[1] Ts'in-lun supplied the information required, and, on seeing some small men of Yi and Hsi[2] which the

---

[1] *See* pp. 20, 168 (Note 3); cf. p. 238.

[2] *Yi* (黟, commonly written 黟), and *Hsi* (歙). Mr. Parker draws my attention to the fact having escaped my notice that these two characters, which I translated by "blackish coloured" (p. 48, H 10), represent geographical terms. The latter is identical with the city of Hui-chou-fu in An-huei (lat. 29° 59', long. 118° 28'), the former is a district city in the immediate neighbourhood of it (lat. 30° 05', long. 117° 58'; *see* Playfair, *The Cities and Towns of China*, Nos. 8579 and 2614).

Chinese of the state of Wu had made prisoners in a campaign against the people of Tan-yang [=part of the present Kiang-nan Province] under the general Chu-ko K'o (a nephew of K'ung-ming, the great supporter of Liu Pei, the Minor Han Emperor), he remarked that such dwarfs would be considered a great curiosity in Ta-ts'in. The Wu Emperor thereupon ordered an official, Liu Hsien, a native of Kuei-chi (the present Chekiang,-Playfair, No. 3817) to accompany Ts'in-lun back to Ta-ts'in with twenty dwarfs, ten male and ten female. The official died en route and Ts'in-lun went home. So far the Chinese records.[1] The mission,

---

[1] See Translations H 8–10. Von Richthofen (*China*, Vol. I, p. 510, note 1) was again misled by a very faulty translation of this passage, and it seems that Julien's "Examen Critique" (*Syntaxe Nouvelle*, Vol. II) has not had the desired effect on some of the scholars dealing with sinological matters as far as Pauthier is concerned. This industrious writer, "dont j'estime le'zèle et dont j'apprécie les efforts"— with Julien, may be useful enough in suggesting that information regarding certain subjects may be found in certain works he has come across; but I would advise all oriental scholars not knowing Chinese not to accept a single sentence out of his translations without having it compared and checked over with the Chinese text by a competent Chinese scholar. The passage referred to (H 8–10) appears as follows in Pauthier's version (*Journ. Asiat.*, IIIe Série, Vol. VIII, p. 281): "La cinquième des années *Hoang-wu* de *Sun-kiouan*, il y eut un marchand du *Ta-thsin*, ou de l'empire romain, du nom de *Thsin-lûn*, *Lûn* le Romain, qui vint dans le *Kiao-tchi* (le Tonquin). Le gouverneur de *Kiao-tchi*, nommé *Ou-mo*, envoya ce marchand, et l'accompagna en personne près du souverain chinois *Kiouan* (devenu *Ta-ti*). Ce dernier l'interrogea sur les chants, les mœurs de son pays. *Lûn* répondit à toutes les questions qui lui furent faites sur les choses. Dans ce temps-là on se donnait de peine pour chercher le breuvage de l'immortalité dans toutes les plantes nourissières. C'étaient de petits hommes dont le teint tirait sur le noir, qui s'occupaient ainsi de

it appears, has never been heard of again in China, which may have suggested the idea of Liu Hsien's death. I am not aware of mention being made of the arrival of any such dwarfs in western authors. Possibly the dwarfs died as well, if Ts'in-lun succeded at all in reaching his home.

---

faire des dupes au grand jour. *Lûn.* en les voyant, dit que ces hommes se montraient rarement dans le *Ta-thsin*. *Kouan* (le roi de *Ou*) chargea des magistrats d'examiner l'affaire de dix de ces hommes avec autant de femmes, après quoi ils furent tous mis à mort. On reconduisit *Lûn* pendant toute la route avec ses bagages, et il s'en retourna alors dans son pays natal." The Chinese text does not contain a word about Ts'in-lun's baggage, the mention of which caused von Richthofen to think of a lengthy over-land journey to Chiao-chih ("was auf eine grössere Landreise deutet").

LINGUISTIC RESULTS.

The foreign names identified in the foregoing researches belong to a variety of very different languages, and some of them have come down to us through channels quite different from those through which they came to China. We ought not, therefore, to expect results as uniform as are those represented in Julien's[1] and Eitel's[2] lists; for, these were based on identifications more certain and less dependent on personal opinion than is the list offered herewith. The degree of certainty with which these foreign and Chinese sounds may be compared to each other depends, in the first instance, on the identifications of localities, etc., put forward, and some of these it will be remembered have been suggested as mere possibilities. However, the Chinese ancient and mediæval literature regarding the west is as yet an unworked mine; and I hope that, after years of patient research, we shall see the day when Western and Central Asiatic geography will be considered a rich source for the study of

---

[1] *Méthode pour déchiffrer et transcrire les Noms Sanscrits qui se rencontrent dans les Livres Chinois.* Paris, 1861.

[2] *Handbook for the Student of Chinese Buddhism.* Hongkong, 1870.

Chinese old sounds, and when this modest list will attain the size of the books of Sanscrit transliterations now on record.

1. a 阿=a in *Alani* (Plin., IV, 12 (25), 80.), p. 139.
2. a 阿=ak in *Akmatan* (Acbatana), p. 154.
3. an 安=an in *Antiochia*, p. 208.
4. an 安=an in *Antoninus*, p. 175.
5. an 安=ar in *Arsak*, p. 139 seq.
6. an 奄=aor in *Aorsi*, Ἄορσοι (Strab. XI, p. 492), p. 139.
7. an 安=ur, er, or in *Uruku, Erek, Orchoë*, pp. 139 and 155 seq.
8. chan 苫=*Shám* or *Shem*, i.e., Syria, p. 56.
9. chia (kia) 加 or 伽, see ka.
10. chia (kia) 袈=ga in *Gaza* (?), p. 259.
11. chien (kien) 鞬=kem in *Rekem*, p. 170.
12. ch'ih 暹=lek (dik) in *A-lek-san*, Alexandria, pp. 181 and 182.
13. fei 吠=be in *belor*, p. 230.
14. fo 佛=but; bud in *Buddha*, p. 289.
15. fu 拂=but; or beth in *Bethlehem*, p. 287 seqq.
16. ha 哈=kha in *khara*, p. 249.
17. ho 曷=grid, klath, in *tigrid, deklath* (Tigris)? p. 198.
18. hu 琥=chu in *chubich*; keher in *keherbaë*, har in *harpax* (?), p. 245.
19. hua 花=wa, ba, wat (?), bat (?), beth (?) in *Bethlehem*, p. 290.
20. hsi (sih) 悉=sa in *jásamin*, p. 270 seq.

21. hsi (sih) 息=sak in *Arsak*, p. 139 seq.
22. hsien (hien) 軒=kem in *Rekem*, p. 170.
23. hsün (hiün) 熏=ghyun in *ghyunluk*, p. 267.
24. ka 加 or 伽=ka in *theriaka*, p. 277.
25. kai 攺=kai in *Kaisar*, p. 300.
26. kan 軒=kam in *Rekam*, p. 170.
27. ku 谷=ku in *Uruku* (=*Orchoë*), p. 139 and 155 seq.
28. la 喇=ra in *Khara*, p. 249.
29. lan 蘭=lan in *Alani* (Plin., IV, 12 (25), 80), p. 139.
30. li 力 { =rik in *bathrik*, p. 294.
 =lek in *melek;* *Melekshah, Milikshah;* p. 298.
31. li 利=leu in *Seleu-cia* (?), p. 198.
32. li 黎 or 犁=re in *Rekam*, p. 170.
33. li 璃=r in *belor*, p. 230.
34. li 離=r in *belor*, p. 230.
35. li 里=r in *Merw*, p. 142.
36. lin 林=lim; lehem in *Bethlehem* (?), p. 290.
37. lin 林, or 麻=lim or lám; lehem in *Bethlehem*, 289 seqq.
38. liu 瑠=lo in *belor*, p. 230.
39. liu 流=lo in *belor*, p. 230.
40. lo 羅=ra in *Hira*, p. 151; leu or leuk in *Seleukia*, p. 197.
41. lo 羅=lem in *Hierusalem* (?), p. 204. The same character is made to represent the syllable *ram* in *Abram* (Abraham) in old

texts handed down at the Jewish temple in K'ai-fêng-fu, in which this name appears as *A-lo* 阿羅. See *Chin. Rep.*, Vol. XX, p. 459.

42. *lu* 鹿=*ru* in *Môuru*, possibly *rg* in *Murg* and *Marg-iana*, p. 142.
43. *lu* 魯=*rw* in *Merw*, or *ru* in *Môuru*, p. 142.
44. *lu* 陸=*luk* in *ghyunluk*, p. 267.
45. *ma* 馬=*môu* in *Môuru*, or *Me* in *Merw*, p. 142.
46. *ma* 麻=*me* in *Merw*, p. 142.
47. *man* 蠻=*matan* in *Akmatan* (Acbatana), p. 154.
48. *mieh* 滅=*me* in melek, p. 298.
49. *ming* 茗=*min* in *jásamin*, p. 270 seq.
50. *mu* 木=*môu* in *Môuru*, p. 142.
51. *na* 那=NO in *Ala*NO (Alani, Plin., IV, 12 (25), 80), p. 139.
52. *p'an* 番=*par* in old Persian *Parthuva*, p. 139.
53. *pi* 璧=*be* in *belor*, p. 230.
54. *pin* 賓=*phon* in *Ktesiphon*, p. 154 seq.
55. *po* 珀=*bi*ch in chu*bi*ch; *baï* in keher*baï*; *pag* in har*pag* (?), p. 245.
56. *po* 波=*per* in *Persia*, p. 198.
57. *po* 波=*ba* in *bathrik*, p. 294.
58. *sa* 薩=*sa* in *Hierusalem* (?), p. 204.
59. *sa* 撒=*sar* in *Kaisar*, p 300.
60. *san* 散=*san* in *A-lek-san*, *Alexandria*, p. 181, 182.
61. *sha* 裟=*za* in *Gaza* (?), p. 259.
62. *su* 宿=*se* in *Seleucia* (?), p. 198.

63. ssŭ 斯 =si in *Ktesiphon*, p. 154 seq.; *se* in *Seleucia*, p. 197; *si* in *Persia*, p. 198.
64. ta 達 =ti in *tigrid* (Tigris) or *de* in *deklath* (Tigris)?, p. 198.
65. ti 底 =the in *theriaka*, p. 277.
66. to 多 =tha in *batharekah, bathrik*, p. 294.
67. tou 兜 =thu or *thuva* in old Persian *Parthuva*, p. 139.
68. tu 都 =tio (του) in *Antiochia*, p. 208.
69. tun 敦 =ton in *Antoninus*, p. 175.
70. ts'ai 蔡 =SO or S in Ἄοϱσοι (*Aorsi*, Strab., XI, p. 492), p. 139.
71. wu 烏 =a in Alexandria, p. 182.
72. wu 兀 =w in *Merw*, p. 142.
73. yang 秧 =hieru in *Hierusalem* (?), p. 204.
74. yeh 耶 =jâ in *jâsamîn*, p. 270 seq.
75. yeh 也 or 野 =ria in *theriaka*, p. 277.
76. yü 于 =hi in *Hira;* ho or *kho* in Hotien, Khoten, p. 151.

GENERAL INDEX.

A.

ACBATANÀ; see A-MAN.

AELANA (Aïla), the port of, 160, 164, 173.

AÏLA; see AELANA.

AKKA nation, the, 203 seq.

A-LAN-NA (a nation=the Alani), 139 (note 1).

ALEXANDRIA ad Margum; see ANTIOCHIA MARGIANA.

ALEXANDRIA, a city near the Chaldæan Lake, possibly the city of T'iao-chih, 150 (note).

ALEXANDRIA Charakos; see CHARAX SPASINU.

ALEXANDRIA in Egypt, a centre of oriental traffic, 158; trade to, known to the Chinese of the Wei period, 180 seqq.; 199.

A-MAN (=Acbatana), 143 (note 1); 154; 195; 224.

AMAZONS, 200 seqq.

AMBASSADORS enjoying postal privileges, 221.

AMBER, found in Syria; the Syrians trading in; etymology of the Chinese word for, 245 (note 1).

AN-HSI (country) identified with Parthia, 138 seq.; described in the Ch'ien-han-shu, 139; described in the Hou han-shu, 141; name, transferred to the Sassanide empire during period of the Three Kingdoms, 198.

ANIMALS in Ta-ts'in, 219 seqq.

AN-KU, city of An-hsi; perhaps Orchoë, 139 (note 1); 155; or Charax Spasinu, 156; overland routes in three directions dividing at, 187; in the neighbourhood of Tsê-san, 190.

ANNAM, the terminus of early missions to the Far East; furnishing articles of tribute offered to the Chinese court by Ta-ts'in travellers, 176 seq.; 274.

AN-TI, the emperor, 180.

ANTIOCH (An-tu), the capital of Ta-ts'in, 207 seq.; plan of the city according to classical sources, 209; its division into four quarters, 210; its circuit at different times, 211; its size, 212; its city walls and east gate; a clepsydra placed on one of its gates, 213; siege of, by the Arabs, 295 seqq.

ANTIOCHIA MARGIANA (=Mu-lu), 141 seqq.; 224.

AN-TS'AI (a nation=the Aorsi), 139 (note 1).

AORSI; see AN-TS'AI.

Aquilaria Agallocha, Roxb., 275 (note 1).

ARABIA PETREA, 195.

GENERAL INDEX.

ARCHIVES, STATE: at all times well cared for in China, 9.
ARISTOTLE on Silk, 258 seq.
ASBESTOS CLOTH, 249 seqq.
ATTALICÆ VESTES, 253 seq.

B.

BABYLONIA; see T'IAO-CHIH.
BABYLONICA (rugs and carpets) 253.
BAKTISHUA; Christian physicians, translating Greek authors into Arab, 304.
BALANOS (fruit), 63 (note 1).
BARTER trade in Ceylon, 279 seqq.
BATUTA, Ibn, 205.
BEAR, The Black, 220.
BELOR, meaning "glass," the word from which Chinese *liu-li* may be derived, 230.
BENK, 278 seq.
BENTRA, Nicolaus de, 65 (note 1).
BERENICE 158.
BERYTUS, city, 158.
BEWSHER, Lieut., survey of Babylonian tracts, 147; 194 (note 1).
BOYM, M., 61 (note 1).
BRETSCHNEIDER, Dr. E., 4; 38 (note 2); 55 (note 2); 61; 62 (note 1); 64 (note 1); 65 (note 1); 67 (note 1); 140 (note 1); 142 (note 2); 170; 184; 198 (note 1); 199; 220 (note 1); 238; 240; 255; 262; 271 (note 1); 272 (note 4); 276 (note 1); 288 (note); 293; 299; *ibid.* (note 1).
BRIDGE, FLYING, 187; 192 seq.
BRIDGMAN, E. C., 46 (note 2); 61 (note 1); 243 (note 1).
BROCA, P., 302.

BUNBURY, E. H., 142 (note 1); 143 (note 1); 144 (note 1); 149 (note 1); 192 (note 1); 194 (note 1); 224 (note 1).
BURCKHARDT, J. L., discovers the ruins of Petra, 161.
BYSSUS, 254; 262.

C.

CANOBUS, 183.
CANTON may have been opened to trade by the mission of A.D. 284, p. 271 seq.; 274.
CARBUNCLES, 243.
CASPIAN called "Western Sea" (*hsi-hai*), 146; small sea (*hsiao hai*), *ibid.* (note 1).
"CATALOGUE, THE," of the Imperial Library, see *Ssu-k'u-ch'üan-shu-tsung-mu.*
CENSUS taken in China A.D. 740, p. 52 (note 2).
CEYLON, 178; the "spirit" or "devil" market at, 279 seq.
CHALDÆA; see T'IAO-CHIH.
CHALDÆAN LAKE, Preface, ix; 147 seqq.
CHANG CH'IEN, the explorer about B.C. 120, pp. 46 (note 1); 137; 169; 279 (note 1).
CHAO JU-KUA, author of the *Chu-fan-chih*: his notes regarding Ta-ts'in mostly not original, 22; conjectures regarding the time during which he wrote, 23 seqq.
CHARAX SPASINU, 156; 190.
CH'Ê-CH'Ü, 79 (note 2).
CH'ÊN-HSIANG, 275 (note 1).
CH'ÊN SHOU, author of the *San-kuo-chih*, 13.
Chêng-tzŭ-t'ung, 273 (note 1).

CHI-CHANG (rugs, curtains?), 255.
CH'IAI-SHU: style of writing in use since ancient times, 9.
CH'IEH-LAN, 193 seq.; 195.
Ch'ien-han-shu (Dynastic History), 3; early editions of, 7; quoted, *passim*.
CH'IEN TA-HSIN, writes on old sounds, 289 (note 1).
CHIH-CHIA; *see* HENNA.
CH'IH-SAN (= Alexandria), 181 seqq.; 199.
CH'IH-SHUI (Red Water), 292 seq.
CH'IH-T'U (country), 215.
Chin-shu (Dynastic History), 16; quoted, *passim*.
Ching-chuan-chi-chieh, 272.
Chiu-t'ang-shu (Dynastic History), 17; quoted, *passim*.
CHLOROPHANE, 243.
Chu-fan-chih, 21 seq.; quoted, *passim*; *see also* CHAO JU-KUA.
CHU-KO K'O, 48; 306.
CH'Ü-SOU (rugs), 255.
Ch'un-ch'iu-shih-lieh, 272.
CITIES, number of, in Ta-ts'in, 218 seq.
CLEPSYDRA at the city of Antioch, 213 seq.
CLOTH, various kinds of, manufactured in Ta-ts'in, 247 seqq.; the Roman Orient known for the manufacture of, 252; Babylonian kinds, 253; Attalic 253 seq.; woven from different materials, 254 seq.; musters described, *ibid.*; silk, 255; Coic, 295 seq.; Hai-hsi-pu, 263.
COCHIN-CHINA; *see* ANNAM.
COICÆ VESTES, 259 seq.
COINS, Parthian, 140; Roman, possibly brought to China by mission of A.D. 166, p. 177.

COLLINGWOOD, Lieut., surveys, 147.
COLOURS, translation of, doubtful, 73 (notes 2 and 3); 255 (note 1).
COPPER, 275.
CORALS and CORAL-FISHING, 246 seq.
COURT CHRONICLERS, 10; *cf.* JIH-LI.
CRYSTAL, Chinese and Roman lore regarding, 233 (note 1); as an architectural ornament, 238 seq.; produced in Syria, 239.

D.

DAILY CHRONICLES; *see* JIH-LI.
DAMASCUS, 195; 301.
DAMASK BLADES, 301.
DAMGHAN, 143 (note 1); 154.
DARMESTETER, J., 142 (note 2).
DE GUIGNES, J., (père), 4; 28; 29; 30; 40 (note 1); 139 (note 1); 140 (note 2); 150 (note); 152 (note 1); 238; 298; 299; 300.
DENNYS, N. B., 63.
DEPENDENT STATES, 189 seqq.
DISTANCES in *li* should be understood to be in stadia, 142; 212; 222 seq.; accuracy of, in Chinese records, illustrated, 224.
DOURSTHER, 223 (note 1).
DWARFS, 202; 305.

E.

'ECEÔN-GEBER, 160.
EDESSA, 193; 298.
EDKINS, DR. J., 4; 18; 170; 202; 273; 288; 289 (note 1).
EDRISI, 16.
EGYPT, comprised under the name Ta-ts'in, 180 seq.; 216.
ÊLATH, *see* AELANA.

EMBASSIES, alleged, from China to Rome, 304 seqq.

EMBASSIES and other Missions from Ta-ts'in to China:—

A.D. 120 (jugglers and musicians), 169.

A.D. 166 (An-tun): in what month arrived, 42 (note 1); opening the sea-route to China, 173; doubtful tradition as to year of arrival according to Sung authors, 174 (note 1); a commercial mission, 175 seqq.

A.D. 226 (Ts'in-lun), 306.

A.D. 284 (the paper mission): may have landed at Canton, 271 (note 2); offering paper as tribute, 272; a private mission, 274.

A.D. 643 (Po-to-li), 293 seqq.

A.D. 667 (the Theriac mission), 276 seqq.

A.D. 719 (priests), 284 (*see* note 2).

A.D. 1081, p. 298 seqq.

A.D. 1368 (?): Nicolaus de Bentra identified with, 65 (note 1).

EMBROIDERING, 253 seqq.

EMERALDS, where found, 244.

EMESA, 194.

Erh-shih-ssŭ-shih; *see* HISTORIES. DYNASTIC.

ERYTHRÆAN PERIPLUS; *see* SEA, WESTERN, and SEA-ROUTE, etc.

EUPHRATES, navigation of the, Preface, ix seq.; 148 seq.; 150 (note); crossed between Hira and Seleucia 197; its being navigated on in skin boats may have recalled the Weak Water legend to the Chinese mind, 291; 293.

F.

FA HSIEN: his account of Ta-ch'in referred to Ta-ts'in by the *T'u-shu-chi-ch'êng*, 26; on the "devil market" in Ceylon, 280.

FAN YEH, author of the *Hou-han-shu*, 6.

FANG CH'IAO, author of the *Chin-shu*, 16.

Fang shu-ch'ien-li: meaning of the phrase, 214 seq.

FICHTE, J. G., 153.

Fo-kuo-chi; see FA HSIEN.

FRAAS, O., Preface, xii; 245 (note 1).

FRANKINCENSE, 266 seqq.

FRANKS, the name, in the sense of Europeans, when first used, 288 (note).

FREYTAG, G. W. F., 223.

FRIEDLAENDER, L., 167; 175 (note 1); 176 (note 1); 212; 221 (note 1); 225 (note 2); 227; 240 (note 1); 245 (note 1); 254 (note 2); 260 (note).

FU-LIN: name when first used, 17; 286 seq.; 288 (note); its territory, 217; accounts analysed, 283 seq.; reports regarding, bear an ecclesiastical stamp, 284 seqq.; identified, 286 seqq.; different Chinese characters used in writing the name, 287 (and *ibid.* note 1); various etymologies suggested by others, (*ibid.* note 2); probable old sound of name, *bat-lim*, 288 seq.; the Nestorians substitute the name Bethlehem for that of Ta-ts'in, 290; conquered by Arabs, 295, seqq.; a Seldjuk province, 297 seq.

FU-NAN (country), 47 (note 1); 215; visited by the Chinese traveller K'ang T'ai, 169 (note).

GENERAL INDEX.

G.

GABELENTZ, G. von der, 29.
GALLE, the port of, in Ceylon 281.
GAROO WOOD, 275 (note 1).
GAUBIL, A., 24.
GAUZE: derivation of the word, 259 (note 1).
GAZA, 162; 259 (note 1).
GEERTS, A. J. C., 46 (note 2); 53 (notes 2 & 3); 57 (note 1); 59 (note 1); 72 (note 2); 229; 233 (note 2); 242.
GEMS; *see* PRECIOUS STONES; LUMINOUS GEMS.
GIBBON, E., 44 (note 2); 168 (note 1); 218; 219 (note 2); 221 (note 2); 288 (note).
GIESELER, J. K. L., 295 (note 1).
GILES, H. A., 26 (note 1); 243 (note 1); 280; 285 (note); 302.
GLASS industry in Ta-ts'in, 228 seqq. ten colours produced, 228; *liu-li* and *po-li*, how distinguished, *ibid.*; originally classed with precious stones, 229 seq.; derivation of the Chinese word for, 230; when first manufactured in China, 230 seqq.; gradually depreciates in the estimation of the Chinese, 233 seq.; replacing crystal and precious stones as an architectural ornament, 239.
GOLD, 275.
GOLD EMBROIDERIES, 253 seq.
GOLD-POWDER, 236 (note 2).
GOLD, YELLOW, etc., 53 (note 3).
GROSIER, l'Abbé, 231.
GUIGNES, J. DE; *see* DE GUIGNES, J.

H.

HA-LA-NI, Chinese name for Russian Cloth, whence derived, 249.
HAI-HSI (country on the west of the sea), 72 (note 1); 163 seq.
Hai-kuo-t'u-chih, quoted, *passim*.
HAI-LIAO, 22 (note 1).
HAI-PEI (country north of the sea = Mesopotamia?), 187 seq.; 219.
HAI-TUNG (countries on the east of the sea), 72 (note 1); 163 seq.
HANBURY, DAN., 5; 264; *ibid.* (note 2); 266 (note 1); 267 (note 1); 275 (note 1).
HANCE, Dr. H. F., 264; 270 (note 1).
HEEREN, A. H. L., 162; 240; 261 (note 3).
HEHN, V., 63 (note 1); 256 (note 2).
HEKATOMPYLOS, capital of Parthia, 139 (note 1); 141; its site near the present Damghan confirmed in Chinese records, 143 (note 1); route from, to the west, 153 seqq.
HEMP, foreign, introduced in China by Chang Ch'ien, 279 (note 1); known in ancient China as a narcotic, *ibid.*
HENNA, 268 seqq.
D'HERBELOT, 278 seq.; 294; 300; 304. *Cf.* VISDELOU.
D'HERVAIS DE ST. DENYS, translator of Ma Tuan-lin's geographical chapters, 20 (note 2).
HILLS, ranges of, 195 seq.
HIRA (=city of T'iao-chih, and Yü-lo), Preface, ix seq.; 148 seqq.; 196 seq.; the kingdom of, its origin, 149 (note 2).
HIRSCH, A., 175 (note 1).

HISTORICAL WRITERS, official: from what materials they drew their information on foreign countries, 10 seqq.

HISTORIES, DYNASTIC, impartiality of, 1 seq.; information regarding Ta-ts'in contained in which, 2 seqq.

HOECK, K. F. C., 227.

HO-TU (=Hekatompylos), 141.

HORSES, WHITE, with red manes, 73 (note 1); 269 (note 1).

Hou-han-shu (Dynastic History), 3 seqq.; its trustworthiness, 7; early editions of, 7 seq.; quoted, *passim*.

HSI-NÜ; see AMAZONS.

HSI-WANG-MU, 292 seq.

HSI-YÜ-CHUAN (chapter on western countries in Dynastic Histories), 4; from what materials compiled, 11.

Hsiao-chin-chi-yüan, a collection of reprints, 21.

HSIAO-JÊN; see PYGMIES.

HSIEH-CHI-HSI (chicken-frightening rhinoceros), 79 (note 1).

HSIEN-TU, 195 seq.

Hsin-t'ang-shu (Dynastic History), 18; preferred by Ma Tuan-lin to *Chiu-t'ang-shu* in quoting, 86 (note 2); quoted, *passim*.

HSÜ CHIA-KUANG, manager of a Chinese Publishing Company, 8 (note 1).

Hsü-wên-hsien-t'ung-k'ao, the continuation of Ma Tuan-lin's work, 23.

HSÜAN-CHUANG's Journeys; see *Ta-t'ang-hsi-yü-chi*.

HSUN-LU (=Frankincense), 263 seqq.; the word, related to Turkish *ghyunluk*, 267.

HU (foreign), the term, 70 (note 1); applied to western silk textures, 259; *Hu* people, 268; 271 seq.

HU-MANG (date), 204.

HUA-LIN, "the flowery groves," in Nestorian Inscription, may stand for Fu-lin, 290 seq.

HUC, Abbé, 21 seq.; 61 (note 1); 92 (note 1).

HUMBOLDT, A. von, 138 (note 1).

HUO-HUAN-PU; see ASBESTOS CLOTH

HYENA (=Ts'ung?) 220.

I.

ICHTHYOPHAGI, 204 seqq.

IMBAULT-HUART, C., 7 (note 2).

INDIA: glass industry said to have been introduced from, 231 (note 1); trade with, 158; 165; 168; 183; 226 seq.

INDIAN OCEAN, average speed of ancient navigation in, 168.

INTERPRETERS, foreign, at the court of China, 11; when appointed by the Roman emperors, 44 (note 2).

IRON, exported from China for the Roman market, 225 (note 2); where produced during Han dynasty, 226 (note).

J.

JACKAL (=Ts'ung?) 220.

JACQUET, M., 287 (note 2).

JADEITE, 46 (note 2); 55 (note 1); 59 (note 2).

Jao-hai, the term, 184 seqq.

Jasminum Sambac, L.; see MO-LI-HUA.

Jasminum Officinale, L.; see YEH-HSI-MING.

JERUSALEM (=Yang-sa-lo?), 204.

GENERAL INDEX.

JIH-LI, or "Daily Chronicles," 1.
JONES, WM., 235; 236.
JO-SHUI, (Weak Water), 291 seqq.
JUGGLERS, 80 (note 2); 169; 179 seq.
JU-HSIANG (= Frankincense), 266 seqq.
JULIEN, Stan., 6; 17 (note 1); 29; 35 (note 1); 181 (note 1); 190 (note 1); 201 (notes 1 and 2); 202 (note 2); 204 (note 1); 259 (note 1); 266 (note 2); 307 (note 1).

K.

KAISAR (Cæsar), the title, used by Arab and Seldjuk kings, 300.
KALLENBERG, C., 247 (note 2).
KA-NA-TIAO-CHOU, a port (?) whence one could reach Ta-ts'in, 169 (note).
KAN YING, special commissioner, sent by Pan Ch'ao to explore Ta-ts'in, 13; 138; reached what point in T'iao-chih, 149; his intended sea-journey, 164 seqq.; the first traveller to the Far West, 305.
K'ANG T'AI, a Chinese traveller of the Wu period, 169 (note)
KAO-TSUNG, emperor, 7.
KARKA (=Charax), 156 (note 1).
KEMPTHORNE, Lieut., 206.
KERBELA, city of, 152.
KHOTEN, the name, 151 (note 1).
KIEPERT, H., 139 (note 1); 142 (note 2); 147; *ibid.* (note 1); 148; 155 (note 1); 156 (note 1); 160 (notes 1 and 2); 191 (note 1); 197 (note 1).
KINGSMILL, T. W., 153 (note); 156; 293.

KIRCHER, Athan., 61 (note 1).
KLAPROTH, J., 79 (note 2); 138 (note 1); 176 (note 1); 245 (note 1).
KLUNZINGER, C. B., 247.
KOCHE (=Seleucia), 197.
KOPTOS, 158; 182.
KOSEIR, the port of, 247.
KRINOS, Prof., 265.
KTESIPHON, land-road from, to Hira, 148; *i. q.*, Ssŭ-pin, 152; 154 seq.; captured by the Romans, 174; having a long range of hills north of it, 195 seq.
Kuei-huan-hsing-ching-chi, wrongly quoted by Ma Tuan-lin for *Tu-huan-hsing-ching-chi* (a work of the T'ang dynasty), 95 (note 1).
KUO-TZŬ-CHIEN, the Imperial Academy of Learning, 7 (note 2).

L.

LAO-PO-SA; *see* ICHTHYOPHAGI.
LAPIS LAZULI (?), 72 (note 2).
Lawsonia inermis, L,; *see* HENNA.
LEGGE, Dr. J., 214 seq.; 291 seq.
LEI-SHU or Cyclopedias: quoting passages relating to Ta-ts'in, 14; 19.
LETRONNE, J. A., 176 (note 1).
LEUKE KOME, a port trading with Petra, 162.
LI (road-measure=stadium), 142; 152, 153 seqq.; 164; 187; 191 seq.; 194; 196; 204; 205 (note 2); 211; 214; 222 seqq.; (=passus), 192; 193 (note).
LIBANON range of hills, 196.

GENERAL INDEX.

LI-KAN, Li-chien, etc. Sound of this name, 77 (note 1); west of An-hsi; not known before A.D. 120, p. 137; various modes of writing the name in Chinese, 170 (note 1); etymologies, *ibid.*; identified with Rekem or Petra, 169 seqq.; a market for silk and landing dépôt for oriental goods, 171; 173; jugglers from, 169; *cf.* 179 seq.

LI-KAN T'IAO-CHIH, as a double name: either Syria and Babylonia, 146, or the country of the Nabathaeans and Chaldaeans, 172.

LIANG CHI, 251.

Liang-shu (Dynastic History), 16; quoted, *passim*.

LING (=damask or gauze), 257 seq.

LINGUISTIC RESULTS; 309 seqq.

LIONS in Ta-ts'in, 187; 219 seq.; 220; 221 (note 1).

LIU-LI; *see* GLASS.

LIU-SHA, or Flying Sands, p. 292 seq.

LOFTUS, W. K., Map of Chaldaea, etc., 147 (note 1); his excavations near Shuster, 198 (note 1).

LUMINOUS GEMS, 242 seq.

LÜ-CHIN-CHING (=gold-powder?), 236 (note 2).

LÜ-FÊN, 191 seqq.

M.

MADAIN, capital of the Sassanide kings, 198.

MAGADHA, the name of Buddha's birth-place, applied to India, 290.

MANNERT, K., 139 (note 1).

MANUSCRIPT LITERATURE: well regulated in China before the period of printing, 9.

MARC AUREL, his alleged embassy to China; *see* EMBASSIES, A.D. 166.

MARQUARDT, J., 227.

MAS'UDI, Preface, ix; 144 (note 1); 150 (note); 208.

MA TUAN-LIN, author of the *Wên-hsien-t'ung-k'ao*: his merits as a geographical writer, 20 seq.; quoted. *passim*.

MAYERS, W. F., 7 (note 2); 13 (note 1); 25 (note 1); 80 (note 1); 233; 272 (note 3); 292; 302.

MELEK, as a title, meaning an under-king during the Seldjuk rule, 298.

MERW, city of, 142 (note 2).

MESNY, Wm., 229.

MESOPOTAMIA, 187 seq.

MI-HSIANG-CHIH (paper), 272 seqq.

MI-HSIANG-SHU (=*Aquillaria Agallocha*, Roxb.?), 272 seqq.

MIEH-LI-I-LING-KAI-SA cannot be the name of Michael VII Parapinaces, but must be the title of a Seldjuk under-king, 298 seqq.

MIEH-LI-SHA (=Milikshah), 298.

MILE, ARABIAN (=*t'ing*) *see* MILLIARY SYSTEM.

MILLIARY SYSTEM: parasangs, Arabian miles, stadia, 222 seqq.; *see* LI.

Ming-shih (Dynastic History), 19.

MOELLENDORFF, Dr. O. F. von, 288 (note).

MO-LI-HUA (*Jasminum Sambac*, L.), 268; 270 seq.

MO-LIN; *see* ICHTHYOPHAGI.

MOLTKE, Count von, 193 (note).

MOMMSEN, TH., 172.

MOSHEIM, J. L. von, 65 (note 1).

Mōuru (=Mu-lu), 141 seq.
Muavia, Governor-General of Syria, 297 (note 1); 301.
Muir, Sir Wm., 150 (note); 151 (note 1); 162 (note 3).
Mulberry, the, in Syria, 256.
Mu-lu, city of, 141 seq.
Mu-nan (a pearl), 59 (note 1); 80 (note 1).
Müller, K., 139 (note 1); 181 (note 2); 191 (note 2); 206 (note 1).
Müller, Otfried, 208.
Musicians from Ta-ts'in, 179 seq.
Muziris, a port in India, 168.
Myos Hormos, 158; 159 (note 1); fleet leaving, for India, 168; possibly the Chinese Wu-tan, 181; country about, inhabited by Ichthyophagi, 205 seq.

N.

Nabathaea, Preface, x (note 1); 159; 161; 172.
Nan-ch'i-shu (Dynastic History), 16.
Nan-fang-ts'ao-mu-chuang, an ancient botanical work, 20; 268 seqq; 270 seq.; 272 seqq.; 275 (note 1).
Navigation, average speed of ancient, in several seas, 167 seq.; 182 seq.
Nedjef, city of, Preface, ix; 148.
Negro Tribes: see Ichthyophagi.
Nesbitt, A., 228 (note 1).
Nestorian Inscription, 5 seq.; its genuineness, 6; characters of—represent the T'ang style of writing, 10; contains an account of Ta-ts'in, 19; says that Nestorians came from Ta-ts'in, 289 seq.; the expression *hua-lin* in, 290 seq.

Nestorians, 5; 284 seqq.; 304.
Neumann, K. F., 6; 10 (note 1); 37 (note 2); 70 (note 1); 140 (note 2); 146 (note 1); 157 (note 1); 199; 272; 288 (note).
Nicephorium, 193.
Nile, the river, 158; 181 seqq.

O.

Ocelis, a port in the Red Sea, 168.
Odorić, Friar, 261 seq.
Olibanum; see Hsün-lu.
Olin, S., 161 (note 2).
O-lo-pên (=Ruben, Rupen?), 285 seq.
Ophir, Solomon's fleet to, started from the Gulf of Akabah, 160.
Opium, possibly first brought to China in the disguise of a medicine, A.D. 667,—p. 278.
Orchoē, city; see An-ku.
Orontes, the river of Antioch, navigable, 214.
Orpiment, 275.
Ostrich-eggs of Rekem, 169.
Ouseley, Sir Wm., 288 (note).
Oxus (Kuei-shui), 139.

P.

Pallacopas Canal, 149.
Palmyra, 194.
Pan Chao, sister of Pan Ku, co-operates in compiling the *Chien-han-shu*, 3.
Pan Ch'ao, the exploring general, 3; 13; 46 (note 1); 138; his designs with regard to Ta-ts'in, peaceful, *ibid*. (note 1).

GENERAL INDEX.

PAN KU, author of the *Chien-han-shu*, 3; 138.

'AN-TOU (capital of An-hsi,=Parthuva), 139 (and note 1).

PAPER presented by Ta-ts'in to the court of China, 272 seqq.

PARASANG (=*chih* or *hou*); see MILLIARY SYSTEM.

PARAVEY, le Cher de, 6; 202 (note 3).

PARDESSUS, J. M., 256 (note 1).

PARKER, E. H., 122; 142 (note 2); 185 seq.; 207; 269 (note 1); 306 (note 2).

PARTHIA (=An-hsi); see AN-HSI; western boundary of, 147; overland route through: Hekatompylos to Chaldaea, 153 seqq.; the same route backwards, 157 (note 1); Roman war with, causing new trade route to China to be opened, 173.

PARTHIANS occupying Syria previous to B.C. 38,-p. 13; jealous of trade with China, 164 seq.

PAUTHIER, G., 6; 18; 22; 29; 30; 44 (note 1); 48 (note 3); 51 (note 2); 52 (note 1); 55 (note 2); 61 (note 1); 92 (note 1); 93 (notes 1 and 2); 170; 208; 261 (note 4); 273 (note 1); 274; 286 (notes 1 and 2); 287 (note 2); 290 (note 1); 293; 299; 307 (note 1).

PEARLS, 247.

PEGU, coast of, as a terminus of oriental trade, 179.

Pei-shih (Dynastic History), a reproduction of the *Wei-shu*, 17; 48; quoted, *passim*.

PEI SUNG-CHIH: compiles a commentary to the *San-kuo-chih*, 14.

Pên-ts'ac-kang-mu, a Chinese pharmacopœia, 14; 266 seqq.; 277; quoted, *passim*.

Pên-ts'ao-pin-hui-ching-yao, a manuscript pharmacopœia of A.D. 1506,-p. 277 (note 2).

PERSIA called An-hsi in Chinese records, 198; when first mentioned separately, *ibid*.

PESCHEL, O., 16; 167.

PETRA, city of, or Rekem, 27; the landing-stage, or port, of Ta-ts'in, 157 seqq.; its local names, 160; accounts of, by Olin and Muir, 160; seqq.; bifurcation of road east and west, 162.

PFIZMAIER, A., 79 (note 2); 229; 241.

PHILLIPS, G., Preface, viii; 24; 55 (note 2); 276; 284; 294.

PHŒNICIAN INDUSTRIES, 158 seq.

PHYSICIANS of Fu-lin, 301 seqq.

PILLARS and WALLS adorned with crystal, glass, and precious stones, a peculiarity of Syria, 240.

PLAGUE, the, under Marc Aurel, may have led to the opening of a direct sea-route to China, 175 (note 1); contemporaneous with an epidemic in China, *ibid*.

PLAYFAIR, G. M. H., 306 (note 2); 307.

PO-LI; *see* GLASS.

POLO, MARCO, 24; 25; 180; 205; 249 (note 1).

PO-SSŬ (=Persia), 199; *see* PERSIA.

POSTAL ARRANGEMENTS, 221 seqq.

PO-TO-LI, king of Fu-lin: name identified with *bathrik* (=patriarch), 293 seqq.

PRIAULX, DE BEAUVOIR, 150 (note); 158 (notes 1 and 2).

PRECIOUS STONES, 234 seqq.; glass imitations of, 237.

GENERAL INDEX.

PURPLE; five and nine colours of, 248.
PYGMIES, 200; 202 seqq.

R.

RAWLINSON, G., 140; *ibid.* (note 3); 224 (note 1).
REALGAR, 275.
REINAUD, J. T., 12; 178 (note 1).
REKEM; *see* PETRA.
RÉMUSAT, A., 20 (notes 1 and 2); 29; 37 (note 2); 65 (note 1); 138 (note 1); 146 (note 1); 157 (note 1).
RENAN, E., 6.
RHINOCEROS, the, in Chaldaea. Preface, x seqq.
RHINOKOLURA, 162.
RICCI, MATTH., 19; 67 (note).
RICHTHOFEN, F. VON, 4; 28; 153 (note); 287 (note 2); 307 (note 1).
RIEHMER, 160 (note 2).
ROADS in Ta-ts'in, 221 seq.
ROAD, the Royal, in Asia, 222 (note 1).
ROBBERS, absence of, in Ta-ts'in, 220.
ROCK, Very Rev., 253.

S.

SACHAROFF, F., 52 (note 2).
SACHAU, ED., 193 (note).
SADDLERY, 300 seq.
SÁDIK ISFAHÁNI, 288 (note).
SAMOSOTA, 193.
San-kuo-chih (Dynastic History), 13.
SCALIGER, J., sen., 261.
SCHATT-EL-AMÁRA, 155.

SCHNEIDER, O., 245 (note 1).
SCHOTT, W., 29.
SCHWEINFURTH, G., 203; 204.
SEA, RED, 49 (note 1); 81 (note 1); ports on its coast, 157 seqq.; 163 (*cf.* note 2); producing corals, 246; 291.
SEA-ROUTE from Babylonia to Petra, length of, 164; average speed of navigation on, compared with navigation in other seas, 167.
"SEA," the term, (*hai*) frequently substituted for "river" (*ho*), 76 (note 1); 192.
SEA, WESTERN (*hsi-hai*), the term, 146; 163; also called "Great Sea" (*ta-hai*) *ibid.* (note 1); navigation of, 157 seqq.; 164 seqq.
SELBY, Commr., survey of Babylonian tracts, 147.
SELDJUKS, the, rule over Fu-lin, 297 seqq.
SELEUCIA (=*Ssŭ-lo*), 151; destroyed by the Romans, 174; its site, 197.
SHÁM (Syria), 56 (note 2).
SHAN, country, 179 seq.; 190 (note 2).
SHÊN Yo, author of the *Sung-shu*, 16.
Shih-chi (Dynastic History), 2; quoted, *passim*.
Shih-chia-chai-yang-hsin-lu, 289 (note 1).
SHIH-KUAN; *see* COURT CHRONICLERS.
SHUI-YANG; *see* WATER-SHEEP.
SIDON, city, 158.
SILK: Li-kan and Ta-ts'in probably known to the Chinese at first as purchasers of this commodity, 137; why landed in Petra, and not in Egyptian ports, 158; dyed and remanufactured in Phœnicia, *ibid.*;

interruption in—trade owing to Parthian war causes the opening of a direct sea-route to China being attempted, 174; weighed up with gold in Rome, 225 (*see* note 2); produced in the north-west of China during the Han dynasty, 226 (note); whether the ancient Syrians could produce it, 255 seqq.; Chinese, unravelled and re-woven into gauzes, 257 seqq.; Coïc gauze, 259 seq.

SILVER, 275.

SINAI, desert of, 204.

SITTAKE, 194.

SIZE of Ta-ts'in, 214.

SKINS, exported from China during Han dynasty, 225 (note 2).

SMITH, PORTER, 37 (note 1).

"SPIRIT MARKETS," 279 seqq.

SPRUNER and MENKE, *Atlas Antiquus*, 150 (note); 208 seq.

SQUIER, E. G., 302.

STADIA; *see* MILLIARY SYSTEM.

STRAUSS, V. VON, 73 (note 2).

SU-LI (=Madain), 198.

SUN-CH'ÜAN, emperor, 16; 306.

SUN SHIH, edits the *Hou-han-shu*, 7.

Sung Shih (Dynastic History), 19; 23; 25; quoted, *passim*.

Sung-shu (Dynastic History), 16; quoted, *passim*.

Ssŭ-ch'ao-shih, historical work of the Sung dynasty, 91 (note 1).

SSŬ-FU, 194; 195.

Ssŭ-k'u-ch'üan-shu-tsung-mu, the "Catalogue of the Imperial Library at Peking," 7; 14; 22; 23.

SSŬ-LO; *see* SELEUCIA.

SSŬ-MA CH'IEN, author of the *Shih-chi*, 2.

SSŬ-PIN; *see* KTESIPHON.

SSŬ-T'AO, 194.

STAR STONES (Asteria), 242.

STONY LAND, The, 195.

STORAX, 263 seqq.

STREETER, on precious stones, 242.

SU-HO; *see* STORAX.

Sui-shu (Dynastic History), 17; quoted, *passim*.

SULTAN, the title, 298 seq.

SUSA, ancient, its site, 198 (note 1).

SWORD-BLADES of Damask, 301.

TA-HO-SHUI (=Tigris), 198.

Ta-t'ang-hsi-yü-chi, 17; 201; 287; 288 (note).

TA-TĔ-SĔNG (priests), 284 (note 2)

T'A-TĔNG (rugs), 255.

TA-TS'IN SHIH, 22.

TA-TS IN: the port of, 157 seqq.; size of the country, 214 seqq.

TA-YÜEH-CHIH, 231.

TAINTOR, E. C., 138 (note 1); 170; 268 (note 2); 270.

TAURUS range of hills, 196; 291.

TABERISTAN, 146 (note 1).

T'ang-pên-ts'ao, 276.

T'ang-shu; *see Chiu-t'ang-shu*; *Hsin-t'ang-shu*.

TAPROBANE; *see* CEYLON.

TENNENT, Sir J. E., 281 seqq.

TERRITORY of Ta-ts'in and Fu-lin: size of, 214 seqq.

TEXTILE FABRICS, 247 seqq.; 252 seqq.

TEXTS, Chinese: their treatment in former periods compared with the history of classical texts, 8-10.

THERIAC; *see* TI-YEH-KA.

GENERAL INDEX. 327

TI-YEH-KA, 276 seqq.

T'IAO-CHIH, country on the coast of the Persian Gulf, 13; formerly believed to be farther away from China than Ta-ts'in. 138; Kan Ying arrives in, *ibid.*; originally more powerful than An-hsi (Parthia), 143; 146; identified with Chaldaea, 144 seqq. cf. Preface, viii seqq.; account of, in the *Ch'ien-han-shu*, 145 (note 1); city of, 147 seq.; former identifications of, 152 (note 1); shipping-port of sea-route to Ta-ts'in, 157; site was south of the city of Madain and down river, 198; occurrence of the rhinoceros in, Preface, x seqq.

TIGERS in Ta-ts'in, 219.

TIGRIS, 155; 197 seq.

T'ING-SHIH, 22.

TO-LO-NI, Chinese name for broad-cloth, whence derived, 249.

T'O-T'O, author of the *Sung-shih*, 19.

TRADE, Indian and Chinese, to Rome, in what respect differing, 158 seq.; 173; profit derived from Chinese and Indian, 165; 225; nature of articles forming Chinese, 225 seqq.; value of Chinese, Indian, etc., import trade, 226 seqq.; articles of trade in China during the Han dynasty, 226 (note); Roman imports from China chiefly paid for in kind, 228; barter trade in Ceylon, 279 seqq.

TRADE ROUTES, 137 seqq.; overland through Parthia, 153 seqq; by sea from Chaldaea to Petra, 157 seqq.; sea-route from the Red Sea to China (or Annam) direct, 173 seqq.; by sea to the coast of Pegu, 179 seq.; overland from Parthia to Syria, 183 seqq.; through Mesopotamia, 187 seq.

TRANSLATING from the Chinese: comparative method of, 18; 21.

TRANSLATIONS of Chinese Notices of Ta-ts'in, 27; von Richthofen misled by de Guignes, 28; necessity for new, 29.

TRANSLATIONS of Chinese texts. 33 seqq.

TRAVELLING, safety of, in Ta-ts'in, 220.

Ts'ê-fu-yüan-kuei, 22.

TSÊ-SAN, tributary state of Ta-ts'in, 156; 190.

TS'IN-LUN, a merchant from Ta-ts'in, reaching China, 16; sent back to Rome with dwarfs, 306.

TS'UNG, a quadruped, 220.

TU-HU (a Chinese governor in Central Asiatic provinces), 139.

Tu-huan-hsing-ching-chi, 95 (note 1); 202.

T'u-shu-chi-ch'êng, the great cyclopedia in 5,000 vols., 25; new edition about to appear, *ibid.*, note; its accounts of Ta-ts'in and Fu-lin, 26.

TU YÜ: presented with paper for literary work, 272.

TUN-HSÜN (country), 216.

T'ung-chien-kang-mu contains an account of the Weak Water legends, 292: no notice regarding arrival of Roman embassy about A.D. 337 contained in, 305.

T'UNG-WÊN-SHU-CHÜ, a Chinese publishing company, 8; 25.

TYRE, city of, 158; 183 (note 1).

U.

URUF- (Orchoe), 155.

V

VARIANTS in Chinese text, 74 (notes 1 to 5); 87 (note 1); 88 (note 1); 90 (note 1); 92 (note 2); 95 (notes 1 and 2); 122; 195.

VEDDAHS, aborigines in Ceylon. identified with "spirits" or "devils" of Chinese records by Tennent, 282.

VISDÉLOU, C., 4; 18; 30; 40 (note 1); 48 (note 3); 49; *ibid.* (note 1); 56 (note 1); 59 (note 1); 61 (note 1); 79 (note 1); 140 (note 2); 152 (note 1); 222 (note 2); 280 (note); 290.

VOLOGESIA: possibly the Parthian name of the city of Hekatompylos, 141 (note 1); city near the Chaldaean lake, possibly the city of T'iao-chih, 150 (note).

VOLTAIRE, M. F., 6.

W.

WANG YU-CHÜN, the calligrapher, 9.

WATER-SHEEP (*shui-yang*), 260 seq.; referred to in *Hou-han-shu*, 54 (note 1).

Wei-lio: an important source of information regarding Ta-ts'in, 14 seqq.; part of Ma Tuan-lin's notes regarding Ta-ts'in may be derived from it, 21; quoted, *passim*.

Wei-shu (Dynastic History), 17; Ta-ts'in account identical with that found in *Pei-shih. ib.*; 48; quoted, *passim*.

Wên-hsien-t'ung-k'ao; *see* MA TUAN-LIN.

WÊN-TI, emperor of the early Sung dynasty, 14.

WILLIAMS, S.W., 72 (note 2); 230; 285 (note).

WU-CH'IH-SAN (= Alexandria), 182 seq.

Wu-shih-wai-kuo-chuan, 20; 168; 238; 306.

WU-TAN (a port in the Red Sea?), 181.

WYLIE, A., 3 (note 1); 6; 13 (note 1); 35 (note 2); 59 (note 1); 61 (note 1); 91 (note 1); 138 (note 1); 140 (notes 1 to 3); 145 (note 1); 225 (note 2).

Y.

YANG-SA-LO; *see* JERUSALEM.

YANG-TI, the emperor, 285.

YEN-TS'AI; *see* AN-TS'AI.

YEH-KUANG-PI, a shining stone (?), 242.

YEH-HSI-MING (*Jasminum officinale*, L.), 268; 270 seqq.

Yen-pao-tan-yü, 287 (note 1).

YÜ HUAN, author of the *Wei-lio*, 14.

Yü-kung, the, containing first mention of the Weak Water, 291 seq.

YÜ-LO, city or kingdom of, identical with T'iao-chih, 145 seq.; a dependency of Ta-ts'in, 146; 151; 197; old sound of this name, 151 (note 1); 154; in the north-east of Ssŭ-fu (?), 196.

YÜ-TIEN (= Khoten), probable sound of the name, 151 (note 1).

Yüan-chien-lei-han; *passim*.

YULE, Col. Hy., 24; Preface, vi seqq.; 144 (note 1); 150 (note); 178 (note 1); 205 (note 1); 208; 256 (note 1); 258; 261; 284 (note 1); 305.

Z.

ZAGROS HILLS, 154; 196.

ZEBU (*Bos Indicus*), 38 (note 2).

ZEUGMA, 191 seqq.; distance from Gulf of Issus to, 191 (note 2); the bridge across the Euphrates at, 192 seq.

ZOTTOLI, A., 29.

ERRATA.

P. 9, near bottom: *for* Ch'ieh-shu *read* Ch'iai-shu.

,, 12, ,, ,, *for* 叉元 *read* 叉云.

,, 17, bottom: for *Ch'iu T'ang-shu* read *Chiu T'ang-shu*.

,, 18, near bottom: *for* eliminating *read* eliciting.

,, 21, bottom: *for* 計 *read* 計.

,, 22, note 1, middle: *for* Yao (秩) *read* Hsien (秩).

,, 26, bottom: for *Fu-kuo-chi* read *Fo-kuo-chi*.

,, 38, note 1, line 3: *for* 陂下者曰隰, pei-hsia-chê-yüeh-shih: "a bank, being low, is called shih" *read*: 陂者曰阪下者曰隰 pei-chê yüeh fan; hsia-chê yüeh shih: "a bank is called fan, and what is low, is called shih." [The former reading appears in K'ang-hsi, the latter, in the *Erh-ya* itself.]

,, 43, near bottom: *for* fei-chiao *read* fei-ch'iao.

,, 44, note 1: *for* *T'ung-tien* (通典) read *Yüan-chien-lei-han*.

,, 46, middle: *for* Buddah *read* Buddha.

,, 48, middle: *for* Hui-chi *read* Kuei-chi.

,, ,, bottom: remove "?" after "Ta-t'ung-fu."

,, ,, note 3: *for* p. 329 *read* p. 392.

,, 54, bottom: *for* and the animal may be taken off, etc., *read* and the animal may be turned to grass.

,, 58, middle: *for* laid up *read* led up.

,, 60, middle: *for* they are taken off the water-plants *read* they are turned to grass.

,, ,, near bottom: *for* ta-yu *read* ta-chiu.

,, 62, line 3: *for* king *read* ching (景).

,, 73 and *passim*: *for* Turtoise *read* Tortoise.

,, 78 (Q 8): *for* a thousand li *read* several thousand li.

,, 80, top: *for* they may be taken off the water plants *read* they are turned to grass.

,, 86, near bottom: *for* ta-yu *read* ta-chiu.

,, 87, near middle: *for* pecks *read* beaks.

,, 102, col. 4: *for* 汎 *read* 汎.

,, 108, col. 9: after 琴 add 小.

,, 141, note 1: *for* A.D. 90 to 107 *read* A.D. 51 to 90.

,, 154, bottom: *for* 36,000 *read* 3,600.

,, 155, bottom: *for* Ὀρχόη *read* Ὀρχόη.

,, 156, middle: after "about the identity" *add* of.

,, 159, note 1, middle: *for* Μυὸς ὄμρον *read* Μυὸς ὅρμον.

,, 276, near top: for *Chin-t'ang-shu* read *Chiu-t'ang-shu*.

,, 302 near top: *for* cured *read* proposed to cure.

www.ingramcontent.com/pod-product-compliance
Lightning Source LLC
Chambersburg PA
CBHW052141300426
44115CB00011B/1471